Politics in Manitoba

Politics in Manitoba
Parties, Leaders, and Voters

Christopher Adams

UNIVERSITY OF MANITOBA PRESS

© 2008 Christopher Adams

University of Manitoba Press
Winnipeg, Manitoba Canada R3T 2M5
www.umanitoba.ca/uofmpress

All rights reserved. No part of this publication may be reproduced or transmitted in any form or by any means, or stored in a database and retrieval system, without the prior written permission of the University of Manitoba Press, or, in the case of photocopying or any other reprographic copying, a licence from ACCESS COPYRIGHT (Canadian Copyright Licencing Agency) 6 Adelaide Street East, Suite 901, Toronto, Ontario M5C 1H6, www.accesscopyright.ca.

Cover and interior design: Doowah Design

Library and Archives Canada Cataloguing in Publication

Adams, Christopher, 1960-
Politics in Manitoba : parties, leaders, and voters / Christopher Adams.
Includes bibliographical references and index.
ISBN 978-0-88755-704-0
1. Political parties--Manitoba--History. 2. Manitoba--Politics and government.
3. Manitoba--Politics and government--Public opinion. 4. Public opinion--Manitoba.
I. Title.
JL299.A45A33 2008   324.27127'009   C2008-906319-8

The University of Manitoba Press gratefully acknowledges the financial support for its publication program provided by the Government of Canada through the Book Publishing Industry Development Program (BPIDP), the Canada Council for the Arts, the Manitoba Arts Council, and the Manitoba Department of Culture, Heritage, Tourism and Sport.

Table of Contents

Introduction vii

Chapter 1: Manitoba's Party Systems 1

Chapter 2: The Progressive Conservative Party 23

Chapter 3: The Liberal Party 65

Chapter 4: The New Democratic Party 99

Conclusion: Understanding Manitoba Party Politics 133

Appendix A: Party Preferences and Survey Data 149

Appendix B: Provincial Election Results, 1870 to 2007 169

Notes 178

Bibliography 215

Index 231

Photographs appear following page 97

Introduction

THE ORIGINAL IDEA BEHIND THIS BOOK WAS TO PROVIDE READERS WITH a study on the attitudes and perceptions of Manitobans regarding social issues and politics. However, as with other things in life, the project evolved as it moved out of infancy. While teaching a course on Canadian party politics at the University of Manitoba, I became aware that there are no books currently available about Manitoba government and party politics. The most recently released book on this theme was Murray Donnelly's superb *The Government of Manitoba*, which was published in 1963.

During the research phase it struck me repeatedly that Manitoba's electoral and political history can be connected to conceptual and analytical themes that have been raised by political scientists in Europe, the United States, and other parts of Canada. In fact, one could use Manitoba as a case study for understanding political parties in Western industrial societies. As the reader will see in this book, the wider themes reflected in Manitoba politics include how the party system evolved within the context of a specific government structure (in this case, the Westminster system of parliamentary government), how economic factors precipitated political change, including the impact of agrarianism and industrialization on provincial party politics and outcomes, how labour-based parties faced similar challenges as elsewhere, how ethnicity and social-class cleavages became transformed into electoral cleavages, how media can influence electoral outcomes and party strategies, the long-term consequences of realigning electorates and "critical" elections, and, finally, how electoral systems and their accompanying rules, including the first-past-the-post system (i.e., single-member plurality) and the determination of electoral boundaries, can significantly shape a party's fortunes.

Another major theme in this book is that Manitoba can be divided roughly into three political regions. These are Winnipeg, the rural southern portion of the province, and the North. Of course there are distinct areas within each of these regions, such as Winnipeg's "North End," the City of Brandon, the Interlake, marginal farmlands, First Nations communities, as well as any or all of the various towns and communities spread across the province. Nevertheless, different parts of the province do collect together under the three regional umbrellas when we examine patterns of support for each of the main parties, allowing us to see the forest rather than each of the trees. In recent decades, voters in both the rural South and wealthier parts of South Winnipeg have tended to support the Progressive Conservative (PC) Party while the New Democratic Party (NDP) has drawn support from the less prosperous parts of Winnipeg, marginal farming areas, and the North.

Much of this book is based on an examination of newspapers dating back to the 1870s, political biographies, published historical studies, journal articles, MA and PhD theses, political party documents, and personal interviews. Of particular use were the chapters focusing on Manitoba in the series *Canadian Annual Review of Politics and Public Affairs* published by the University of Toronto Press. Small portions of research from my doctoral dissertation regarding grain politics and agricultural interest groups also found their way into this project.¹

The Structure of the Book

The main body of the book includes an introductory chapter regarding historical trends in Manitoba party politics and the forces shaping the political system. This is followed by three chapters, each pertaining to the history of the three main parties: the Progressive Conservatives, the Liberals, and the New Democratic Party.² Attention is paid to how social and economic forces, leadership, campaign strategies and platforms, and organizational resources together shaped the parties' electoral fortunes. In order to contain the scope of this project, some areas of discussion have been left for a later project or for others to explore. These include the changing nature and growth of the civil service in Manitoba, the nature and characteristics of the provincial policy process, the many federal politicians who have served Manitoba in Parliament, and municipal politics. Therefore, those such as Clifford Sifton, Stanley Knowles, Steve Juba, and Lloyd Axworthy enter into this book only to the extent to which they influenced provincial party politics.

The book's conclusion provides an overview of the different factors that shape party politics in Manitoba. This includes the enduring influence of political geography and political culture, as well as the impact of leadership, campaign strategies, organizational resources, and the media on voter preferences.

Appendix A provides an examination of recent public opinion data regarding each party's socio-demographic basis of support. While the three parties aim to draw support from all parts of society, and therefore sometimes have overlapping policies and platforms, there are discernible patterns in the opinion data by which we can differentiate the PCs, Liberals, and NDP. It is hoped that this examination will help confirm some of the current notions that many of us hold about partisanship in Manitoba, while dispelling certain misconceptions that we might be hesitant to discard.

This information is drawn from a unique and comprehensive public opinion database. Every three months Probe Research launches a province-wide omnibus survey of 1000 interviews on a range of issues including the economy, community-related concerns, the Internet, tobacco usage, health issues, and anything else that is of interest to Manitobans. Included also in this survey, with results often published in the *Winnipeg Free Press*, are the results from a question that asks Manitobans about their provincial party preferences. For this book, the results from over 20,000 interviews with individual Manitobans between 2000 and 2007 were compiled and analyzed. No other company, organization, or research firm has such a rich source of publicly available information about the political preferences of Manitobans as Probe Research, and it is a pleasure to have the opportunity to present some of the findings here.

A compilation of Manitoba provincial election results (1870 to 2007), prepared especially for this publication, can be found in Appendix B. These tables of election results have their roots in the work of a group of individuals including my brother, Paul Adams. In the 1970s, while working for the provincial government, he was part of a small team that was responsible for preparing for the first time a comprehensive set of historical tables on election results. These riding-by-riding results, which are now regularly updated and published by Elections Manitoba following each election, were indispensable for the preparation of this book. Some small differences exist between these tables (especially pertaining to the province's early decades), the work of others who have written about particular elections, and the figures presented in this book. Where discrepancies occur, I have resorted to historical documents and newspaper coverage and have duly noted the sources for my factual corrections.

Acknowledgements

There are a number of individuals who deserve deeply felt thanks for their help. First, I would like to thank Scott MacKay and Probe Research for permission to use the firm's public opinion results dating back to the 1990s. I also appreciate the ongoing support that Scott has shown during the length of this project. Kevin McDougald at Probe Research provided thoughtful comments, points of discussion, and corrections on the chapter drafts. I owe him many thanks. My colleague Lloyd Fridfinnson, who has written on Manitoba's political history for the three-volume *Manitoba 125* series published by Great Plains Publications, put up with what must have seemed to be endless conversations in the office regarding Walter Weir, Edward Schreyer, and the 1969 election. His good hearted-patience did not go unnoticed. I would also like to thank Terry Barna, who was a colleague of mine at the Angus Reid Group in the 1990s, for contributing his personal time to amalgamate the quarterly databases and providing the occasional expert advice. His fine work in this regard helped immensely.

A number of individuals who were directly involved in provincial politics were also gracious enough to provide input on my interpretation of events, and to successfully disabuse me of a few mistaken notions. Of particular help were three former premiers. Edward Schreyer discussed his perspectives on the provincial elections of 1969, 1973, and 1977 and his tenure in office over a very pleasant lunch. Duff Roblin kindly responded to questions regarding his early years as an MLA in a multi-member constituency, and Gary Filmon set aside time to discuss the period in which he served as party leader and provincial premier. Others who were helpful and generously gave their time for interviews were Stuart Murray, Harvey Bostrom, Allison Molgat, Markus Buchart, and Paul Edwards.

A word of thanks is also due to all my current and former students from Carleton University, the University of Ottawa, the University of Winnipeg, and the University of Manitoba. Many of the ideas found in this book regarding elections and state-society relations were initially bounced around in their classes. Bob Cox at the *Winnipeg Free Press* graciously gave permission to use some of the photographs appearing in this book while Sharon Foley provided important assistance for digging up historical materials at the Manitoba Public Archives. David Carr at the University of Manitoba Press provided kind and thoughtful words of encouragement during this project's formative period, and then as the project proceeded through its various stages to completion. I would like to thank the anonymous reviewers and Paul Thomas for their valuably insightful comments. Glenn Bergen at the University of Manitoba Press provided valuable changes to final drafts of the text while Steven Rosenberg created the charts for the book. Of course, all errors and shortcomings remain mine.

On a personal note, I owe a great deal of gratitude to numerous professors who, in their own particular way, introduced me to the study of party politics, elections, ideologies, and the intricacies of government. They include Paul Thomas, Geoff Lambert, Tom Peterson, Wally Fox-Decent, Alain Gagnon, Jon Pammett, Jane Jenson, and the late Ken McVicar. These are only a few of the professors under whom I have had the honour to study.

Sue Adams and each of our children supported this project by continual displays of affection and patience. Finally, I want to thank my parents, Paul and Louise Adams, for all the good things they have done for both their children and the community. Through example they taught us that intellectual pursuits have an honest value of their own. It is to them that this book is dedicated.

Chapter 1

Manitoba's Party Systems

SINCE JOINING CANADA IN 1870, MANITOBA HAS OPERATED WITHIN A number of distinct political-party systems.[1] These can be enumerated as follows: an embryonic formative system (1870 to 1878), a traditional two-party system (1879 to 1922), a quasi-party system[2] (1922 to 1958), a transitional three-party system (1958 to 1969), and the province's currently operating two-and-a-half-party system (1969 onward). Until the 1880s, candidates chiefly aligned themselves both in the legislature and in elections as either being "Government" (another term used was "Ministerial") or "Opposition." As in many other pre-twentieth-century developing democracies with their own nascent democratic institutions, elected representatives first grouped themselves into loosely structured "factions" before parties entered the scene.[3]

The shift from a non-party formative system to the two-party system occurred between 1878 and 1883. Due to the support John Norquay received from John A. Macdonald's federal Conservatives (operating then under the "Liberal-Conservative" label), the 1878 and 1879 provincial elections are considered by some to be the first in which candidates formally battled along party lines in the province.[4] However, and in spite of his loose association with Macdonald's federal Conservatives, Norquay declared himself non-partisan and candidates continued to position themselves as supporting either the Government or the Opposition. This is demonstrated by the *Manitoba Free Press* coverage leading up to the 1879 election: "Winnipeg is the only constituency in which Dominion party lines have been made an issue—either Liberal or Conservative—and we, therefore, hope that the day is yet remote when it shall split our Local House."[5]

There appears to have been debate at the time on whether or not candidates had been running on party lines during the December election. The *Manitoba Free Press* severely criticized the *Winnipeg Daily Times* for identifying in its 19 December 1879 edition candidates according to party labels. The *Manitoba Free Press* argued that Manitobans are "a people that has thoroughly identified themselves with the best interests of the country at large, unconstrained and unbiased by party spirit or party bigotry."[6]

Party identities became clearer in 1883 when an early version of the Liberal Party (or "Grits") appeared in the form of a loose collection of Liberal and "Provincial Rights" candidates in opposition to Government candidates. Indicative that a new era of partisan politics had arrived is the following report from the *Manitoba Free Press*: "The nomination of candidates in the different constituencies throughout the province takes place at noon today, and a bid fair to be an event of more than ordinary interest. As the day of battle draws near the winnowing process is thinning the number of candidates down, and by the time the contest takes place, there will probably be an average of two candidates in each of the constituencies representing respectively the issues that divide the two great political parties."[7] Both parties supported policies that would promote investment, transportation, settlement, agriculture, and trade. The main issue was over the federally supported Canadian Pacific Railway monopoly and the right of the Province to allow competing railway lines. In other words, the two parties were ideologically indistinguishable and therefore marked by what Maurice Duverger, in his political science classic *Political Parties*, terms a "technical dualism" rather than a "metaphysical dualism."[8] That is, the two provincial parties aimed to win control over the administrative levers of government, rather than to radically redistribute power according to social groups or economic classes.

Bubbling under this two-party arrangement, however, were those who did want to see power and wealth redistributed. These represented the specific class interests of urban labour and agrarianism. As Winnipeg's industrial economy quickly expanded, labour-based urban parties made some inroads within the urban electorate. Yet, and in a similar manner as Alberta and Ontario,[9] it would be the farmers who swept aside the cozy Liberal-Conservative arrangement and introduced to the province its third political-party system in 1922. Once in government, and with John Bracken as their new leader, the United Farmers of Manitoba transformed itself into a solidly based coalition of elected representatives with continual backing from urban business leaders and rural farmers. It would become the Progressive Party (a label already used by farmers at the national level as well as by the United Farmers of Manitoba's Winnipeg branch[10]) and then Liberal-Progressive upon being merged with the provincial Liberal Party in 1932.

One could say that Bracken's leadership style was an outgrowth of his personality and background. According to Gerald Friesen, "Bracken was a no-nonsense farm boy from eastern Ontario who had become an agricultural extension officer and eventually a professor of agriculture. He had absorbed the strict teaching of a Methodist household and combined them with an unusual flair for organization and exposition, on the one hand, and for instilling loyalty and a sense of common purpose, on the other."[11] In the 1940s, and with a wartime coalition encompassing Liberal-Progressives, Conservatives, the Co-operative Commonwealth Federation (CCF), and Social Credit, candidates continued to run in elections under distinct party banners yet were also expected to declare whether or not they were supporting the governing coalition. The effect was that party distinctions became less than clear.

During the 1950s and with the accompanying rise to power of Duff Roblin's Progressive Conservatives (the renamed Conservative Party), Manitoba's system of one-party dominance dissolved into a three-party system. As the Liberals (having dropped their "Progressive" moniker after the 1958 provincial election) fell into a long-term decline, the system eventually evolved into the province's fifth and current party system: two main parties with a minor third party, or, as the British political system is described, a two-and-a-half-party system.[12] However, it was in this new era that the provincial parties began to increasingly move towards what would be termed in other countries the "catch-all party" model, in that they jockeyed to win government power by recruiting new members from a wide range of social sectors. Across both Western Europe and countries elsewhere in the industrial West in the post-war era, political scientists observed the increasing predominance of "catch-all" political organizations. Parties that were previously aligned with specific sectors were, according to Otto Kirchheimer, "turning more fully to the electoral scene, trying to exchange effectiveness in depth for a wider audience and more immediate electoral success."[13] The Progressive Conservatives expanded their search to include business interests as well as farmers and workers, while the CCF worked to reach out to white-collar service-sector voters, farmers, and small-business owners.

For modern political parties, a large membership base signifies a sound financial base for the organization, volunteer armies to operate invigorated campaigns, and increasingly high levels of voter commitment. The Liberal Party of Canada is an example of how this was effectively done at the national level. Christina McCall-Newman revealed in her account of the national party how its success was largely tied to an ability to shift its organizational basis from business elites to a more broadly based organizational structure during the 1960s as it cultivated support among the urban middle class and growing numbers of first-generation Canadians.[14] In Manitoba, as the old Liberal-Progressive quasi-party system was replaced by a more competitive party system, provincial party organizations were shifting from being primarily elite-driven to mass-oriented entities.

Manitoba's Political Geography

Serving as the province's only major urban centre, with a population of 695,000 persons in a province of 1.15 million, Winnipeg is the province's critical electoral battleground.[15] An apt metaphor for Winnipeg might be the eye of a Cyclops. No other province has such a large territory tied so dependently to one major city. Historically, it might also be described as a "vertical mosaic"[16] of people who are defined by both ethnicity and social class, and according to the neighbourhoods in which they reside. The city's North End was originally settled in the first half of the twentieth century by low-income labourers, many of whom were of eastern European origin and who served as the backbone for much of the city's working class.[17] As the city has grown outward, the traditional North End has become chiefly part of the city's downtown core area and has been populated by more recent waves of immigrants arriving from the Philippines, Africa, South Asia, and China (120,000 of Winnipeg residents were classified as "First Generation" Canadians in the 2006 census). Winnipeg is now also a major centre for the country's Aboriginal population. In the 2006 census, 68,385 Winnipeg residents reported being of Native ancestry. Many of the new arrivals, from both overseas and elsewhere in the province, have moved into the very same houses and apartments originally occupied by the previous century's urban immigrants.

In contrast, Winnipeg's South End developed with a disproportionate number of Ontarians of English and Scott ancestry.[18] With better educational opportunities and fraternal connections, members of these ethnic groups generally dominated the city's business and professional sector. The visible impact of social class and ethnicity was unavoidable when looking at the composition of professional and recreational clubs in Manitoba, such as the ethnically exclusive Manitoba Club and the St. Charles Country Club, and even distinguished different summer cottage areas according to ethnicity and class.[19] This link between location of residence and social class continues in the present era as members of the professional and managerial classes move further away from what is now labelled the "core area" into newer neighbourhoods in the southern portions of the city including Tuxedo, Linden Woods, St. Vital, and Charleswood. Beyond these two major socio-economic "halves" of the city, there are of course other segments, including the historically significant francophone population in St. Boniface.

Manitoba's political culture and history have also been heavily influenced by the province's once-dominant rural southern region in which many farms were settled in the late 1800s by people of British ancestry arriving via Ontario as the fur trade receded. Nelson Wiseman argues that as the Métis and French Canadian populations became increasingly marginalized by this population influx, a "grit agrarianism"—which was another term for farmer-oriented liberal individualism—was stamped onto the province's political psyche. Wiseman writes: "Ontarians occupied the best agricultural lands and secured homesteads along the new Canadian Pacific Railway. Their power was profound in Manitoba which, having entered Confederation in 1870, offered the first and most accessible frontier for westward immigration.... In Manitoba the grit agrarianism of Ontario express[ed] itself in the selection of every premier from the 1880s until Ed Schreyer in 1969."[20]

While the southern rural region's relative importance to other sectors in the provincial economy has declined, it remains important for both agricultural production, food processing, and manufacturing, as signified by the economic growth of such towns as Morden and Winkler.[21] This region also includes the province's second-largest population centre, Brandon, with a 2006 census population of 48,000 in the city and immediately surrounding area. It operates with its own manufacturing, food processing, and service sector and includes also two post-secondary institutions: Assiniboine

Community College and Brandon University. Brandon therefore has its own brand of politics and is socio-economically divided along an east-west axis.

The third major region is Manitoba's North, which broadly contains three types of socio-economic groupings. Each of these groups is linked in a particular manner to the "rock and water"-filled Canadian Shield, a region that has been transformed from what northern historian Jim Mochoruk describes as "the fur-trading preserve of the Hudson's Bay Company into an industrial hinterland."[22] The first two types of groupings are First Nations communities, many predating the arrival of the European fur traders, and, secondly, communities that have grown around the resource sector including nickel and copper mining and hydroelectricity. The third grouping is chiefly associated with marginal farming activity in areas straddling the geographic line where the Canadian Shield meets the agrarian South.[23]

A helpful approach for examining Manitoba party politics is to use the historically comparative analysis of Seymour Martin Lipset and Stein Rokkan who connect together party politics and the development of two major social and economic class cleavages in modernizing societies. In the European-based industrial era, political parties and electoral outcomes can be examined along the following axis: 1) the land-industry (rural-urban) cleavage and 2) the ownership-worker (class) divide. That is, with the evolution of party systems, one is able to identify parties along one axis or both of these axes.[24] As shown in the accompanying chart (Figure 1.1), this conceptual schema works very well for studying the link between territorial politics, social class, and electoral party support in Manitoba's political history. Leaving aside Winnipeg, the provincial electoral axes generally follow a diagonal line coinciding with the southern edge of the Canadian Shield. This runs from the northwest where the Swan River Valley is located to the Lake of the Woods in the southeast.[25] This link between geography and party support is no coincidence in that this line distinguishes between fruitful southern farming areas and marginal farmlands (as well as the northern hinterland). This translates into the longstanding and current pattern in which southern farmers generally elect PC candidates while the NDP draws support from marginal farming communities, northern labourers, and those residing in Aboriginal communities.

A second critical and enduring line in Manitoba politics is that which divides the City of Winnipeg into two territorial halves. With social and class divisions reaching back to the city's early years, this pattern continues, with the PCs drawing support from many business and white-collar professionals who reside on the city's south side while the NDP remains strongest in working-class neighbourhoods. (Admittedly, and as will be discussed in Chapter 4, in recent years this division has become less pronounced, with popular support for Gary Doer's NDP during the 2003 and 2007 election causing many voters in traditional PC southern Winnipeg ridings to elect NDP MLAs.) Overall, with the two major parties occupying generally well-defined positions along these two axes across the entire province, as well as in Winnipeg, combined with how the first-past-the-post system for electing MLAs adversely affects smaller parties that are unable to win pluralities in many areas, the Liberal Party continues in its struggle to spatially locate itself and thereby win a significant number of seats in the legislature.

Manitoba's Early Political-Party System

The first provincial election was held on 27 December 1870, the year Manitoba entered Confederation. This new legislature established by the Manitoba Act of 15 July 1870 replaced Louis Riel's short-lived provisional government and its Legislative Assembly of Assiniboia.[26] The vote was restricted to property-owning males, and candidates were elected by public declarations of support at constituency meetings. It was not until 1888 that the property restriction was removed and voting was conducted via private ballot, and only in 1916 were women granted the right to vote.[27] A total of 1057 votes were cast in the first provincial election, and in all but one riding (Winnipeg and St. John) less than one hundred votes needed to be counted. The first government was operated under inauspicious conditions: it assembled in a log cabin with a royal mace (used to represent the Crown's sovereignty) constructed from a locally obtained ox-cart wheel.[28] Consisting of

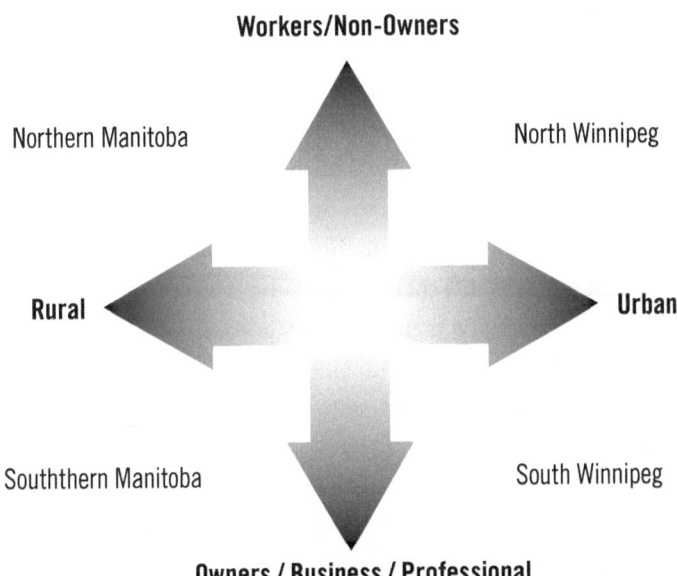
Figure 1.1

twenty-four elected members, the legislative assembly was much smaller than the fifty-seven-member assembly of today. Furthermore, representation was balanced between French-speaking citizens and English-speaking citizens with twelve seats assigned to each group.[29]

The Lieutenant-Governor played a central role in these early years. The first two, Adams G. Archibald and Alexander Morris, served as the Crown's symbolic representative and as direct leaders of the provincial government. Their activities included general administration, putting forward legislation, amending provincial bills, and reserving legislation for review by Ottawa.[30] W.L. Morton summarized their role as serving as "their own prime ministers."[31] The legislative wing of the government in these early years was led by Alfred Boyd, Marc-Amable Girard, Henry Joseph Clarke, and Robert Atkinson Davis.[32] At the same time each MLA identified himself as either a government supporter or opponent, rather than along identifiable party lines. One additional curious feature to the structure of government was the existence of the Legislative Council. This was the province's "upper house" consisting of seven lifetime-appointed members. This local version of the Canadian Senate was disbanded in 1876 due to cost considerations.[33]

The early growth of political parties in Manitoba can be linked to what was occurring throughout other parts of the Western world; that is, as the voting franchise expanded, political parties pulled citizens into the electoral process. They helped to inform voters about candidates and party platforms while encouraging newly enfranchised citizens to cast their ballot on election day.[34] The specific characteristics of Manitoba's new provincial parties were, according to Andy Anstett and Paul Thomas, shaped by the arrival of many Ontario settlers who "brought with them attachments to Liberal and Conservative labels."[35]

Table 1.1 shows how the Conservatives and Liberals dominated the provincial electoral landscape from 1879 to 1915 (however, party identities were often indiscernible for elections prior to 1883). Table 1.2 shows how strong electoral support for the two parties translated into a dominance within the assembly. Between these two parties, three premiers were prominent during this era: John Norquay (Conservative), Thomas Greenway (Liberal), and Rodmond Roblin (Conservative). Their dominance is demonstrated by the fact that eleven of the twelve elections held in the province prior to 1915 were won by these three men. It is also worth noting that during this period the same two parties dominated the federal landscape in Manitoba as well. Of particular significance was Clifford Sifton, who served in Greenway's cabinet and then moved into federal politics as an influential cabinet minister under Wilfrid Laurier and was responsible for settlement policies. Prior to 1920, and with only one exception with regard to one seat in 1891, Liberal and Conservative candidates won every federal seat in the province.[36]

Winnipeg's Odd Electoral System

In 1914 and 1915 a complicated voting system was used in Winnipeg that differed from the standard first-past-the-post system used elsewhere across the province. The city was divided into "North," "South," and "Centre" areas, with voters in each area having two ballots to cast: one for a candidate in an "A" seat and the second for a candidate in a "B" seat. The parties took great care to explain to their supporters how the system worked and how they should mark their ballots and avoid vote spoilage.[37] Because it was still a riding-based ballot (rather than city-wide), and with candidates prevented from running on both of the two ballots within their respective city region, the process was neither an example of transferable voting (that is, where voters identify a list of preferences by which extra votes can be transferred to the next preferred candidate) nor proportional representation.

Table 1.1: Voter Support in Manitoba's Two Party System: 1879-1920

	Conservative	Liberal	Other
1879	34	7	59
1883	55	45	0
1886	51	48	1
1888	34	57	10
1892	41	50	9
1896	40	50	10
1899	44	50	7
1903	48	45	8
1907	51	48	2
1910	51	44	5
1914	47	43	11
1915	33	55	12
1920	19	35	47

Source, Based on Elections Manitoba, "Historical Summaries," with adjustments based on newspaper coverage.

The system was replaced in 1920 with city-wide proportional representation (PR), which has been said to be the first time that PR was used in an election in North America.[38] Winnipeg was treated as one large constituency that was represented by ten MLAs, and voters cast their ballots by rating their preferences for all the candidates offered.[39] Counting the ballots proved to be an overwhelming and confusing task for the electoral officers in the first election in which the system was used. However, problems relating to ballot counting were rectified in time for the 1922 election.[40] This system of electing candidates in Winnipeg ridings would survive until 1949. But even then electoral experimentation continued. The single ten-member constituency system was replaced by three constituencies with four MLAs elected in each and by using the preferential ballot. St. Boniface, which was not part of Winnipeg at the time, had two MLAs representing the riding. This system would be in effect until 1958 when Winnipeg was divided into twenty single-member constituencies and St. Boniface's representation reduced to a single MLA.[41]

It is important to note that until the 1960s Manitoba's electoral system was heavily weighted to give more representation to rural voters than urban voters. This gave a strong advantage to rural-based parties while hampering those based on labour. Murray Donnelly calculated that in 1952 there were seventeen MLAs representing a total of 228,280 registered urban voters, while forty MLAs represented 224,083 registered rural voters.[42] This discrepancy became more extreme when comparing specific ridings. In the urban riding of Kildonan-Transcona, for example, one MLA represented six times as many voters as those in the small rural riding of St. George.[43] In 1955, with the support of all parties, the legislature passed a bill regarding the establishment of an independent boundaries commission. In 1957 the Electoral Divisions Boundaries Commission submitted its first report to Premier Campbell, including a recommendation that the rural-urban ratio be set at seven to four. The new system was passed by the legislature.[44] In 1968, the independent boundaries commission put forward new adjustments to the new system (ridings could vary only by 25 percent from the norm to represent rural areas), which further reduced the relative weight of rural ridings and thereby resulted in almost half of the province's ridings being located in Winnipeg and its suburbs just prior to the 1969 election.[45]

Table 1.2: Seats Held in the Provincial Assembly: 1879-1920

	Conservative	Liberal	Other
1879	14	2	8
1883	20	10	0
1886	21	14	0
1888	5	32	1
1892	9	24	7
1896	5	32	3
1899	18	17	5
1903	29	9	2
1907	28	13	0
1910	28	13	0
1914	28	20	1
1915	5	40	2
1920	9	21	25

Source, Elections Manitoba, "Historical Summaries"

The Quasi-Party System

During the 1920s, Canada's national two-party system was severely challenged by the Progressive Party with its agrarian-based attacks on party politics and party-led governments. As a result, the Progressives acquired more House of Commons seats than did the Conservatives in the 1921 federal election. Farmer politics were having a similar effect in the provincial arena. In 1922, the United Farmers of Manitoba (UFM) were elected to power. As was the platform of their federal agrarian counterparts, the

UFM maintained that all votes in the assembly should be "free votes" rather than having MLAs forced to vote along party lines. According to Thomas and Anstett, "the UFM group was led by John Bracken, who believed in co-operative group government as a way to ensure honesty and economy. A non-partisan approach would also end cabinet domination of the Assembly. Except for financial measures which would involve the life of the government, all legislative votes would be free votes."[46]

Table 1.3: Voter Support in Manitoba's Quasi-Party system: 1922-49

	Conserv.	Liberal	UFM/Prog/ Lib-Prog	Lab/CCF	Social Credit	Other
1922	16	23	33	16		13
1927	27	21	32	11		9
1932	35		40	17		9
1936	28		35	12	9	14
1941	20		35	17	8	19
1945	16		32	34	2	16
1949	19		38	26		17

Source, Elections Manitoba, "Historical Summaries"

The UFM took on a new name, the Progressive Party, in time for the election of 1927. Continuing their self-proclaimed non-partisan approach, Bracken's Progressives promoted both their leader and the idea of a non-party-based functioning government. They labelled themselves the "Bracken Party" while running under the following slogan: "A Business (not a party) Government."[47] While the practitioners of Bracken's non-party government claimed that legislative non-partisanship would allow MLAs to act according to what they thought was best for their constituents, it effectively reduced the extent to which government decision makers could be challenged by opposition parties. In other words, the Westminster government model, which is the basis for Manitoba's system of government, is based on having government and opposition groupings within the assembly that are able to debate with each other. Parties therefore play a central role in helping the system function. Undercutting their activities benefits those who hold power, rather than the opposition. This is not limited to the case of Manitoba, or those that operate with the Westminster model. For example, over forty years ago Richard Dawson and James Robinson made the case that in the US competitive party systems further the policy needs of the "have less," while non-partisan governments tend to serve the interests of socio-economic elites.[48] In the Manitoba context, one can argue that non-partisanship served to maintain the Winnipeg business and southern farmer status quo to the detriment of urban labour and socially disadvantaged segments of the population. This condition would last for many years to come.

Table 1.4: Seats Held in the Provincial Assembly: 1922-1949

	Liberal	Conser.	UFM/Prog/ Lib-Prog	Lab/CCF	Social Credit	Other
1922	8	7	28	6		6
1927	7	15	29	3		1
1932		10	38	6		1
1936		16	23	7	5	4
1941		15	27	3	3	7
1945		13	25	10	2	5
1949		13	30	7		7

Source, Elections Manitoba, "Historical Summaries"

By the 1940s, the competitive party system had almost evaporated, both in the assembly and within the electoral system. The numbers in Figure 1.4 are misleading since candidates would run under their own party banners, yet, once elected could opt to support or oppose John Bracken's Liberal-Progressive government. The stultifying impact was evident by the fact that many seats were won through acclamation. Prior to the 1940s, no provincial election in the twentieth century had more than three ridings won through acclamation. Yet in the 1941 election, of the forty-five non-Winnipeg ridings, sixteen were won without any challengers. In 1945, seven of the forty-five ridings were awarded in this fashion and, in 1949, fifteen of the forty-five ridings were won through acclamation. Some years later Duff Roblin would reflect on his experiences as an MLA in the 1940s and the negative consequences of non-partisanship: "When war ended, drawbacks of the coalition system became clear. It gave a strong tendency to reinforce the status quo in the legislature and in the constituencies. Coalition nominations were seldom contested, and a nomination in that system was the equivalent of election. The Progressive Conservative and Liberal Progressive [sic] party organizations generally co-operated in supporting whoever happened to be the sitting member of the time, so this was pretty much a closed system. In the legislature, the government proceeded serenely, not much disturbed by the views of the few members who were in the opposition."[49]

Table 1.5: Composition of Pro-Government Coalition by Seats: 1941-49

	Conser.	Liberal-Progressive	CCF	Social Credit	Ind/Other
1941	12	27	3	3	5
1945	13	25		2	3
1949	9	30			5

Source, Elections Manitoba, "Historical Summaries," with adjustments[50]

The Three-Party System

Manitoba returned to a more normalized party system during the 1950s. That is, candidates battled against each other according to distinct party platforms, both on election day and in the legislature. The party with the most seats was expected to form the government, while those elected to other parties would serve in opposition; there would be no non-partisan coalitions. In this new era, winning by acclamation had become a thing of the past. Only one riding in 1953 was won through acclamation (by Liberal-Progressive William Morton in Gladstone) and no candidate has since been acclaimed in the province. However, while the parties operated differently in this new era, Bracken's old Liberal-Progressive Party, then under the leadership of Douglas Campbell, lingered on, continuing to hold power until Duff Roblin's Progressive Conservatives were able to form a minority government in 1958.

Apparently, old habits die hard. In light of the 1958 results, the Liberal-Progressives attempted to hammer together a new coalition with the Co-operative Commonwealth Federation. These talks failed, and, in discussion with Lieutenant-Governor J.S. McDiarmid, Roblin agreed to form a minority government on condition that McDiarmid grant dissolution if the government failed on a confidence motion, rather than allow for renewed discussions to occur between the other two parties; a deal of questionable constitutionality.[51]

Table 1.6: Party Seats: 1953-1966

	Liberal	Progressive Conservative	CCF/NDP	Other
1953	33	12	5	7
1958	19	26	11	1
1959	11	36	10	0
1962	13	36	7	0
1966	14	31	11	1

Source, Elections Manitoba, "Historical Summaries"

With the CCF also in the mix with eleven seats in 1958 and ten in 1959, albeit as a weaker party compared to the other two, the regularized party system was essentially a classical three-party system, with all three of the major provincial parties jockeying for power. In retrospect, this party system served as a transition towards the current two-and-a-half-party system (discussed in the following section) and is marked by the Liberal Party's (which would shed its "Progressive" moniker during this period) decline from 39 percent of the provincial vote in 1953 to 33 percent in 1966, and then to 24 percent when the NDP came to power in 1969.

Table 1.7: Voter Support: 1953-66

	Liberal	Progressive Conservative	CCF/NDP	Social Credit	Other
1953	39	21	16	13	11
1958	35	40	20	0	4
1959	30	46	22	0	1
1962	36	45	15	3	0
1966	33	40	23	4	0

Source, Elections Manitoba, "Historical Summaries"

The Two-and-a-Half-Party System: 1969 onward

Throughout the 1950s and 1960s, the CCF and its successor, the New Democratic Party, was a third-place party with popular support ranging from 15 percent to 23 percent. Little did voters realize when visiting the voting station in 1969 that they were creating not just a potential change in government but also a new party system. Once the ballots were counted the effect was far from certain or immediate. The fact was that with only a slight plurality of the electorate (38 percent of the vote versus the PCs' 35 percent) Edward Schreyer's NDP had won less than half the seats in the legislature (twenty-eight out of fifty-seven) which was momentarily insufficient to form a new government. It was an inauspicious beginning to a new era, in that different scenarios were possible from the 1969 outcome. Some pondered the idea of having the Liberals and PCs forming a coalition government with support from the lone Social Credit MLA (J.M. Froese from Rhineland) and independent MLA Gordon Beard from Churchill. However, when St. Boniface Liberal Larry Desjardins crossed the floor to serve as a "Liberal Democrat" to support the new NDP minority government, the opposition's back broke, with long-term consequences for the provincial party system.[52]

Table 1.8: Popular suport: 1969-2007

	Liberal	Progressive Conservative	NDP	Other
1969	24	35	38	2
1973	19	37	42	2
1977	12	49	38	
1981	7	44	47	2
1986	14	40	41	4
1988	35	38	24	2
1990	28	42	29	1
1995	24	43	33	1
1999	13	41	44	1
2003	13	36	49	1
2007	12	38	48	1

Source, Compiled from Elections Manitoba, "Historical Summaries" and *Winnipeg Free Press* 2007 election coverage

The 1969 election shook up Manitoba party politics with what political scientists would call an electoral "realignment," which can be defined as "a significant shift" in popular support with long-term consequences.[53] After 1969, and with the exception of the 1988 election in which the Liberals formed the official opposition with twenty candidates elected with 35 percent of the vote, the battles for control of the provincial government have primarily occurred between the NDP and the PCs. The Liberals would have trouble breaking the 20 percent popular-vote mark in most elections after

1969. In this sense, the three-party system of the 1950s and 1960s had evolved into a two-and-a-half-party system.[54] Every subsequent government has been won by either the NDP or the PCs. Under Premier Schreyer, the NDP ruled Manitoba from 1969 to 1977, and then under Howard Pawley from 1981 to 1988. Sterling Lyon led a one-term PC government from 1977 to 1981 and, under the leadership of Gary Filmon, the PCs held power through three terms, from 1988 to 1999. In 1999, Gary Doer's NDP was elected to power with 44 percent of the vote and thirty-two seats in the assembly. In the 2003 election, Doer was able to further solidify the NDP's base of support by garnering 49 percent of the vote and thirty-five seats, which was increased to thirty-six seats in 2007 (with 48 percent of the vote).[55] The significance of each of these elections as they pertain to each of the three parties will be discussed in the upcoming chapters.

Table 1.9: Party Seats 1969 -2007

	Liberal	Progressive Conservative	NDP	Other
1969	5	22	28	2
1973	5	21	31	
1977	1	33	23	
1981	0	23	34	
1986	1	26	30	
1988	20	25	12	
1990	7	30	20	
1995	3	31	23	
1999	1	24	32	
2003	2	20	35	
2007	2	19	36	

Source, Compiled from Elections Manitoba, "Historical Summaries" and *Winnipeg Free Press* 2007 election coverage

Conclusion

Geographical patterns have provided an enduring influence on Manitoba's political parties. This is largely due to the interconnection between socio-economic differences and geography, both across the province and within Winnipeg. Yet parties and their leaders are not always bound up in a straitjacket of structures. Opportunities arise due to major events and changing social and economic forces, including those relating to immigration, social mobility, economic crises, new modes of transportation, the media, and new forms of communication. In response, successful parties and their leaders continually seek to capture the changing moods of voters while putting forward strategies and platforms that reach beyond their traditional bases of support. As will be seen in the following chapters, the political fortunes of Manitoba's parties and their leaders are shaped by both long-term forces and short-term factors and strategies.

Chapter 2

The Progressive Conservative Party

THE HISTORY OF MANITOBA'S CONSERVATIVE PARTY, NOW OPERATING under the Progressive Conservative label,[1] reaches back to the province's early years. Since its inception it has stood for many of the same things as the federal branch of the party, at least until the latter part of the twentieth century. This includes maintaining Canada's connection to the Crown and Great Britain, a respect for social rank and class privilege, and the belief that governments should play a role in furthering the interests of business and economic development.[2] For John A. Macdonald's national Conservatives (originally, and somewhat confusingly, called Liberal-Conservatives), this was best represented by the National Policy, which included nation building, railway construction, and the establishment of protective national trade barriers to promote Canadian industry.[3]

In Manitoba, the Conservative Party's strongest allies have been the business sector and farmers. This basis of support, especially since the

1950s, is at the root of two (and sometimes opposing) tendencies within the party. For example, Duff Roblin and Gary Filmon tended to reflect the party's urban and pragmatic elements while Walter Weir and Sterling Lyon drew much of their support from rural and more right-wing members. At least since the 1960s, the party's orientation has swung like a pendulum between these two tendencies. The party has been most successful when it has reached beyond farmers and business people to gain the appeal of blue-collar and white-collar service-sector workers.

The Party's Formative Years

Often thought of as Manitoba's first Conservative premier, John Norquay was first elected to the provincial assembly in 1870 as the MLA for the riding of High Bluff.[4] He was fluent in English and French as well as Cree and Saulteaux.[5] In one account, Norquay was described as "a 300-pound Métis who could astonish English visitors with a high-kicking Red River jig"[6] and was said to carry "extra moccasins to a dance because he was certain to wear out more than one pair."[7] He became government leader in November 1878 and won the provincial election of December 1878. However, he was considered a Conservative due to his support for John A. Macdonald's national Conservatives, not due to being part of any provincial party organization. In fact, he was opposed by certain Conservative elements in the province, specifically many of the newly arriving "Conservative Orangemen" from Ontario who objected to a person of mixed blood leading the province. According to historian Gerald Friesen,

> Only the strong hand of Macdonald could quell the annual revolts from among the Manitoba Conservatives; only a command from his office could call out the troops to support Norquay in election campaigns. In 1883 Macdonald prevented the distribution of 10,000 protest leaflets, sponsored by the Orange order, which might have overturned the government ... In 1885 a crucial ministerial by-election was saved by Macdonald's telegram to prominent local Tories. According to Manitoba's lieutenant governor, James Cox Aikins, the public meeting held when Macdonald passed through Winnipeg in 1886 on his CPR junket rekindled local Tory enthusiasm and rescued Norquay from certain defeat in the general election.[8]

However, disagreements between Ottawa and the Province over railway policy, especially with regard to the idea of building the Red River Valley railway to better link the province to the US, caused a rift between Norquay and Macdonald. The prime minister used his influence to prevent Manitoba from selling bonds in London and New York. Eventually provincial debt, personal problems, and battles over railway building forced Norquay into resigning from the premiership in 1887.[9]

Norquay's rise and decline reflects the region's changing social order as it moved from the Red River Settlement era into a period marked by the expansion of its borders in 1871 (from its original "postage stamp" size to an area covering half of its current territory) and growing numbers of settlers arriving from Ontario with their own particular ideas of society and politics. According to Friesen, "the Norquay era in provincial politics saw the utter collapse of metis defences against manipulation of their land grants. Some metis moved west to follow the buffalo herds in the 1870s; many more followed in search of new lands for farming in the last years of the decade and in the early 1880s. Manitoba by then ceased to be a metis community."[10] In another work, Friesen recounts that, in Norquay's home community, "by the 1940s some St. Andrews descendants were denying that their families had ever had any contact with Aboriginal people, let alone were descended from marriages between European fur traders and Aboriginal or partly Aboriginal women."[11] When a plaque honouring Norquay was unveiled in the legislature, loud objections were raised to wording that included references to the premier's mixed ancestry.[12] Since Norquay, to date no leader of any of Manitoba's major parties is known to have Aboriginal ancestors. He would also be the last Manitoba-born person to lead the province until the Douglas Campbell in 1948.

Upon Norquay's departure from office, the premiership went to Ontario-born David Harrison, who was sworn into office on 26 December 1887. However, the new premier lacked sufficient support when the legislative session began on 17 January 1888. Harrison resigned a week later, and upon the election of Thomas Greenway's Liberal Party government, Norquay became leader of the opposition caucus. It would be a long hiatus on the opposition benches for the provincial Conservatives while Greenway was in power. The Liberals were able to win government power in the elections of 1888, 1892, and 1896, with popular support ranging from 50 to 57 percent.

The Roblin Era

Following Norquay's death in 1889, the Conservative Party underwent a decade-long period of general incoherence. More a faction than a party, opposition members were led by Rodmond Roblin from 1890 to 1892, William Alexander Macdonald in 1893, and John Andrew Davidson in 1894. The high turnover was mostly due to the unlucky electoral fortunes of each of these individuals. Roblin lost his seat in the election of 1892 while the latter two lost their ridings due to each having the results declared void. From 1894 to 1896, James Fisher was generally recognized as the opposition's leader in the house and, with Roblin's re-entry into the legislature in 1896, Roblin resumed this role. However, it was not until 1899 that the Conservative Party became an official organization, and this occurred with the linking of the provincial and federal wings of the Conservative Party under the leadership of Hugh John Macdonald, the son of John A. Macdonald.[13] The younger Macdonald's first visit to the western region was as a soldier taking part in Ottawa's action to quell the Red River Rebellion. He returned to Winnipeg after the death of his first wife and reluctantly entered federal politics—after much local prompting—prior to becoming leader of the provincial Conservatives. He was a lawyer by trade and had served as the MP for Winnipeg after being elected to the House of Commons in 1891 (but had soon lost the seat due to the results being challenged). With their new leader and the backing of the federal Conservative Party, the 1899 election provided a breakthrough opportunity. Macdonald was elected as premier with the Conservatives winning eighteen seats to the Liberals' seventeen seats. However, his stay in provincial politics would be brief. Before the end of his first year in office, Macdonald left the provincial scene (in part due to clashes with Roblin over prohibition legislation) to run federally against Clifford

Sifton in the riding of Brandon. According to John Dafoe, the prominent local Liberal and editor of the *Winnipeg Free Press*, it was "at the call of his father's colleague Sir Charles Tupper, and under pressure from some of his immediate political associates, whose advice was not wholly disinterested, [that] he gave up the Premiership," to enter the campaign.[14] After losing the election he returned to practising law and then became police magistrate for the City of Winnipeg.[15]

Organizationally, the Conservative Party under its new leader Rodmond Roblin[16] was, to use Murray Donnelly's description, a "political machine." Its success was demonstrated by winning successive elections and governing the province for a decade and a half.[17] As did Greenway's Liberals in previous years, the Conservatives drew support from the business establishment as well as farmers, but it also effectively won support from the various groups of newly arriving immigrants to Winnipeg. The city's total population had tripled from 42,340 in 1901 to 136,053 in 1911, and non-British immigrants formed part of this growth as a potentially important voting

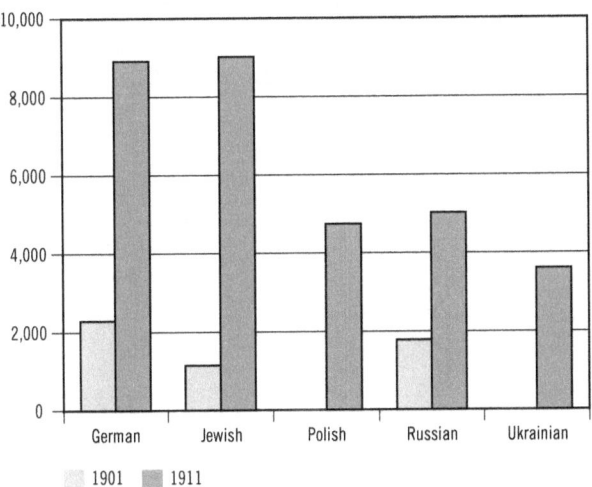

Figure 2.1: Dominion of Canada Census Figures, 1901, 1911

bloc (Figure 2.1).[18] The party's ability to capture this segment of the population led University of Manitoba political scientist Tom Peterson to compare Roblin's Conservatives to the American Democratic Party's "Tammany Hall," the prototypical big-city machine used for securing immigrant voter support in the American northeast.[19]

The Conservatives won majority governments in the elections of 1903, 1907, 1910, and 1914 with popular support ranging from 45 to 51 percent. During this period the Conservative government created North America's first large-scale publicly owned telephone system,[20] promoted the grain trade and railway development, and oversaw the construction of a new legislative building on Broadway. Furthermore, the provincial boundaries were expanded in 1912 to include an additional 168,000 square miles, the now existing northern portion of Manitoba. As the government expanded its activities, the seeds were planted for its downfall. In the first session following the Conservative victory of 1914, the Liberals called for an investigation into public expenditures involving the legislative building and accused the government of defrauding the public of $800,000. A Royal Commission, chaired by Hugh John Macdonald, soon found, among other things, that the

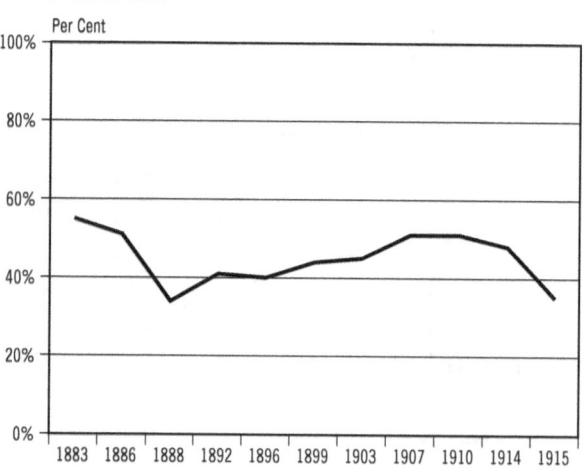

Figure 2.2: Compiled from Election Manitoba Historical Tables and *Manitoba Free Press*

Liberal charges were correct. Roblin announced his government's resignation and charges were laid.

James Aikins, known by many as "Jam" Aikins, a former Conservative MP for Brandon and the son of Lieutenant-Governor James C. Aikins, was chosen by 1500 party delegates on 14 July 1915 to serve as their new leader. Attempting to separate themselves from the previously discredited organization, Aikins's Conservatives ran as "Independent Conservatives" in 1915 and put forward a reformist platform, including the establishment of an independent Auditor General's office, temperance measures, and women's suffrage.[21] However, the voters wanted change, and the Conservatives went down to defeat at the hands of T.C. Norris's Liberals, gaining just 35 percent of the popular vote.

Two years after his resignation, criminal charges against Roblin and two other ministers were dismissed.[22] But, according to historian W.L. Morton, the consequences of the scandal were far-reaching, both for the Conservatives and for Manitoba politics in general. Morton writes that the scandal "involved more than a change of administration and the discrediting of the Roblin government. The revelations of the moral obtuseness of party workers and even ministers of the Crown, of the things which were done to raise funds to fight the blindly partisan elections of the day, discredited the party system in Manitoba. It was apparent that the Roblin government had been subdued to what it worked in, coarse and completely immoral party politics, and that the Conservative party had been captured by its machine."[23] More than forty years would have to pass before the Conservatives would again achieve government power. Oddly, the party would be led by Duff Roblin, the grandson of Rodmond Roblin.

The Winter Years
Following the 1915 defeat, which included also party leader Aikins's defeat in the riding of Brandon, a quick succession of leaders soon followed. Albert Prefontaine, who was known to speak out against the Liberal government measures to further reduce French-language rights in the province, led the

Conservatives from 1916 to 1920.[24] R.G. Willis, a politician described as having an "old country schoolhouse style of speaking" who would "flay away, hammer and tongs"[25] at his opposition, became the new leader in April 1920, just prior to the June 1920 election. To win the leadership, Willis had to first defeat future leader Fawcett Taylor, a local war hero and former mayor of Portage la Prairie. Four other candidates, including Prefontaine, withdrew from the leadership race prior to the vote. Prefontaine later switched parties and went on to serve in the United Farmers of Manitoba (which later reformed as the Progressives) government following the election of 1922 and served in Premier John Bracken's cabinet as minister of agriculture.[26]

Whatever pleasures Willis took by winning the leadership were short-lived. In the 1920 election he lost his own riding and the Conservatives won only 19 percent of the provincial vote.[27] John Haig took over the leadership from 1920 to 1922. Depicted by some as a capable orator who was able to capture public attention by his numerous speeches in the legislature, it was also said that he "often opened his mouth only to go away and leave it running."[28] In April 1922, he was replaced by Taylor.[29] The party performed

Figure 2.3:
Compiled from Elections Manitoba, "Historical Summaries"

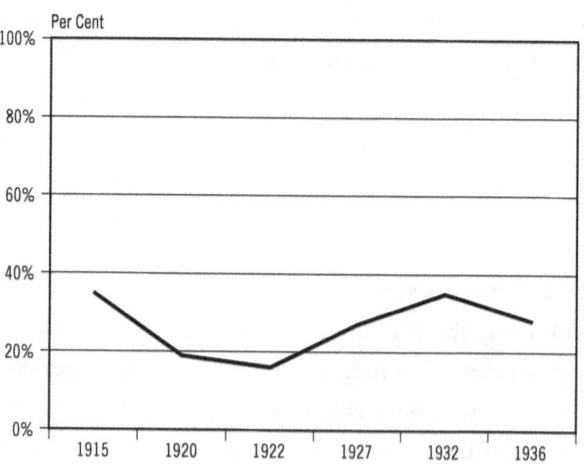

Provincial Conservative Party Support 1915 to 1936

poorly in the 1922 election by taking only seven seats in the face of the surging United Farmers (which took twenty-eight seats).

By 1927, the party's fortunes were improving and it became the official opposition. Memories of the previous decade's scandals were receding and the party organization was reported to be in good health.[30] The Conservatives' vote grew to 27 percent in the 1927 election, up from 16 percent in 1922. This provided fifteen seats compared to the third-place Liberals, who won only seven seats. However, through the machinations of the Liberals and their "fusion" with Premier Bracken's Progressives in the early 1930s, the Conservatives were kept from power even while their popular support increased to 35 percent in 1932. The Liberal-Progressives took three of the ten Winnipeg seats (compared to the same number for the Conservatives) and took 40 percent of the provincial vote, a level not achieved by any party since 1915. After eleven years at the helm, Taylor resigned as party leader in 1933 and was appointed to the Manitoba Court of King's Bench.

Following Taylor's resignation, Sanford Evans was chosen by the caucus to lead the party. He came with strong credentials. A respected member of the business community, Evans had been the editor for the *Winnipeg Telegram*, mayor of Winnipeg from 1905 to 1911, an investment broker, and an MLA since 1922, which included time as finance critic. However, Evans was viewed by some as too much part of the city's commercial elite[31] and "far less flamboyant and aggressive than Taylor." As a result, he was forced into retirement by the rural wing of the party prior to the 1936 election.[32] He was replaced by Errick Willis, a forty-year-old farmer from Boissevain and the son of R.G. Willis, who represented a return to the party's agrarian base. According to historian John Kendle: "With his folksy, down-to-earth style, Willis had a considerable appeal in the rural south and southwest where he concentrated his campaigning."[33]

Shortly after the 1936 election, in which Bracken's majority was reduced to a minority government, the premier invited Willis to fuse his Conservative Party with the governing Liberal-Progressives. The offer involved an odd arrangement in which Conservatives would enter the new cabinet with Bracken serving as premier for the first two years of the agreement and Willis taking over the office for the final two years. It was declined by Willis after a majority in his caucus voiced their opposition.[34] However, Bracken was able to salvage the situation by obtaining the support of the five elected Social Credit MLAs.[35] Four years later conditions would change. In 1940, Bracken claimed that a non-partisan government would be needed while Canada was at war with Germany and, perhaps more importantly, to have a united voice at the federal-provincial table as the Royal Commission on Dominion-Provincial Relations (commonly called the Rowell-Sirois Commission) was preparing to make its recommendations regarding the financial difficulties of such provinces as Manitoba.

Bracken succeeded in getting Willis's Conservatives to join his 1940 all-party coalition government, which would include in the cabinet three Conservatives (including Willis as minister of public works), one CCF, and one Social Credit representative. As part of the new plan, Bracken's idea was to have all sitting members acclaimed in the upcoming 1941 election. In a letter dated 25 October 1940, from the premier to Willis and the leaders of the other opposing parties, Bracken wrote, "In whatever we may do in this connection, if anything, there is involved no sacrifice or compromise of principles on your party or our own ... We are not today only CCF-Labor [sic] or Liberal-Progressive or Conservative or Social Credit, but rather Canadians and democrats and freemen. Our cause, even Manitoba's cause, is at this time greater than your party or our own."[36] The Conservatives accepted the offer and joined the coalition and Bracken's cabinet. In the 1941 election Willis led his party's slate of candidates as part of a pro-government campaign. Yet there were a few dissenting Conservatives who ran as opposition candidates, three of whom were elected to the legislature.

Some political scientists, such as Murray Donnelly, have since argued that participating in the coalition damaged the party in that it led to a loss of Conservative identity and organizational deterioration.[37] However, to put the provincial party's situation into context, it was a tough time to be a Conservative anywhere in Canada and the party appeared to be nearing extinction. Following the national election of 1940, the party held only forty seats in the House of Commons, and its leader, R.J. Manion, had gone down to defeat in his own riding. None of the provinces were operating under Conservative governments. Only five provinces contained a Conservative Party with an identifiable leader while the provincial Conservatives had virtually disappeared in Quebec, Alberta, and Saskatchewan.[38]

Duff Roblin and the Progressive Conservatives

With Errick Willis as their leader, and as part of the Liberal-Progressive coalition government, Conservative Party candidates ran as "Progressive Conservatives" for the first time in the 1945 provincial election. The national Conservative Party underwent a name change in response to concerns that it was increasingly seen as being out of step with the times. There were real fears that it would be replaced by the CCF as the electoral alternative to the Liberals if the Conservatives continued to operate with right-of-centre platforms. At a meeting held in Port Hope, Ontario, influential members within the party (what some called the "Hopefuls") recommended putting forward a "progressive" platform. Party leader Arthur Meighen (who operated without a seat in Parliament) then pushed for Bracken to be nominated as the new leader. Bracken ran for the leadership with the condition that the party would adopt the new name at its December 1942 convention, which was to be held in Winnipeg. The party agreed, but his election almost didn't occur. According to Bracken's wife in a letter to her sons: "everything had conspired to hold them up that night. Every traffic signal was against them, they got into a traffic jam, and arrived at one of the doors at five minutes to eight [the deadline for filing nomination papers], but it was not at the right entrance and had a reporter that knew Jack not been there it is doubtful if the committee would have gotten him in time to sign his nomination papers. As it was he had just one minute to spare when the signatures were attached."[39]

The provincial organization officially adopted the national party's new name at its 1946 annual conference in conjunction with a redesigned platform that was better suited to the post-war era. It called for an increase in old-age pensions, tariff reduction, and northern development.[40] Willis resigned from the cabinet in August 1950, and the governing coalition broke up, with three of the four Conservative members of the cabinet switching allegiance to the Liberal-Progressives. Willis remained loyal to his party and was confirmed as the party leader later that year.[41] However, the 1953 election was a disappointment for both the leader and his party. Only twelve PCs were elected, with 21 percent of the vote, compared to thirty-three Liberal-Progressives who, with 39 percent of the vote, continued to draw large amounts of support from southern farmers and South Winnipeg. Not helpful to their cause was the presence of Social Credit which drew 13 percent of the provincial vote, took Dauphin from the PCs, split the vote in the previously held PC ridings of Lansdowne, Portage La Prairie, and Rhineland, which were won by Liberal-Progressives, and drew sufficient numbers to damage the PCs in Minnedosa and Hamiota. It was clear that a new leader was needed.

Politics produce many coincidences, one of which is the fact that two Roblins, a grandfather and grandson, serve as historical bookends to the party's absence from power. For the most part, while they did elect candidates in Winnipeg, the Conservatives had been led by rurally oriented individuals. This would change with the arrival of Duff Roblin, who was first elected in 1949 as one of four members representing the riding of South Winnipeg in the legislature. Unlike most other Conservatives who supported the governing coalition, he ran as an "Independent PC" and sat with the opposition.

In 1954, Roblin and J. Arthur Ross, the MLA for the constituency of Arthur who had also served previously as the MP for Souris, challenged Willis for the leadership in what the *Winnipeg Free Press* would call "three months of bitter campaigning."[42] In light of Willis's "record of umpteen difficult years of somewhat limited success," Roblin reported that "I rated my prospects as promising."[43] The convention took place at the Royal Alexandra Hotel, where Willis led on the first ballot in the three-way race. On the second ballot Roblin won by 160 votes over Willis's 123 votes. Of those 160 votes for Roblin, 137 came from rural delegates, many of whom were Ross supporters, signifying that the Winnipeg-based MLA could bridge the party's rural-urban divide.[44] Aside from Sanford Evans's brief tenure as party leader, it was the first time since Hugh John Macdonald (from 1899 to 1900) that the party had a Winnipeg MLA as their leader.

Roblin soon found that many parts of the province lacked a local PC constituency organization. In one constituency, "wiseacres advised me to visit the graveyard because there I would find the only known Progressive Conservative supporters."[45] There were three elements in his strategy to rejuvenate the party: attract new and qualified candidates, reach beyond the party's WASPish base for support, and rejuvenate local constituency associations with new funds (which initially came partly from the Ontario PCs).[46] Murray Donnelly writes how Roblin energetically started to rebuild his party:

> His rule was to find the best possible man to run in each riding, get him nominated, and build the organization around him. The situation in Gimli was fairly typical. The Conservative organization there had been dead for forty years. Roblin simply went and inquired who was best known to the inhabitants of the area and, learning that it was Dr. George Johnson, sought him out and convinced him that he ought to accept nomination. Johnson was nominated, ran, won, and became minister of health in the Conservative government that took office in 1958. In June 1960 the Progressive Conservative party had an organization in every constituency.[47]

Now it was a good time to be a Conservative in Canada. In 1957, John Diefenbaker broke the national spell by defeating the long-ruling federal Liberals and winning a minority government, and followed this with his 31 March 1958 landslide victory. All fourteen Manitoba seats went to the PCs as part of the national sweep, in which 208 of 245 seats were taken. The lesson was not lost on the provincial PCs,[48] and in the June 1958 election, Roblin's PCs took power by obtaining 40 percent of the vote and twenty-six seats compared to the Liberal-Progressives' popular support figure of 35 percent, which garnered nineteen seats. Because the CCF held eleven seats (and with one seat going to Stephen Juba, who represented the riding of

Logan while also serving as the mayor of Winnipeg), the PCs had won a minority government.

One factor that contributed to the PCs' success under its more urban-oriented leader was that in 1957 the Manitoba legislature implemented a number of measures based on recommendations from the Electoral Divisions Boundaries Commission. These were aimed at correcting some of the more extreme disparities between rural and urban representation that benefitted the Liberal-Progressives. In 1953, for example, the Liberal-Progressives had won a majority government based chiefly on rural victories, with only three Winnipeg ridings and the multi-member riding of St. Boniface, which had elected two Liberal-Progressive MLAs. The 1957 correction was less than a complete solution, with the rural-urban bias partially resolved at a seven-to-four ratio, yet it was sufficient to help the PCs squeak into power the following year.[49]

Under its more youthful and photogenic leader (at least compared to both his predecessor Willis and his opponent, Premier Campbell), in 1958

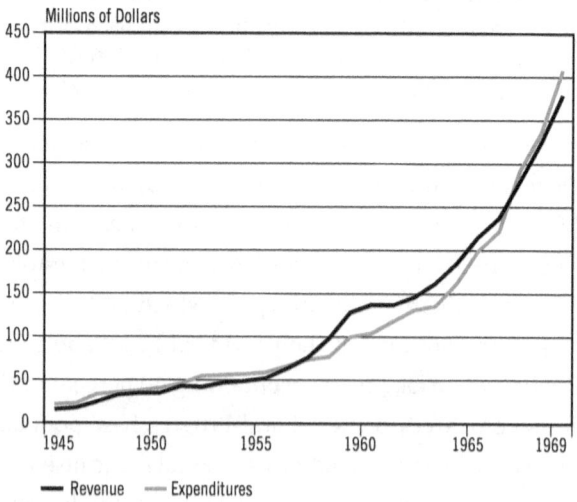

Figure 2.4:
Based on F.H. Leacy, Ed., *Historical Statistics of Canada*, 2nd Ed., Tables H124-135, H197-208

the PCs took ten Winnipeg ridings, mostly in the southern half of the city, including Fort Garry, in which a young Sterling Lyon was elected for the first time (he would serve in Roblin's cabinet and later become party leader and premier). The PCs also won in areas that would later become NDP strongholds: Seven Oaks, Wellington, Winnipeg Centre, and St. Matthews. With the exception of St. Boniface, the Liberal-Progressives were shut out of the city. The PCs were also successful in the North by taking the newly created seat of Churchill as well as Rupertsland and The Pas, which had previously been held by the Liberal-Progressives. The party also took Dauphin, which was the lone seat won by Social Credit in 1953, which effectively but temporarily wiped the Socreds from the electoral map. While the Social Credit vote damaged the PCs in 1953 by drawing 35,750 votes (13 percent) province-wide, it faded into a whimper in 1958 with only 5174 votes, less than 2 percent of the total popular vote.

Table 2.1: Percent Changes in Manitoba Government Expenditures by Sector, 1958 to 1969

Policy Sector	Percent Change
Health, Social Welfare	367
Education	591
Transportation and Communication	56
Natural Resources and Primary Industry	302
Other (including debt changes and transfers to municipalities)	309

Source: Dominion Bureau of Statistics, Provincial Government Finance, 1957, 1968[50]

The Manitoba PCs gained even more support following Diefenbaker's national landslide in 1958. In the 1959 provincial election, the party obtained 46 percent of the vote and a majority victory of thirty-six seats. The PCs won the northern riding of Flin Flon, which had previously been held by the Liberal-Progressives, as well as Churchill, and Rupertsland (which had their elections deferred from the 14 May election day to 11 June 1959). In Winnipeg, they again drew support from across all parts of the city, including Wellington and Winnipeg Centre. But it was in the rural parts of the province where the PCs did significant damage to the Liberal-Progressives by taking from them the ridings of Birtle-Russell, Dufferin, Lac du Bonnet, Minnedosa, Rockwood-Iberville, and Springfield. Clearly, by the late 1950s the PCs had moved beyond their southern rural and South Winnipeg business bases of support and looked poised to become the governing party of Manitoba for decades to come.

With the power of a majority government, Premier Roblin's government expanded the role of the provincial state by tripling public spending from 1958 to 1969, with much of it devoted to health care, social welfare, and education. In large part this corrected the previous Liberal-Progressive government's propensity to under spend. According to political scientist William Neville, "in the 11 years following Roblin's 1958 victory, public spending in Manitoba almost tripled; but spending on health and welfare increased by almost 370% and that on education by nearly 600%. Education's share, as a percentage of total public spending rose from 23% in 1958 to nearly 39% in 1969."[51] Figure 2.4 shows how provincial government spending (and revenues) escalated rapidly from the late 1950s onwards. Table 2.1 contains

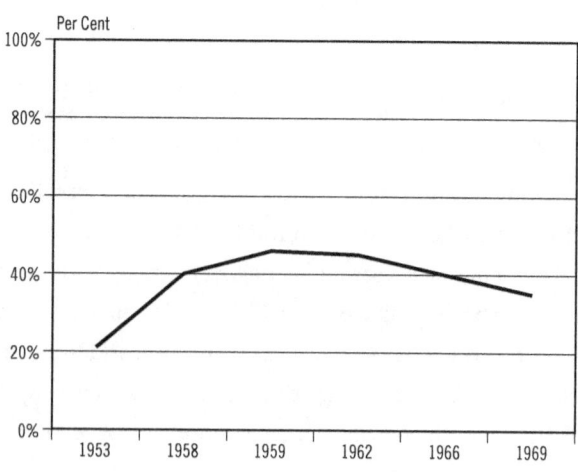

Figure 2.5: Source, Elections Manitoba, "Historical Summaries"

Provincial Conservative Party Support 1953 to 1969

greater detail by showing how provincial government expenditures grew exponentially in health and social welfare, education, and resource development. From 1958 to 1967, the Roblin government built 225 new schools, of which more than half were built between 1959 and 1961, during the early years of his administration.[52] It also established the Manitoba Development Fund (MDF) in 1958 to promote foreign investment. Unfortunately, $92 million of MDF funds were lost to the Churchill Forest Industries project when its Austrian investors disappeared with the money, a problem that Schreyer's NDP government was later to inherit in 1969.[53] Perhaps the most significant action taken by the Roblin government was to bring about the construction of the Winnipeg Floodway. Derisively called "Duff's Folly" by the opposition, the province committed itself to $26 million for its share of the cost (at a time in which the total provincial budget was $653 million). Added to this was a federal-provincial arrangement in which Ottawa contributed 55 percent of the cost, which had been negotiated in what Roblin recounts as a "small pokey hotel bedroom in Winnipeg" between Diefenbaker and himself.[54] Digging began on 6 October 1962, two months before the provincial election. Manitobans demonstrated their approval for the new direction that Roblin was taking both his party and the province. In contrast to the national party's fate, in which Diefenbaker dropped in national popular support from 54 percent to 37 percent between 1958 and 1962, Roblin and his provincial party maintained popular support during this same period. In December 1962, the Manitoba PCs were re-elected with 45 percent of the vote and thirty-six seats. Again, this was based on victories in all the major regions of the province.

In the 1966 provincial election, the PCs won their third majority victory in a row with 40 percent of the vote, producing 31 seats.[55] The PCs remained strong in the North and rural areas, while in Winnipeg support was receding in working-class neighbourhoods. The riding of Wellington, which was PC in 1959 and 1962, elected NDP candidate Philip Petursson, while in Winnipeg Centre the incumbent PC candidate, James Cowan, held onto his seat although NDP support jumped by 40 percent. In Kildonan, a riding that

PC candidate James Mills took by a mere four votes from the NDP in 1962 (and which had elected a CCF candidate in 1959), voters elected Peter Fox for the NDP by a margin of 836 votes.

Table 2.2: Selected North and Central Winnipeg Ridings: 1959 to 1969

	1959	1962	1966	1969
Kildonan	CCF	PC	NDP	NDP
St. Matthews	PC	PC	PC	NDP
Wellington	PC	PC	NDP	NDP
Winnipeg Centre	PC	PC	NDP	NDP

When Duff Roblin retired from the provincial scene to run for the federal party leadership in 1967 (coming in second to Robert Stanfield), he was replaced by Walter Weir who—after winning the party leadership against Sterling Lyon, Stewart McLean, and George Johnson—became the province's new premier on 25 November 1967. The PCs' choice of leader, a funeral director by occupation who was first elected in the riding of Minnedosa in 1959, signalled a shift back to the more rurally based "small government, low tax" orientation for the party. According to Roblin, who applauded Weir's record as a cabinet minister, "like the rest of us, he was a creature of his own background. He had little feel for urban affairs, particularly for urban politics, and he surrounded himself with men of his own stamp."[56] The new premier quickly reversed his predecessor's bilingualism policies and slowed down medical care reform.[57] Many of these policy reversals were aimed at controlling taxation rates that were heightened by his predecessor's propensity to spend. The party's new direction was noted by a *Winnipeg Free Press* editorial that stated "it will be a refreshing change to have a premier who is intent on keeping taxes down."[58]

In early 1969, Weir looked like he would win the next provincial election. The party had been in power since the 1950s and had scored a number of recent by-election victories, and polls were showing the PCs leading both the Liberals and the NDP. To quote Proverbs, "pride comes before a fall." Weir called an election for 25 June 1969, while both opposition parties were in the process of choosing new leaders. According to political scientist Tom Peterson's account of the election, Weir spent much of his campaign travelling to the province's southwest, where traditional Tory support was already strong. Weir's low-key approach caused the *Winnipeg Free Press* to report that the PC campaign "has been conspicuous by its apparent absence."[59] This ill-conceived strategy was in contrast to the highly televised NDP leadership campaign that was underway between Edward Schreyer and Sidney Green. The victor, Schreyer, was able to reach out to many of the province's various ethnic groups while also bridging the urban-rural divide of the province by attracting farmers in the marginal farming areas as well as the North. On election day, the PCs' popular support fell to 35 percent (from 40 percent in 1966), leaving the party with twenty-two seats. This was six seats less than the NDP's twenty-eight seats based on 38 percent of the vote (which was up from the NDP's 23 percent in 1966).

The 1970s and the Lyon's Roar

The 1969 defeat brought to the fore the rural-urban division within the party. Walter Weir represented the traditional WASPish, rural and small-town side of the party membership, which appeared to be increasingly disconnected from the party's urban wing. He would be replaced by Sidney Spivak, an urban MLA (for the riding of River Heights) who had served in Roblin's cabinet. He was also known as a respected lawyer, successful businessman, and the son of lawyer Malek Spivak. The elder Spivak had been an early supporter of Roblin in helping marshal Jewish support for the party. Years later Roblin revealed his admiration for the son: "He came to the legislature and to his portfolio of industry and commerce with a fresh look and new enthusiasm marked by innovative ideas and energetic applications. He soon proved [to be] an engaging debater with a deceptively smiling demeanour … He was later a strong and successful candidate to replace Walter Weir as leader of the party."[60] However, Weir and many of his supporters were not yet ready to relinquish the leadership. At the November 1969 PC annual meeting, it was reported that Spivak was seeking the leader's position but "lacked support from the party's rural British base."[61] He therefore settled for the position of party president. At the February 1971 leadership convention, representing the urban and more moderate wing of the party against the more right-wing rural MLA Harry Enns, Spivak became the new leader by a vote of 261 to 215.[62] The difference in style between the two candidates was noted by the *Winnipeg Tribune*: "Mr. Spivak's campaign was peppered with issues and proposals while his opponent maintained 'the best policies in the world aren't worth a damn if we don't get elected.'"[63]

Unfortunately for Spivak, he was at the right place but at the wrong time. Manitobans had never rejected a governing party that was seeking a second term, which was what Schreyer and his NDP were trying to do in 1973. Schreyer's popularity was high across most parts of the province. The result was that Spivak and his PCs were able to increase their popular vote by only two percentage points over the 1969 results. They won 37 percent of the vote, which produced twenty-one seats (compared to the NDP's twenty-three seats) with support confined to southern rural ridings and South Winnipeg.[64] Not since 1953, when they took only twelve seats, had the PCs won so few seats. And it would not be until 2003 that they would be held to twenty seats again. However, the 1973 election results did not produce the type of victory for which NDP supporters were hoping. According to the post-election coverage in the *Winnipeg Tribune*, "It's a very strange election when the winner should be disappointed while the loser is a kind of winner. The PCs won a moral victory by simply standing still. Why? Because they faced a government with as good a record as any in Canada, a government that had kept its promises and maintained a close human relationship with the electorate."[65]

Following the election, disgruntlement quickly arose among members of the rural wing who had never felt attached to Spivak's moderate urban pragmatism or his Jewish background. Added to this was the fact that a new strain of neo-conservatism was growing within the party's membership in response to widespread concerns regarding inflation, unemployment, and a problematic provincial investment climate.[66] Across the industrial West, governments came to be seen as the problem rather than the solution. Compared to successful neo-conservative leaders such as Margaret Thatcher (who became the leader of the British Conservatives in 1975), and, later, American President Ronald Reagan, Manitoba's "Red Tories," including Duff Roblin and Spivak, appeared out of step with the times.

During the mid-1970s, Sterling Lyon became a perfect fit for the new times by forging together support from the PCs' rural wing and urban neo-conservatives. Lyon was first elected in 1958 for the urban riding of Fort Garry and served in Roblin's cabinet throughout the 1960s. In 1967, he finished second by lasting until the third ballot at the leadership convention in which Weir was made party leader. He did not run in the 1969 election, but in the 1974 federal election resurfaced to challenge (unsuccessfully) Jim Richardson in Winnipeg South and then returned to the provincial scene by challenging Spivak's leadership in 1975. The bitter lead-up to the convention included legal battles over delegate selection procedures, accusations of anti-Semitism,[67] and even fist fights. With support from nineteen of the twenty-three sitting PC MLAs, eight of the nine federal PC MPs, as well as rural delegates, urban neo-conservatives, and business interests, Lyon took the leadership from Spivak at the 1975 convention by a vote of 264 to 207.[68]

In the 1977 election, the PCs under Lyon smashed the NDP and Liberals with 49 percent of the vote, something not seen by any party since 1915. The PCs had thirty-three seats to the NDP's twenty-three seats, and the Liberals were reduced to a lone member (Lloyd Axworthy). In large part it was the Liberal collapse that helped the PCs. According to the *Winnipeg Tribune*'s post-election analysis: "The Progressive Conservatives won a majority government Tuesday night because of the collapse of the Liberal party and a re-alignment in Manitoba politics. The right wing in Manitoba has coalesced. The left wing remains divided. Liberal leader Charles Huband's strong campaign wasn't enough to save his party from the ravages of polarization. But it was enough, and of an urban social reform nature, to retain the small-l liberals and account for much of the NDP's popular vote drop."⁶⁹ But something more significant had occurred. The PCs had been elected with a platform that included pro-business policies, government cutbacks, and lower taxes. However, the party had been sufficiently astute to avoid making any threats to pharmacare for the elderly or the generally popular public automobile insurance program.⁷⁰ For Manitobans it was a throwback to the Weir interlude as well as the pre-Roblin Liberal-Progressive era. Others, such as *Winnipeg Tribune* columnist Vic Grant, used the language of the day by describing it as a success for "free enterprise" over the NDP's socialism.⁷¹ It was no surprise, therefore, that the new government proceeded quickly to instigate a number of cutbacks and dismissals of civil servants. Murray Donnelly in his review of the political events of 1977 would wryly remark that "all this, with the prospect of more to come, made New Year's celebrations at the Manitoba Club unusually cheerful."⁷²

The celebrations were short-lived. Manitoba's economy continued to falter, in contrast to those of Saskatchewan and Alberta, which were enjoying the benefits of an energy boom. In April 1981, towards the end of the government's first term in office, Finance Minister Brian Ransom

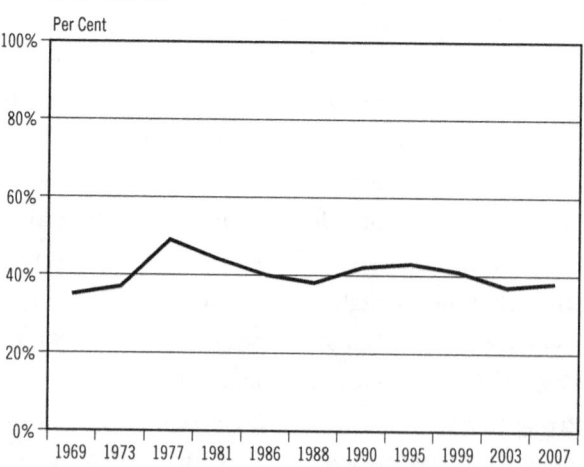

Figure 2.6:
Compiled from Elections Manitoba, "Historical Summaries"

presented a budget containing an operating deficit of $219.8 million. For a province of one million citizens, this signified $219.80 per individual, and while such provincial shortfalls could be traced to broader economic problems in Canada and in other countries, it was an embarrassment for a party that had campaigned on the issue of fiscal restraint. In spite of the province's economic woes, the Fall 1981 election began with the PCs leading the polls,[73] but a number of factors would lead to the PCs' defeat as the campaign proceeded. Lyon, a strong opponent to the impending constitutional entrenchment of the Charter of Rights and Freedoms, was distracted by a federal-provincial conference that overlapped with the campaign's commencement. Lyon's strong personality was off-putting to some, especially women who remembered his flippant remark that "women make good breeders" when defending his government's actions regarding new family-law legislation. In contrast to Lyon's pugilistic demeanour, NDP leader Howard Pawley appeared bland yet predictably decent. The PCs campaign slogan and TV advertisements shouting "Don't Stop Us Now!"—a reference to economic development through "megaprojects"—unsettled those who also took this to mean ongoing government cutbacks and underfunded social programs. Moreover, the PCs appeared ill-prepared compared to the NDP, which had candidates already nominated in important ridings while enjoying a surge in membership.[74]

In the 1981 election, PC support dropped to 44 percent of the popular vote, a figure which is usually sufficient to win power in Manitoba. Yet with support overly concentrated in southern rural ridings, it proved insufficient to counter the NDP's 47 percent province-wide share of the vote. The PCs' geographic imbalance allowed the NDP to more effectively translate its own support into seats, and with only a three-percentage-point gap between the two front-running parties, the NDP took thirty-four seats to the PCs' twenty-three seats, while the Liberals received only 7 percent of the popular vote and no seats in the legislature. The *Winnipeg Free Press* would write the next day in its post-election editorial: "The decisive victory of Howard Pawley and the New Democratic Party in yesterday's general election was a tribute to splendid organization, a skilful campaign and moderate leadership. It reflects as well four years of a Conservative approach to government which effectively narrowed that party's appeal in the province, and to a dismal election campaign that did nothing to broaden that appeal. There is persuasive evidence that a substantial number of Manitobans now regard the New Democrats as the party of moderation."[75] Yet the editorial missed a more significant point by focussing on seat results rather than vote totals, results which signified a mounting polarization between the two major parties: a left-of-centre social democratic party and the right-of-centre PCs. It also signalled a growing urban-rural divide. Contrary to what editorial writers at the *Winnipeg Free Press* thought, what would follow would reveal that the 1981 results were no harbinger of a moderating political climate in Manitoba.

The Filmon Era

Lyon did not quickly retire after the 1981 defeat, and as leader of the opposition led a vitriolic attack against the NDP government's measures to introduce legislation regarding bilingualism and French-language services in Manitoba.[76] Using excessive language to attack Pawley's government, including accusations of "tyranny," "zealotry," and of creating a state of "chaos," the negative tone of debate made for an uncomfortable atmosphere in the legislature while doing nothing to moderate the PCs' right-of-centre image.[77] It would take a new leader to do this, and the opportunity came in 1983 when Lyon announced that he would resign so that a successor could be chosen at a December leadership convention.

The party was at a crossroads, with three candidates representing different elements within the party. Brian Ransom, the MLA for Turtle Mountain who had served as Lyon's finance minister, chiefly represented the small-c rural wing and was seen by many to be the front runner with support from many who had supported Lyon against Spivak in 1976. Gary Filmon, an engineer by training and an MLA for the Winnipeg riding of Tuxedo, who had served briefly as a junior minister in Lyon's cabinet, represented the more pragmatic urban wing and thereby drew support from those who had previously supported Spivak in 1976. Placed at a distant third in the race was Clayton Manness, a young MLA representing the rural riding of Morris, who drew support from both neo-conservatives and rural delegates.

Filmon was elected on the second ballot by a vote of 297 to Ransom's 251 and Manness's seventy-one.[78] In retrospect, it was a wise choice for a party needing to reach beyond South Winnipeg and southern Manitoba. Although Filmon represented the affluent riding of Tuxedo, he played up his North End background and eastern European heritage, thus attracting voters across different social classes and neighbourhoods. Furthermore, unlike Weir, Lyon, or Ransom, he could be described as a "pluralist" rather than small-c conservative in that he understood society as containing a wide array of social groupings and economic interests, each having its own legitimate concerns. Filmon believed that voters in Manitoba wanted moderate leaders and moderate parties. "The vast majority of Manitobans are at the centre of the political spectrum," he said.[79] On the day after the convention, Frances Russell summed up his victory as follows: "in 1975, the establishment triumphed, while on Saturday, it was the reformers' turn."[80] Evidence that Filmon represented moderate urban members was further demonstrated by the support he received from Spivak, who was quoted in the *Winnipeg Free Press* as saying that Filmon "has fresher and newer people with him who will bring forth new ideas and energy," and city councillor and political scientist William Neville's view that Filmon represented a coalition of disaffected conservatives, new Canadians, and northerners.[81]

Research at the time by the author revealed the geographic divisions among Manitoba's Progressive Conservatives. Three other political science graduate students at the University of Manitoba (Shona Connelly, Eugene Hazen, and Anna-Marie Konopelny) and I conducted a confidential survey based on one hundred interviews of the party's delegates prior to the December 1983 convention. Our results revealed stark geographic divisions. Ransom was strongly supported by delegates representing the rural riding associations while Filmon drew support from among the urban associations. Manness placed a distant third yet was supported as the second choice of most delegates, revealing the deep rift that existed between the two front-runners.

Filmon was resolved to demonstrate a freshly moderate approach in his early days as leader of the opposition, especially over the bitterly fought issue of French-language services. However, he needed to deal with opponents within his own caucus. According to one *Winnipeg Free Press* report: "Twice prior to the [legislative] session's opening, Filmon opened the door to some accommodation with the government and twice had his caucus tear his olive branch apart."[82] The new leader was undeterred and by 1986, with the departure of Lyon and Ransom promoted a generally pragmatic platform based on the need for a less costly yet well-functioning pro-business government. By doing so, he was able to bridge the gulf between the intra-party factions. However, these two were replaced by other but perhaps less powerful dissenters within the party caucus, including Don Orchard and Clayton Manness, who party insiders believed were leading a "Roman Guard" bent upon slaying their leader.

In the 1986 election the PCs came close to defeating the NDP by winning 40 percent of the popular vote compared to the NDP's 41 percent. Again, by more efficiently translating popular support into seats, the NDP was re-elected with thirty seats to the PCs' twenty-six, while the Liberals regained a presence in the legislature with Sharon Carstairs winning River Heights. John Laschinger, a long-time Ontario PC campaign strategist who was brought into Manitoba to help the Filmon campaign, provides an interesting backroom perspective. He recounts how on the Friday prior to the Tuesday election a PC poll conducted by Decima Research had the PCs leading by 3.5 percent over the NDP. Later that day Angus Reid released a poll showing the NDP *ahead* by a whopping 9 percent. "Then on Monday," writes Laschinger, "Howard Pawley's father died and Conservative attempts to control the damage of the Reid poll were swept away on a wave of public sympathy for the NDP premier and his family."[83] (Laschinger appears unaware that Schreyer's father died one week prior to the 1977 election, an event which had no discernible effect on the outcome.)

Two years later, the PCs finally took power, largely due to the NDP's collapse. By 1988, Pawley and the NDP were exhausted from dealing with dissent from within its own caucus, fallout from the French-language issue, internal divisions regarding the legalization of abortion clinics, growing budget deficits, and anger over escalating public automobile insurance rates.[84] Furthermore, the NDP, under its new leader, Gary Doer, was fighting a two-front battle in Winnipeg: against a moderated PC party under Filmon and the re-energized Liberals under Carstairs. Many PCs were disappointed when, in 1988, they were contained to a minority government based on 38 percent of the vote with twenty-five seats in the legislature, one less than in 1986. However, they did better when compared to the NDP's twelve, and were shocked to see the Liberals become the new official opposition with twenty candidates elected (with the exception of Selkirk, all were elected in Winnipeg ridings).

The minority government, which lasted from 1988 to 1990, gave both Filmon and his PCs an opportunity to show themselves as pragmatic moderates rather than the neo-conservative ideologues of the previous era. To help heal social divisions within the province, not to mention the rift between the PCs and the Franco-Manitoban community, the very first action performed by the Filmon government in the legislature in 1988 was to have Denis Rocan become Speaker of the House. It was a deeply symbolic gesture for the new premier. In addressing the assembly, Filmon stated that "as the first Franco-Manitoban Speaker of our Legislature, the Honourable Members' selection will serve to recognize the contribution that all Franco-Manitobans have provided to our province in the past and will provide, indeed, in the years to come."[85]

The first PC government budget was a pragmatic policy instrument based chiefly on the 1988 campaign platform: no new taxes, deficit reduction, expanded spending on health and community services, drought relief spending to help farmers, and the phasing out of the payroll tax which was introduced by the NDP and despised by the business community.⁸⁶ On 6 November 1989, Filmon's government tabled legislation dictating that "services provided by the Government of Manitoba shall be offered, to the extent possible, in both official languages in areas where the French-speaking population is concentrated."⁸⁷ This was, according to political scientist Raymond Hébert, "a stronger policy than that of the Pawley government, although it was applied somewhat haphazardly through the 1990s."⁸⁸ In the meantime, Premier Filmon continued to pull together the different factions within his caucus, including neo-conservative and rural elements. Towards this end, he appointed Clayton Manness to cabinet as government house leader and minister of finance.

Unplanned circumstances came to the aid of the Filmon minority government and helped the premier appear as a national figure, which in turn promoted the PCs' chances to build voter support at home. Prior to the 1988 Manitoba provincial election, Prime Minister Brian Mulroney attempted to revise the Constitution by negotiating with the provinces, including the Manitoba government under Pawley, which resulted in the Meech Lake Accord. Upon taking power, Premier Filmon endorsed the accord by presenting it to the legislature on 16 December 1988. However, he quickly reversed his support after the Quebec government invoked the notwithstanding clause to restrict English language rights. Filmon argued that Quebec's action was "not in the spirit of the Meech Lake Accord." In her summary of events that transpired, Ingeborg Boyens writes that "[Quebec Premier] Bourassa's decision to appease Quebec nationalists provoked particular anger amongst English-speaking Manitobans who had endured their own political convulsions over minority language rights. Filmon knew his sudden about-face would be popular with voters. He also knew his opportunistic reversal would irrevocably damage his relationship with Brian Mulroney."⁸⁹ Filmon appointed a well-respected labour mediator and political scientist, Wally Fox-Decent, to chair the all-party Manitoba task force that would hold public hearings regarding the accord. Over 300 presentations were made by groups and individuals to the task force.⁹⁰

Concerns about the accord began to be raised elsewhere in the country, and in the spring of 1990 the prime minister invited all the premiers to a First Ministers meeting in Ottawa. In order to provide a united front, Filmon brought Carstairs and Doer to the discussions. Behind the scenes, and within all three parties, much political manoeuvring was occurring, including debates over procedures, accusations that legislative hearings were being packed in order to frustrate the resolution's passage, and lobbying by federal party officials as well as activists within the provincial-party ranks.[91] After what was described as "relentless federal pressure," and fears that rejecting the accord would lead to the breakup of Canada, all three provincial leaders gave their endorsement. However, if a resolution of endorsement were to meet the accord's expiration deadline of 23 June 1990, the provincial government needed to sidestep the lengthy process that occurs prior to a bill being passed in the legislature.

Suspending the rules of the House required the unanimous consent of all fifty-seven MLAS, which was denied by NDP MLA Elijah Harper, who argued that the accord had been negotiated without proper consultations with the Aboriginal community. In his account of this period in the Manitoba legislature, Lloyd Fridfinnson captures the drama of the moment when Harper blocked the accord's passage:

> Given that all three party leader leaders had endorsed the deal, agreement was considered likely. Several backbenchers from each party had expressed reservations about the accord, but they were expected to fall into line. It seemed no one took seriously the concerns of Elijah Harper, the lone aboriginal MLA, who felt Meech Lake was fundamentally flawed in that aboriginals were excluded from the constitutional negotiations.... On June 12, and in the days to follow, Premier Filmon asked members of the legislature for leave to proceed with a motion on the constitutional amendments. Harper steadfastly denied the unanimous consent of the legislature. On June 22, the final day before the deadline, a packed house watched as Harper held a symbolic eagle feather, leaned into the microphone and uttered the dramatic refusal: "No, Mr. Speaker" for the seventh and final time. A native trapper from northern Manitoba had killed Prime Minister Mulroney's deal.[92]

Of all three party leaders, the premier gained the most by events leading up to the accord's defeat: the pressure-filled Ottawa meetings, calls from the prime minister, and media scrums, all of which were endured by Filmon who appeared, to use the words of political scientist Geoffrey Lambert, as "a pragmatist and problem-solver, as perhaps befits a professional engineer... In the aftermath of Meech Lake ... his reassuring public persona was of considerable benefit to his party."[93] This contrasted with the Liberals' Carstairs, who appeared volatile and vulnerable. The outcome of all this was that the PCs began hovering above 50 percent in the provincial polls, just in time for the provincial election of 1990.[94] As the party moved into the campaign they faced a weakened Liberal leader and an NDP that was still rebuilding itself.

Due to Brian Mulroney's unpopularity in Manitoba, the provincial party distanced itself from the PC label in the 1990 election. It did so by running candidates under the "Filmon Team" banner. Similar to how the federal Liberals caused problems for the Manitoba Liberals in the 1970s, Mulroney and the federal PCs made life difficult for the Manitoba PCs in the 1980s and early 1990s due to actions taken on a number of sensitive issues. Against the wishes of Manitoba's PC MPs, Mulroney supported a policy of official bilingualism in Manitoba. Prime Minister Trudeau set an early trap for the new Leader of the Opposition by introducing a resolution in the House of Commons that called for the Manitoba government to hold an immediate vote on the French-language services legislation rather than allow the bill to die on the order papers. Temporarily defusing an open battle between his Manitoban MPs and those of other regions, Mulroney asked those representing Manitoba ridings to be absent from Ottawa during the debate and ensuing vote. Addressing the House of Commons, Mulroney said, "I acknowledge, Mr. Speaker, that the view in some areas of western Canada is different ... It is neither pernicious nor benighted. It is simply different. It is different because the evolution of western Canada did not in some very important respects parallel the evolution in the east."[95]

Regional divisions exploded later when, as prime minister, Mulroney supported a decision to award a $2 billion CF-18 fighter jet maintenance contract to Quebec's Canadair rather than to Winnipeg's Bristol Aerospace, the latter having what was considered by many to have submitted a technically superior and lower-cost proposal. Although the federal government's decision occurred in 1986 while the NDP was still in power in Manitoba, it threw a bad light on the federal PCs throughout the West and served as a rallying cry for those seeking to build a new regional party.[96] According to Murray Dobbin, the PC government's behaviour surrounding the CF-18 contract "signalled to many westerners that Quebec interests would override those of the West."[97] Adding fuel to the fire, Mulroney's introduction of the new Goods and Services Tax (GST) produced anti-PC rallies, including a Winnipeg rally hosted by the Reform Party which drew 1000 angry attendees.[98]

While Filmon and the provincial PCs were distancing themselves from the federal party in public, behind the scenes they relied on the federal party for a "direct mail and computerized soliciting systems that gave voters the impression they were receiving a personalized letter from Filmon."[99] In the end, the combined use of federal party resources with a campaign that downplayed the PC Party label produced a win with thirty seats based on 42 percent of the popular vote. An examination of the 1990 results shows that the Filmon breakthrough was very different from Roblin's majority victories in that the Filmon victory was based on solid wins across southern Manitoba and the southern half of Winnipeg. The PCs were shut out from the northern half of the province, where the NDP held onto its northern base of support by winning Flin Flon, Rupertsland, The Pas, and Thompson, and Winnipeg's North End, where the NDP recaptured many of the seats it lost in 1988. Although the victory was less than sweeping, it was a majority government win, and the PCs were now free of the demands of the other parties in the legislature. New problems surfaced, however, in the early 1990s due to an underperforming economy and federal government cutbacks. In order to avoid increasing the provincial debt, the provincial government needed to implement austerity measures in a number of sectors, including health care and education.

The 1995 campaign operated with the same strategy as that which was used in 1990. This time the words were reversed and candidates ran under the "Team Filmon" banner (instead of "The Filmon Team"), again with few references to the PC Party label. According to one poll at the time, Filmon was receiving 70 percent approval ratings across the province, leading his chief strategist, Taras Sokolyk, to argue that the "Team Filmon" strategy made sense in that his party "is wider than the PC party in the past ... the premier has done this on his own popularity and integrity."[100] The PCs won 43 percent of the popular vote and thirty-one seats, and had now won three successive elections, including two majority governments. It appeared that the next election would also go their way, as indicated by an early 1998 Angus Reid provincial poll showing that 52 percent approved of the PC government's performance since 1995 and that "the Progressive Conservatives are in a strong first place position" for the next election with an 11 percent lead over the NDP.[101]

1999 and After

Support for the PCs would not hold true. In the 1999 election, the PCs lost power by winning only twenty-four seats compared to the NDP's thirty-two seats. In large part the defeat was due to a swing of urban voters from both the PCs and Liberals to the NDP. PC popular support declined slightly, from 43 percent to 41 percent between 1995 and 1999, the NDP went from 33 percent to 44 percent, and the Liberals achieved only 13 percent. With only a three-point difference between the two front-runners, the NDP had used its support more efficiently by linking together that of northern regions and Winnipeg's North End. The NDP took all of the northern portions of Winnipeg, the North, and ridings straddling the South and North: the Interlake and Dauphin-Roblin. The NDP also pushed the PCs back in four southern Winnipeg ridings, St. Vital, Lord Roberts, Riel, and Fort Rouge, which signalled what would become a long-term trend.

There were two strong factors that caused PC-voter defections. One was of the party's own making while the other was not. The first factor was a scandal involving the Premier's chief of staff, Taras Sokolyk, and Julian Benson, who was secretary to the Treasury Board. When the story broke on the CBC on 22 June 1998, the public learned that PC funds had been secretly and illegally used to support three Aboriginal candidates (two of whom ran under the First Peoples' Party banner) in an unsuccessful attempt to split the NDP vote.[102] The issue dogged the premier with questions raised about his government's ethics, not to mention the cynical exploitation of Aboriginal voters.[103] According to polls and commentary, a number of Manitobans thought that Filmon had been aware of his staff's scandalous activities.[104]

Retired Manitoba Chief Justice Judge Alfred Monnin, who headed the inquiry into the matter, concluded that "Premier Gary Filmon testified that he was not aware of the plot or the cover-up and I find his evidence to be credible."[105] Many were relieved, yet Filmon's situation could be compared to that of Prime Minister Paul Martin, who was unable to sufficiently distance himself from those who had been responsible for the Liberal Party's advertising scandal in Quebec. Martin's dilemma led to his government's defeat in 2006. In Manitoba, the statute of limitations prevented legal action being taken against the perpetrators, yet the government and the PC Party's reputation were damaged, especially when Monnin was quoted widely from the inquiry's report saying that "in all my years on the bench, I never encountered as many liars in one proceeding as I did in this inquiry."[106]

The second factor in the 1999 defeat was largely due to federal government fiscal policy. From 1996 to 1999 the federal Liberals reduced social transfers to the provinces by a total of $6 billion.[107] Rather than increase taxes or run budget deficits to meet budgetary shortfalls, the Filmon government took a turn to the ideological right by cutting social spending and selling the province's publicly owned telephone system. The Manitoba Telephone System (MTS) thereby became a publicly traded corporation at the beginning of 1997, while "hallway medicine," a term used for leaving patients in the corridors, sometimes unattended, became a widespread concern. Six months prior to the 1999 election, a poll of 600 Winnipeg voters revealed that 30 percent thought that health care was a major issue facing the province, while 36 percent of those aged fifty-five and over (and who exhibit higher voter turnout rates) identified this as a major area of concern.[108]

What was Filmon's legacy? The day after the PCs' defeat, a sympathetic *Winnipeg Free Press* reported, "Despite the challenges, Filmon's government has proven to be a strong manager of the province's finances, with balanced budget legislation and careful attention to debt reduction."[109] Yet Filmon accomplished much more than this. Under their leader's guidance, the PCs were able to reduce the deep divisions that had occurred over the French-language crisis (albeit partly of their own making under Lyon), steered the province through the troubled waters of constitutionalism, coped with the effects of federal-government cutbacks, and managed the day-to-day operations of the provincial government.

The Post-Filmon Era

On the night of his government's defeat, Filmon announced his retirement from politics. Needless to say, the PCs were left with a number of challenges. First, the party would need to distance itself from the vote-splitting scandal that had factored into the 1999 defeat. Secondly, the PCs needed to recapture the support of urban-based swing voters, many of whom had become disaffected over spending cutbacks in health and education and the impact of the party's emphasis on balanced budgets. Thirdly, it had to competently perform as the official opposition. Fourthly, it would have to develop new and effective campaign strategies to replace the "Filmon Team" approach.

One way to do these things was to find a new and effective leader who could win support across all parts of the province. The party membership thought that it had found one when Stuart Murray put his name forward. Having been raised on a Saskatchewan farm, educated at the University of Manitoba and Ryerson Polytechnical Institute in Toronto, then later becoming CEO of Domo Gasoline, Murray initially drew support among both rural and urban members. Although never elected, he had a strong record as a party organizer, including work for the federal PCs in the mid-1980s and directing various aspects of the provincial PC campaigns in 1990, 1995, and 1999. When he announced his candidacy for the leadership, he was endorsed by the party establishment, including influential Winnipeg business leaders Hartley Richardson, Sandy Riley, and Bob Kozminski. His one would-be challenger, Darren Praznik, the long-time MLA for Lac du Bonnet who had come close to losing his riding in 1999 (he won by 149 votes), withdrew from the race six months prior to the convention claiming, in the words of one organizer, that "there was a group of people who wanted to control the party at any cost. What they basically did was cut off the taps ... People said they had been told not to support us."[110] Regardless of some bad feelings within certain quarters of the party, Murray was acclaimed on 4 November 2000, and subsequently entered the legislature as the MLA for Kirkfield Park in a by-election of that same year.[111] At the time it appeared as if the party had made a smart move by avoiding a full-blown leadership contest with its predictable bloodbath. In retrospect, it was a mistake in that an opportunity was missed for re-energizing the membership and for testing the mettle of whomever would become the new leader.

The first years in opposition were problematic for Murray and the PCs, in part due to a lack of sufficiently skilled advisors. In addition to losing Sokolyk and Benson (due to the vote-splitting scandal), many of Filmon's advisors departed following the 1999 defeat, including chief of staff Hugh McFadyen (who would later take over the leadership in 2006) and communications director Bonnie Staples-Lyon. Conditions worsened when provincial polls revealed a steady decline in support between the 1999 defeat, in which the party won 41 percent of the vote, and March 2002, in which support dropped to 30 percent (with the Liberals at 21 percent). In an attempt to address the situation, Murray compounded his problems by hiring Sokolyk as a consultant to help create policy and party positioning strategies. Claims were made in the press that Murray had done the hiring in secret without consulting with his caucus, a fact that Murray strongly disputes.[112] However, it resurrected for the public the PCs' vote-splitting scandal and would haunt the leader for the remainder of his tenure.[113]

In the 2003 election, the PCs under Murray faced off against a popular centrist NDP government. However, the PCs appeared old-fashioned by campaigning on government spending issues and tax cuts. Among their promises was the removal of post-secondary tuition freezes, an unpopular platform for many middle-class voters who were funding their children's studies. The party was also hampered by new financing laws for provincial parties, introduced in 2001, that banned corporate and union contributions while reducing annual individual contributions to $3000. With the PCs strongly dependent on the business community, the impact was enormous. This was soon made apparent when, just after the rules were put into place, party revenues dropped from $1.28 million in 2000 to just under $400,000 ($393,674) in 2001.[114] In the 2003 election, funding shortages meant that the PCs were unable to purchase sufficient media to mount a strongly visible campaign.[115]

The PCs' popular vote in the 2003 election was reduced from 41 percent to 36 percent, yet it was not much less than Filmon's 1988 victory, in which

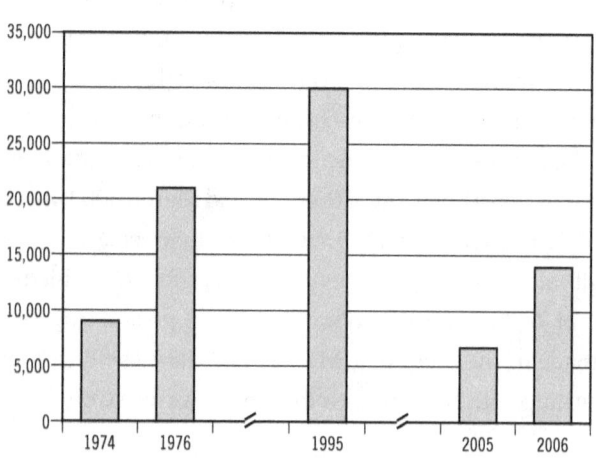

Figure 2.7:
Compiled from various sources[118]

PC MEMBERSHIP
1974 to 2006

38 percent voted PC. The outcome for the party was twenty seats, which was its worst showing since 1953. However, some were relieved that it was a better figure than the twelve seats that were predicted during the campaign. Two pre-election polls, including one by Probe Research, had reported that the NDP would receive more than half of the popular vote. However, a major decline in voter turnout—from 71 percent to 55 percent—probably caused the decline in NDP support to 49 percent on election day.[116] Once again the provincial map was PC blue in the rural south but in their other traditional stronghold of southern Winnipeg they were pushed back to the southeast and southwest corners of the city. The NDP took Fort Garry, St. Norbert, and Seine River in southern Winnipeg, signifying that the PCs were continuing to lose middle-class urban support and drifting further towards being a purely rural party. Calls quickly arose for a leadership review, both among party members and within the press.[117]

By 2005, party membership had dropped to 6700 from the 30,000 figure that the party enjoyed in the mid-1990s (Figure 2.7). Popular support across the province was also stalled in the mid-30s. Because most governments in Manitoba are formed by parties that achieve at least 40 percent of the vote, the PCs were clearly in crisis. By the summer of 2005 an organized campaign was underway for a leadership review. At the annual meeting that was held on 5 November 2005, only 55 percent were willing to support Murray by voting against having the review, a figure deemed insufficient by Murray, who announced two days later that he would resign. It was then announced that a PC leadership convention would be held on 29 April 2006, a meeting that the retiring leader would not attend.

New rules were used to choose the party's new leader. Previous leadership contests had operated by having each constituency association select delegates to represent the riding's members at the leadership convention. Along with MLAs and other senior party officials, the delegates would then choose the new leader. The older system was subject to problems including "stacked" meetings and the uneven application of rules by biased local party officials. For example, in the 1975 battle between Spivak and

Lyon, accusations were made regarding ineligible voters being bused into local meetings and even that some members were residents of nearby cemeteries. During the 1983 battle between Filmon and Brian Ransom, in one riding (Transcona) there were more votes cast for the Filmon slate of delegates than the total number of party members who were eligible to vote (the results were later overturned by the party).[119] The new rules resolved such problems by making *all* members eligible for the leadership vote. They could do so by mailing in their ballot (and having them received by noon on the first day of the convention), voting in their own ridings, or by appearing at the convention itself. As before, the winning candidate required a 50 percent majority.[120] However, one drawback to the new system was that in the event that no candidate was able to reach the majority threshold on the first ballot, a second vote would need to be counted two weeks later, an event which did not occur in 2006.[121]

The 2006 leadership race included three candidates, Hugh McFadyen, Ron Schuler, and Ken Waddell. McFadyen drew support from across the province, including Winnipeg members and party elites, while Schuler and Waddell were supported by mostly rural members. McFadyen had emerged from the party backrooms, after serving in senior advisor roles for both Filmon and Winnipeg Mayor Sam Katz, to be elected in the southwest Winnipeg riding of Fort Whyte in a December 2005 by-election. From the start he was seen as the front runner and, two weeks prior to the convention, obtained the endorsement of fourteen MLAs.[122] The new system for choosing the leader was a technical and organizational success. Two-thirds of the members cast their ballots, of which 8100 were returned by mail. On 29 April, when the votes were counted, McFadyen had won a total of 6091 votes over Schuler's 1953 and Waddell's 1099 votes.[123] However, one has to question whether or not the new system is good for a political party in opposition: that is, do the new types of leadership selection systems promote the type of extended media coverage that traditional leadership conventions might typically draw? Although there was less fanfare at the 2006 convention compared to earlier conventions such as those in which Roblin, Lyon, or Filmon were chosen, it drew more media attention than when Murray was acclaimed. Its positive impact was made evident by a series of *Winnipeg Free Press* polls conducted afterward by Probe Research that showed the party hovering above the 40 percent mark.[124]

An interesting path led Hugh McFadyen to the provincial assembly. In 2004 Rod Bruinooge ran against Liberal Party heavy hitter Reg Alcock in the federal riding of Winnipeg South and lost. He was therefore seen as the most likely candidate to run again in the federal riding. Regardless of who was running, it was generally seen as a very safe seat for Alcock. However, at the 2005 nomination meeting, Bruinooge was ousted by McFadyen. Some months later the provincial riding of Fort Whyte (a generally affluent riding in the southwest corner of Winnipeg) was vacated by MLA John Loewen, who left Murray's caucus and jumped parties to run as a federal Liberal candidate in Charleswood. Since having been bumped from his federal candidacy, Bruinooge announced that he would be seeking the PC nomination in the now vacant Fort Whyte. McFadyen then announced that he was abandoning his plans for the upcoming Winnipeg South campaign to seek the Fort Whyte PC nomination. For the second time in one year, Bruinooge's aspirations had been quashed by McFadyen. Bruinooge, much to his credit, again put his name forward to run in Winnipeg South, where he upset Alcock by a handful of votes in the 2006 federal election.[125]

Under McFadyen's leadership, the PCs developed a platform for the 2007 election that appeared better suited to the provincial mood. It included controlling crime, promoting health-care and education spending, reduced sales taxes, downtown development, and creating a positive investment climate to keep young people in the province. The party was also in better financial health, having raised $1,033,051 in 2006, a 75 percent increase over 2005.[126] For the first time since its 1999 defeat, the PCs surpassed the $1 million threshold. This exceeded the NDP's fundraising of $867,144 and the Liberals' $151,632. Yet the PCs were unable to overcome Gary Doer's widespread popularity, or to make significant inroads among middle-class voters. This was demonstrated by a pre-election poll that revealed that 46 percent of those in households with incomes of $30,000 to $59,000 (a rough measure of the middle-class category) supported the NDP while only 38 percent supported the PCS.[127] Furthermore, as in previous years, the PCS were unable to bridge the party's gender gap, with only 34 percent of women saying they supported the PCS compared to 40 percent of men.[128]

The PC campaign was marked also by what would quickly become recognized as a strategic blunder: McFadyen promised that a PC government would bring the long-departed Winnipeg Jets hockey team back to the city. According to campaign director Jonathan Scarth, "We wanted to talk about creating opportunities ... We wanted to say to voters, 'we can be a major league province and a major league city once again.'" However, according to the NDP's chief strategist, Michael Balagus, in focus groups with the general public, "participants were universally negative about the suggestion that government money be used to lure an NHL team."[129] The unintended consequence was that the PC campaign became tied to a single issue. While knocking on doors in their ridings, candidates started finding that they were confronting voters regarding the announcement.[130] What started on a positive note ended with terrible results. The election produced for the NDP thirty-six seats across the province to the PCS' nineteen and the Liberals' two. Under their new leader, PC popular support had only inched forward from 37 percent in 2003 to 38 percent in 2007, while the NDP drew 48 percent. More disheartening was the loss of two more PC seats in southern Winnipeg (Southdale and Kirkfield Park), an area in which McFadyen was supposed to make gains rather than losses for the party. In Winnipeg, the PCS won only 29 percent of the popular vote.

Not since 1953 had the party dropped below the twenty-seat threshold, yet there were some positive signs on the horizon. Pre-election polling revealed that PC support was growing among younger voters (41 percent of those under age thirty-five reported supporting the PCS compared to 37 percent for the NDP[131]). Furthermore, some believe that Doer's anticipated retirement will open up new opportunities for the PCS to reacquire voter support among middle-class swing voters.

Conclusion

The PCs in Manitoba have historically faced two challenges. The first has been to unite its urban and rural wings, each of which in recent decades accentuates two ideological tendencies: the moderate pluralism as exhibited by Duff Roblin, Sidney Spivak, and Gary Filmon, and the more right-of-centre conservatism represented by Walter Weir, Sterling Lyon, and Stuart Murray. Of these two tendencies, Hugh McFadyen appears closer to the former than the latter. The PCs have been most successful when led by urban-based moderate conservatives who were able to win support from the rural wing as demonstrated by Duff Roblin and Filmon, each of whom won multiple terms in power. Both Weir and Lyon became party leaders and then premiers based chiefly on support from the party's right-of-centre and rural elements. Yet these two exceptions proved the rule: Weir was defeated in 1969 shortly after replacing Roblin, and Lyon lasted only one term in office, which is the only time in the province's history that an elected premier was defeated in an election after having served a single term.

The dilemma for the PCs is as follows. To retake the second "s" in the s-plus-s electoral formula (southern Manitoba and South Winnipeg) by winning the middle-class swing vote, the PCs need to assure the electorate that, if elected, they will protect important social, education and health care programs. However, this "march to the centre" makes it hard for the party to differentiate itself from the other parties, of which one (the NDP) now has a proven track record of protecting the interests of this large social segment. On the other hand, if the PCs staked out their ground more clearly by putting forward a more traditional platform covering crime control, low taxes, and government cutbacks, this would signal a retreat towards their rural and business bases of support. Historically speaking, the pragmatic centre appears to hold the most hope for the party's electoral prospects. Shifting economic conditions, a change in the NDP's leadership, and a belief among voters that democratically elected governments ought to be changed on occasion might nudge the NDP from power.

Chapter 3

The Liberal Party

THE LIBERAL PARTY IN MANITOBA HAS OPERATED AS THREE DIFFERENT entities. Within the two-party system which lasted until 1922, the Liberals formed majority governments under Thomas Greenway and T.C. Norris. During the farmer-oriented "quasi-party" system that followed, the Liberals merged with John Bracken's Progressive Party in the early 1930s to become part of the Liberal-Progressive Party. The hyphenated name was dropped following the 1959 election, and the party's decline during the 1960s precipitated the NDP's breakthrough in 1969. The Liberal Party subsequently became transformed into a Winnipeg-oriented centre party: what can be called the "one-half" in the current two-and-a-half-party system.

The Party's First Decades
The Liberal Party first began operating at the provincial level in 1883 against John Norquay's Government slate which was loosely connected to John A.

Macdonald's federal Conservatives.¹ Often called "Grits" or "Reformers," this was a loose collection consisting of nine "Liberal" candidates, who generally identified themselves with the federal Liberal Party, and sixteen "Provincial Rights" candidates.² As an opposition, their primary aim was to attack Norquay's alliance with a federal government that was preventing the establishment of provincially sanctioned railways. These were seen as competitors for the federally chartered monopoly of the Canadian Pacific Railway (CPR). Hence, the two parties were divided over whether or not Manitoba should have powers regarding intra-provincial railway development.

Thomas Greenway was Manitoba's first Liberal leader. He ran under the Provincial Rights banner and as an unofficial leader of the opposition in the 1883 election (the party had yet to operate with a formal means for choosing its leader). Before coming to Manitoba, Greenway had served as an Independent Conservative Member of Parliament for the Ontario federal riding of South Huron before switching over to the Liberals. His main reason for changing parties was that he strongly objected to John A. Macdonald's protectionist tariff policies. He then withdrew his candidacy for the nomination at the 1878 Reform Party convention ("Reform" being another name for Liberals at the time) to make way for Malcolm Cameron, who had previously run in the riding on the Reform ticket. After departing from federal politics, he became heavily involved in land speculation and the resettlement of Ontarians, including himself, to rural Manitoba.³ According to his biographer, Joseph Hilts, Greenway's status as the leader among the early coalition of Liberal candidates was that "it was he who challenged Premier Norquay to a public debate on the issues, a challenge which was not accepted."⁴ He campaigned on the allowance of local railways, the breakup of the Canadian Pacific Railway's monopoly, and obtaining for the province higher subsidies from the federal government for the use of public lands. However, the 1883 results were disappointing: ten opposition candidates were elected to Norquay's twenty.

Within the Liberal Party there existed an urban-rural divide between the growing number of newly arriving farmers from Ontario and the growing population centre of Winnipeg. Problems between the two groups appeared during the 1886 Provincial Reform Association convention when an attempt was made by urban supporters to remove Greenway as leader and replace him with James Fisher. Largely due to support among rural members, Greenway survived the challenge and led the party into the December 1886 election.

A review of newspaper coverage from the 1886 election reveals a growing acceptance for party labels in the province, and the Liberal and Provincial Rights labels were used often for identifying opposition candidates. However, references to "Government" and "Opposition" candidates continued to be used with regard to activities in the legislative assembly and in newspaper campaign coverage.[5] Regardless of how it was labelled, Greenway's party was defeated. Norquay won twenty seats to the Liberals' fourteen.[6] The party's fortunes changed with Premier Norquay's resignation in late 1887 and the failure by his successor, David Harrison, to maintain a majority in the legislature when the House met on 16 January 1888. Lieutenant-Governor

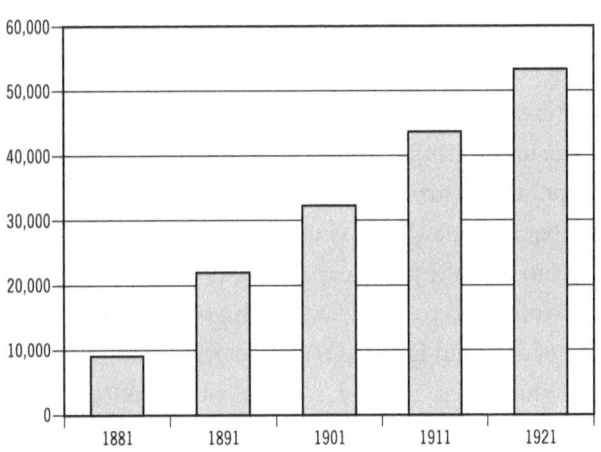

Farm Holdings in Manitoba
1881 to 1921

Figure 3.1:
Source, M.C. Leacy, ed., *Historical Statistics of Canada*, 2ⁿᵈ Edition, Table M12-22.

James Aikins turned to Greenway to form the government. Three days later (19 January), the opposition leader was able to muster a sufficient number of MLAs and thereby created the first Liberal government in Manitoba.[7] It signalled a new era for the province. As Norquay represented the province's political culture of his time, Premier Greenway represented the large number of farmers of British extraction who were arriving via Ontario. A new economic phase was underway, fuelled largely by a doubling of the farm sector between 1881 and 1891 by which time 22,000 farms were operating in the province (as shown in Figure 3.1).[8]

Greenway and his Liberals ran against Norquay and his Conservatives (running under the label "Norquayites") again in 1888. This time the Liberals were successful. On the 11 July election night the new era was marked by celebrations as described by the pro-Liberal *Manitoba Free Press*:

> A double row of carriages half the length of Main street, several hundreds of men shouldering brooms in the middle of the road, another contingent dragging the carriage of the Ministers with ropes, both sidewalks thronged with men, women and children following the Grits' triumphal procession last evening as it passed up and down Main street and Portage avenue, headed by a band and a Provincial Rights banner ... When it became dusk the brooms were lighted and so converted into torches. Finally a halt was made in front of city hall and Mr. Greenway stood up in his carriage and addressed the crowd.[9]

Greenway was able to hold power for a total of three terms based on at least 50 percent of the popular vote in each election (shown in Figure 3.2). Furthermore, by becoming premier, he was able to convert dissenting Winnipeg Liberals in the urban wing of the party to his side through cabinet appointments and political patronage.[10] Some attribute strong support for Greenway and his Liberals to newly arriving Ontarians,[11] yet the party's successes were also tied to a healthy and expanding provincial economy. The "good times" were connected to many factors: high wheat prices, the successful introduction of dry-land farming technologies, readily available investment capital and the lowest interest rates in two hundred years, railway development and new transportation systems, the revoking of the

CPR's monopoly in 1888, the growth of urban centres to service agricultural development, and the near completion of settlement in the western US, which in turn, led many to become interested in the Canadian Prairies.[12] The province's good fortunes were also connected to the Liberal government's promotion of supportive agricultural policies, immigration and settlement, fiscal prudence, and railway development.[13]

The Manitoba Schools Question and French Language Rights

While Premier Greenway and his Liberals successfully managed the province's expanding economy, they also introduced measures that would have profound consequences for both the national politics of the day and future provincial governments. These involved the termination of the delicate arrangements that had been made regarding language rights originally negotiated between the Red River Settlement's founding populations: French-speaking settlers, English-speaking settlers, and the Métis.[14] In 1890, with Clifford Sifton[15] as its minister of education, the provincial government passed legislation withdrawing public funds from Catholic schools and revoking official bilingualism, both of which were constitutionally rooted in the Manitoba Act of 1870.[16]

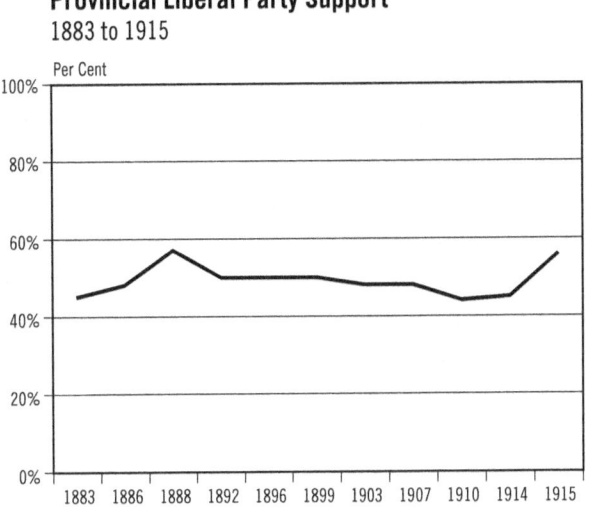

Figure 3.2: Derived from Elections Manitoba, "Historical Summaries"

This action split the legislature's two parties into three factions. This included, first, English-speaking members of Greenway's Liberal caucus. The second consisted of Conservative MLAs, some of whom thought the Liberals were moving too slowly on the matter and whose party had formally supported removing public support for denominational schools at its 1892 convention. The third consisted of a small breakaway group of francophone and English-speaking Catholic MLAs under James Prendergast, who had served in Greenway's government as provincial secretary and resigned over the new legislation. In effect, this third group served as the opposition on this issue.[17]

The Manitoba Schools Question also fuelled nation-wide fires. Uncompromising positions were held over whether or not Canada should be a bilingual country rooted in different cultural identities and religion. It pitted Quebec-based French Canadians against Ontario-based provincial-rights advocates,[18] contributed to the downfall of Charles Tupper's Conservative government, and became a central issue in the 1896 federal election. The Liberals were elected under Laurier, and a compromise was then negotiated between Greenway and the federal government, which was enacted in 1897. Catholic teachers would be employed where sufficient numbers of Catholic children warranted it, religious instruction would be provided if a sufficient number of parents made the request, and bilingual instruction would be provided where a sufficient number of non-English-speaking children (francophone and other ethnic groups) were attending school.[19] However, the compromise was later revoked by the provincial government under Liberal Premier T.C. Norris in 1916, with the abolition of bilingual schools, many of which operated in languages other than English or French. Many believed that the public-school system should be used as a means for assimilating the children of the non-English-speaking population. Such concerns were exacerbated by World War I and a resulting rise in xenophobia.[20] Teaching in a language other than English was thereby outlawed.[21]

The constitutionality of the actions taken by both the Greenway and Norris governments with regard to French-language rights was highly questionable, yet for subsequent decades many Manitobans viewed the subject of French-language rights as an historical artifact. Beneath a generally calm surface it simmered for decades within the Franco-Manitoban community, and turned into an open flame in 1980, with negative consequences for the governing NDP.

T.C Norris and the New Era

Having served three terms in government based on the successful elections of 1888, 1892, and 1896, the Liberals lost power to the Conservatives in the 1899 election. In part this was due to the issue of prohibition. Many thought the government was moving too slowly on the issue, while Hugh John Macdonald's Conservatives were promising strong action.[22] The Liberals remained in opposition for the next fifteen years until scandal brought down the Conservatives. In the provincial election of 1915, Liberal leader T.C. Norris, a Brandon-area farmer and auctioneer, forged an unusual coalition of social forces. Rather than simply relying on southern farmers and urban businessmen, Norris drew together farmers, workers, suffragettes, and various social-reform groups, including the temperance movement, the League for the Taxation of Land Values, and the Direct Legislation League, as well as the social gospel movement with its links to Protestant churches.[23] It was a strategy built upon both the changing dynamics of Manitoba's society (especially in Winnipeg) and a broader North American phenomenon. Three years earlier, in the 1912 US presidential election, Teddy Roosevelt's "Bull Moose" Progressives garnered over 4 million votes with its industrial-reform platform, which included a comprehensive worker's compensation act, anti-trust laws, and limitations on the use of child labour.[24]

While Manitoba Liberals grabbed onto the social-reform movement, the Conservatives were under fire for mishandling public funds. The confluence was remarkable. The Liberals won 55 percent of the vote and forty out of forty-seven ridings.[25] Since 1915, no single party in Manitoba has been able to surpass these results, either in popular support or in the number of seats won. On election night a cheering crowd of 6000 individuals gathered in front of the *Manitoba Free Press* building where three large "phonograph horns" were mounted. As the newspaper reported, "The return from the first poll had hardly been received in the *Free Press* office before the horns spoke—clearly, distinctly, loudly. Everyone could hear, no matter in what part of the street they had taken their stand or had been jostled to. The horns kept on speaking and telling the story of the Liberal landslide."[26]

While much has been said about Norris's ability to win support from progressive urban forces, its importance might be overestimated as a winning factor for gaining majority power. The Liberals' Winnipeg seats grew from two out of four in 1910, in Winnipeg North and Winnipeg West; to three out of six in 1914, in Winnipeg Centre "A" and Winnipeg South "A" and "B"; and then to four out of six in 1915, when Winnipeg North "B" was added to its list of wins. With the legislature consisting of forty-seven members in 1915, it was the collapse of the Conservatives outside Winnipeg that explains the outcome.

Table 3.1: Provincial Elections, 1915 to 1922[28]

	1915		1920		1922	
	Popular Vote	Seats	Popular Vote (%)	Seats	Popular Vote (%)	Seats
Liberal	55%	40	35%	21	23%	8
Conservative	33%	5	19%	9	16%	7
Farmer	N/A	N/A	14%	9	33%	28
Labour/Socialist	3%	0	21%	12	16%	6
Independent	9%	2	12%	4	13%	6

Looking outside the provincial capital, the Liberals took twenty seats from the Conservatives. Of these twenty seats, fifteen had been held by the Conservatives for at least two terms, two had been held for one term, and three had been created since 1910. In effect, rural Manitoba was expressing what the American political scientist V.O. Key would call a landslide election based on a "vote of lack of confidence."[27] Norris, however, was unable to convert the Liberals' massive victory into subsequent majority governments.

Problematic post-war economic conditions, including unemployment and inflation, along with attacks from both the farm sector and urban labour for how the government had handled the Winnipeg General Strike of 1919,[29] contributed to a drop in Liberal support of over twenty percentage points to 35 percent in the 1920 election and a reduction to minority government status with only twenty-one seats. It was the party's worst showing since 1879, with votes leaking to a range of parties. Of the twenty seats taken from the Conservatives outside Winnipeg in 1915, only five were held onto by the Liberals. Three switched back to the Conservatives,[30] five switched to Labour candidates,[31] five switched to Farmer candidates (predecessors to the United Farmers of Manitoba),[32] and one switched to an independent candidate, while one riding (Elmwood) was merged into Winnipeg.[33]

The fortunes of the Liberal Party would continue to fall with the 1922 election. When the election was called, many thought that either the Liberals or Conservatives would form the next government. The sentiment was shared by the *Manitoba Free Press*: "With only two weeks to go before polling, the final spurts are being put to what has been a painfully dull campaign ... The increase [in registered voters] is ample to put either of the two principal contestants in with a majority."[34] On election day, Liberal support slipped to 23 percent, resulting in a defeat at the hands of the United Farmers of Manitoba.

But what was this new political force? The UFM was part of the progressive movement that was growing across North America. Progressivism was based on the notion that farming was more than an occupation or business, it was a way of life that was connected to honest toil, the purity of nature, a respect for God, and selflessness. In contrast, urban life, industrial monopolies, corrupt party politics, and large governments were seen as sources of social and political decay. Hence, it was a reform movement. In Canada, progressivism took on two distinct forms. The more radical variant of the two was pushed forward by those such as United Farmers of Alberta leader H.W. Wood, who called for radical changes to party politics, the economic system, and government institutions. The second and less radical type was more typically found in Manitoba and Saskatchewan. The views of this second group, articulated by individuals such as John Dafoe of the *Winnipeg Free Press* and T.A. Crerar, the leader of the federal Progressives, who had resigned in 1919 from serving in the Union Government as the federal minister of agriculture over the issue of tariffs. Such spokespersons pushed for western-oriented reforms including lower tariffs and limiting the control of eastern business interests in party politics and government.[35]

By the early 1920s the movement had become a considerable force. In 1919, the United Farmers formed the provincial government in Ontario, followed by their success in Alberta in the 1921 provincial election. In the federal election of 1921, the Progressives took sixty-five seats and became the second-largest party in the House of Commons.[36] In Manitoba, the United Farmers first entered the electoral scene without a leader when the organization allowed local representatives to run as "Farmer" candidates.

It is worthwhile to look at shifts in the electorate between 1915 and 1922. Of the five Conservative seats that the Liberals took in 1915 and which they were able to hold in 1920, four fell to the UFM in 1922 (Dufferin, Gilbert Plains, Lakeside, and The Pas), with the other going back into the Conservative fold (Turtle Mountain). For the Liberals, therefore, the UFM's growth from its entry into the political scene in 1920, followed by its 1922 breakthrough, signalled a major realignment. However, beneath the surface of changing party fortunes, the 1922 election revealed that the pro-farmer and pro-South Winnipeg business formula, used previously by Greenway and Roblin, continued to be in operation, only now it was to the benefit of the UFM. In addition to support from farmers, in Winnipeg the UFM attracted financial and moral support from J.H. Ashdown and individuals among the investment community, the commodity exchange, and retailers. Ashdown's support was significant; he had served as Winnipeg's mayor, owned Winnipeg's largest hardware department store, and was generally recognized as the leader and spokesperson for the business community.[37] After all the votes were tallied, with three seats still to be determined due to having their elections deferred, the UFM held twenty-five seats, the Liberals eight, and the Conservatives seven, with the remainder going to Labour and independent candidates. By the year's end, all three of the deferred elections produced UFM MLAs, putting the UFM's total to twenty-eight, of whom only one was located in Winnipeg (Richard Craig).

The UFM clearly gained from the electoral rules of the day, especially the Redistribution Act of 1920, which followed the 1917 Elections Act. It confirmed the long-standing formula by which one rural voter equaled two urban voters for allocating seats in the provincial assembly. As such, the UFM was able to take 50 percent of the seats based on 33 percent of the vote, compared to the Liberals winning only 14 percent of seats based on 23 percent of the vote and the Conservatives' 13 percent of seats based on 16 percent of the vote (Labour won 11 percent of seats based on 16 percent of the provincial vote; however, its candidates were absent outside Winnipeg and Brandon). In the end, the results revealed that the provincial Liberals were clearly on the outs with both rural voters and urban backers in the business community.

The Farmers and Eventual Party Merger

The 1922 election produced an awkward situation for the victors. The electorate had chosen a leaderless party to run its government. The UFM was left with three options: they could select a leader from among their newly elected caucus, attract a member from the federal wing of their party (the Progressive Party), or look elsewhere. It is worth quoting at length John Kendle's surreal account of the UFM's first post-election meeting and how the party came to choose John Bracken, a political outsider and the president of the Manitoba Agricultural College, to be their new leader:

> As the largest group in the legislature the UFM would be obliged to form a government. Since the farmers had no recognized leader, the initial task would be to find one. The farm group had met for the first time on Thursday, 20 July, at 8:00 PM, in the basement of the Odd Fellows Hall on Kennedy Street. The meeting had been convened by W.R. Wood and George Chipman

who, after opening the proceedings, left. Since very few of the twenty-four farm MLAs knew each other, there was initial uncertainty about a chairman but Clifford Barclay from Springfield was finally chosen. Barclay began the proceedings by pointing out that although they did not have a majority they were the largest group and would be called on to form a government. They therefore had to choose a leader. Was there anyone present who thought he should be leader? No one volunteered. Would anyone present put forward someone else in the room? Again, no one spoke. Then, said Barclay, they would have to look outside. The group began considering possible candidates on the understanding that the individual finally selected should have their unanimous approval. Barclay allowed a general discussion but once a name encountered opposition it was temporarily dropped ... By midnight only three names had not been eliminated—Crerar, Hoey, and Bracken. All three were phoned immediately although it was now after midnight. Crerar was asked to come by at 9:00 AM, Hoey at 9:30, and Bracken at 10:00.[38]

At the morning meeting, both Progressive Party national leader Thomas Crerar, and Bob Hoey, the Progressive Member of Parliament for Springfield, gave advice to the newly elected farmers yet declined their nominations.[39] By default Bracken was offered the leadership yet he was reluctant to accept, as was demonstrated by the fact that it took three meetings for the UFM to persuade him to take the job. He later said that he finally accepted the job offer because he feared the UFM would fall apart otherwise.[40] Without a seat in the legislature, Bracken successfully ran in the sparsely populated northern riding of The Pas, which had its election deferred to October of that year. He obtained 472 votes of the 699 votes cast.[41] With a new leader and support from across the province, there were few signs that the UFM's victory would be short-lived. However, there were now three parties competing for the prized southern rural and business vote: the UFM, the Conservatives, and the Liberals. Discussions were emerging among the party's elite that something needed to be done if the Liberals were to ever find their way back into government.

The merging of the Liberal Party—or what was called at the time "fusion" —with Bracken's Progressives (the UFM label having since been dropped[42]) occurred over a number of years. At the national level, and in part due to the activities of the highly influential Liberal strategist and editor of the *Winnipeg Free Press*, John Dafoe, the Progressives were heavily courted by Mackenzie King. Seven MPs were elected as "Liberal-Progressives" for Manitoba in the 1926 federal election.[43] Yet there would be two distinct phases in the coming together of the provincial Liberals and Progressives. In Manitoba the first real opportunity arose with the departure of Norris, who opposed any form of alliance with Bracken, and the choice of Hugh Robson as the new Liberal leader in 1927. Robson, a former judge and Manitoba's first public-utilities commissioner, let his name stand for leader only fifteen minutes before nominations closed, gaining the support of the Young Liberals who erroneously believed he favoured cooperation with Bracken.[44] Two years later, with little progress made towards merging the two parties, Liberal Prime Minister Mackenzie King wrote to his provincial-party counterpart: "The Progressives in Manitoba *need* your help today, and as a consequence you should be able to make your own terms with them. You should make them in the name of Liberalism, as opposed to Toryism. To keep the Conservative Party out of control in Manitoba is an all-sufficient ground for you, as a Liberal, finding means of honourable cooperation with those members of the legislature who are opposed to the Conservative Party."[45]

The Progressives were also interested in seeing this merger of the two parties occur; especially when two cabinet ministers, W.R. Clubb and Bill Major, resigned when news broke out that they had held stocks in the Winnipeg Electric Company while the province was negotiating development plans for hydroelectricity production at the Seven Sisters site.

Hoping that the support of Robson and his Liberals would help his government ride out the Seven Sisters scandal, Bracken offered the Liberal leader the position of Attorney General. In a letter to Robson, the premier wrote that "the situation ought now to be considered carefully with the object of determining whether a greater measure of cooperation between our two groups cannot be worked out, upon terms honourable to both Parties and the Public interest."[46] However, personal friction between the two leaders prevented the idea from bearing fruit. Progress towards a merger was finally made in 1931 with Robson retiring from politics and being appointed to the Manitoba Court of Appeal. This opened up a new and positive phase of activity towards fusion, and as the Depression deepened, Bracken issued an appeal to all the other parties to join him in forming an all-party coalition. In favour of the idea was the new Liberal leader who had replaced Robson, Murdoch MacKay, a practising medical doctor from the town of Transcona (now a Winnipeg suburb). Events moved quickly and an agreement was reached in February 1932. On 27 May 1932, three Liberals, J.S. McDiarmid, Ewen McPherson, and Murdoch MacKay, joined the Bracken cabinet. During the June election of that same year, the two parties were fused with candidates running as "Liberal-Progressives."

Once again only two major parties would be battling over the critically important farmer and business votes. The 1932 election produced thirty-eight seats for the Liberal-Progressives based on 40 percent of the vote. The opposition divided its vote, with the Conservatives drawing the strongest share at 35 percent, producing only ten seats for the party. It was outside Winnipeg where the Liberal-Progressives reaped their rewards with 48 percent of the vote compared to the Conservatives, who had 35 percent. The result was that the rural bias in the electoral system, and the fusion of their main competitors, caused the Conservatives to be kept from the premiership for another quarter-century.

The two-party merger was based on electoral strategy, yet it was also a product of economic conditions. During the 1930s, as the worldwide Depression deepened and farmers faced catastrophic crop conditions, the Manitoba government teetered on the brink of bankruptcy. By 1940, in order to pressure the national government into addressing the public fiscal crisis and to demonstrate wartime solidarity, Bracken was again calling upon all the parties to join a non-partisan government. He successfully brought into the cabinet three Conservatives and one representative each from the CCF and Social Credit to serve alongside his Liberal-Progressive colleagues. Throughout this period, Bracken worked alongside Stuart Garson, who would eventually replace him as premier.

Table 3.2: Provincial Government Coalitions[47]

1941 Government Coalition

	Seats	Popular Vote
Liberal-Progressive	27	35%
Conservative	12	16%
CCF	3	17%
Social Credit	3	2%
Independent	5	11%

1941 Anti-Coalition

Conservative	3	4%
Social Credit	0	6%
Independent	1	8%
Communist	1	3%

1945 Government Coalition

Liberal-Progressive	25	32%
Progressive Conservative	13	16%
Social Credit	2	1%
Independent	3	5%

1945 Anti-Coalition

CCF	9	34%
Social Credit	0	1%
Labour-Progressive	1	5%
Independent/Ind. CCF	2	6%

1949 Government Coalition

Liberal-Progressive[48]	30	38%
Progressive Conservative	9	12%
Ind. Lib/Lib. Prog.	1	4%
Independent	4	4%

1949 Anti-Coalition

CCF	7	26%
Cons and Ind. PC	4	7%
Ind. Lib/Lib. Prog.	1	3%
Others	1	6%

Garson had an impact on both the provincial and federal level. Much like those of Manitoba's preceding premiers, Garson's roots were in Ontario, having been born in St. Catharines, Ontario, in 1898. In 1927, while working as a lawyer in the town of Ashern, he impressed Bracken with a speech at a rural meeting. The premier subsequently persuaded Garson to switch from law to politics, and Garson was elected in the riding of Fairford in that same year. Due to the shortage of cabinet posts caused by the Liberal-Progressive merger, Garson had to wait for close to ten years to become a minister. He became the provincial treasurer in 1936 and proved to be "an extremely able man, hard working, highly intelligent, and quick"[49] while at the same time keeping government spending to a minimum. Due to the financial condition of the province, as well as those of other provinces, Bracken and Garson allied with other provincial leaders to push Ottawa on finding ways to resolve their financial shortfalls (to use modern parlance, "the fiscal imbalance"). The result was that in 1937 the federal government established the Royal Commission on Dominion Provincial Relations (otherwise known as the Rowell-Sirois Commission).

According to historian and federal Liberal cabinet minister Jack Pickersgill, Garson thereby became known later as the "father of equalization."[50] This was due to his work in developing Manitoba's leadership role in the ensuing federal-provincial discussions that led to, in 1942, Ottawa entering into an arrangement with the provinces that involved fiscal transfers from the federal government. Subsequently, in 1946, Ottawa and Manitoba (along with other provinces) came to an agreement that Ottawa would collect taxes while providing fiscal transfers to the provinces. Other elements in the new arrangement included a provision for senior-citizen pensions and funds towards the development of frontier and mining regions. Half of the province's debt to the federal government was also cancelled. The new federal-provincial fiscal arrangements garnered what was a very large sum at the time, of approximately $5.5 million in annual revenues for the province.[51]

It was during this period that Bracken stepped down as premier. Due to a growing national reputation and the urging of former prime minister Arthur Meighen, in December 1942, Bracken declared to the delegates at the national Conservative Party meeting that if "the convention were prepared to give visible evidence of its progressive intent by association of these two names, Progressive and Conservative, I would be willing to become a candidate for the leadership."[52] He was chosen, and upon his departure from provincial politics Stuart Garson became the new Liberal-Progressive premier of Manitoba in 1943.[53]

In 1948 Garson followed Bracken's example by entering federal politics, though as a federal Liberal rather than as a Progressive Conservative.[54] Under Louis St. Laurent he became the minister of justice and Attorney General of Canada and remained in cabinet during each successive Liberal government until his (and the national Liberals') defeat in 1957. Douglas Campbell succeeded Garson as premier from 1948 to 1958. Born in 1895 in the small Manitoba community of High Bluff (which is on the CPR line and near Portage la Prairie), he was first elected as a UFM candidate in 1922 and served as the MLA for the rural riding of Lakeside for forty-seven years.[55] In 1934 he became minister of agriculture and, upon taking over the premiership in 1948, continued to work on drawing both business and rural support for his party. In coalition with MLAs from other parties, his Liberal-Progressive-led government was re-elected in 1949. This would be the last coalition government election. However, the Liberal-Progressives remained the most popular of the parties when re-elected as a majority government in 1953 with 39 percent of the vote and thirty-three seats. Described as "articulate, reasonable, and a shrewd judge of people,"[56] Premier Campbell promoted rural development, pro-farm policies, and the fiscal conservative policies of his predecessors, including reduced government spending and low taxes.[57] Rural electrification and balanced budgets are considered the trademarks of his administration.[58] Perhaps more significant was the further development of hydroelectricity within a publicly owned system during his years as premier.[59]

The last time that the "Liberal-Progressive" label appeared on a Manitoba ballot was in the 1958 election, when Campbell lost to Duff Roblin and his Progressive Conservatives. Thirty-five percent of voters voted Liberal-Progressive, garnering nineteen seats, which was less than the 40 percent who voted PC and allowed them to capture twenty-six seats. Yet the old guard would not go easily, as demonstrated by attempts by Campbell to get CCF leader Lloyd Stinson to join him in a governing coalition. In exchange for support from Stinson and his eleven-member caucus, two cabinet seats, and the position of Speaker of the legislature were offered. The usually tight-spending small-government Liberal-Progressive leader even offered to consider a number of CCF conditions to the deal, including a new public hospital plan, new labour policies, and public ownership for natural gas distribution in the province. But nothing came from these discussions. Stinson reported later that "almost unanimously the CCF on my recommendation rejected both coalition and any form of working arrangement with the Liberals. Our decision was ... confirmed by me over the telephone to Mr. Campbell early Monday morning. He asked me if we would reconsider. I said it was final."[60]

Another indication of Campbell's psychological ill-preparedness for change was recounted in Roblin's memoirs:

> On June 30, 1958, we formed the government. When governments change in some jurisdictions, formal handovers are arranged from the old to the new.... The day that I was sworn in, early that morning, I took over the premier's office. Sterling Lyon was with me going over the orders-in-council to appoint the new cabinet. I heard a little scratching noise at an outside door. As Sterling went to investigate, a key was turned, the door opened, and the former Premier, Douglas Campbell, appeared. He seemed rather nonplussed to find us already, so soon, behind his former desk and, with a muttered remark, "Oh, you're here already," disappeared. That was the handover between governments in the province of Manitoba.[61]

And as such began the Liberals' long-term decline. Campbell's last election as party leader was in 1959, which would be the first time since 1927 that candidates would again campaign in a provincial election under the unhyphenated "Liberal" banner. The 1959 results were worse than those of the previous year, with a loss of eight seats and voter support dropping to 30 percent from the previous year's level of 35 percent. It was a thirty-year low. The last time support had dipped below 32 percent was in the 1927 election during the pre-merger era, when the Liberals received 21 percent of the vote.

It appeared time to find a new leader and to shed the outdated "Progressive" component in the party's name. Never used by the federal Liberal Party, the label was now being used by the Progressive Conservatives in Manitoba and across the country. On 20 April 1961, at the party's first leadership convention in the modern era, Gildas Molgat beat Stan Roberts (who would later become one of the founders of the national Reform Party) for the leadership by a vote of 475 to 279.[62] Molgat was a well-respected rural Franco-Manitoban who represented the constituency of Ste. Rose, which was also his birthplace.[63] His political career began unexpectedly while working on the campaign trail for incumbent Liberal candidate Dane MacCarthy, who died the night before the 8 June 1953 provincial election. With the election for Ste. Rose deferred to 6 July, and with little time to find a more seasoned candidate, at the age of twenty-six Molgat was pressured to become the new Liberal-Progressive candidate, which he did with reported reluctance.[64]

Under his leadership the party was able to recoup some of its losses by winning 36 percent of the vote in the 1962 provincial election. In terms of aggregated votes, such gains were at the expense of the NDP, which had declined from 22 percent (under the CCF banner in 1959) to 15 percent in the 1962 election, while the PCs remained extremely strong with only a 1 percent change over the period from 1959 (46 percent) to 1962 (45 percent). The Liberals were able to win numerous ridings in southern Manitoba, including Emerson, Ethelbert Plains, and Gladstone; however, its decline in Winnipeg was apparent by being restricted to only two seats: Burrows in the North End and St. Boniface. This signalled that the Liberals were struggling to fight on two fronts: against the PCs in the rural areas and against the NDP in Winnipeg.

In 1966, Liberal support slipped to 33 percent while the PCs held their own at 40 percent and the NDP rebounded to 23 percent. Much attention has been paid to the impact of the 1969 election on the Liberals, yet it was in the previous 1962 and 1966 elections where the root of the damage occurred. Molgat was unable to make inroads into rural Conservative support, while urban Liberals complained about his rural-oriented leadership.[65] With the exception of St. Boniface, in 1966 the Liberals were shut out of the Winnipeg region by losing two seats to the NDP. The loss also included an unsuccessful bid by twenty-seven-year-old Lloyd Axworthy to unseat PC MLA D.M. Stanes.[66] At the time it appeared that few were discerning the significance of this long-term electoral trend. On the day after the election, Molgat viewed his NDP challengers simply as "spoilers" rather than the supplanters they would become three years later.[67]

The 1969 election was a back-breaking event which caused Liberal support to drop further to 24 percent. After Molgat's resignation from the leadership (but remaining a candidate in his riding[68]), Robert "Bobby" Bend won the party leadership on 10 May 1969 by a vote of 877 to Duncan Edmonds's 483. He had less than two months to prepare for the election. While many delegates thought that Bend's record would be a strong selling point, having served as an MLA from 1949 to 1959, and as minister of health and public welfare from 1955 to 1958, he appeared to many voters as an aging rural hold-over from the Liberal-Progressive era.[69] Compounding the party's difficulties were two other elements: an ill-prepared organization and internal divisions mainly between rural and urban members but also between the francophone and non-francophone members.[70] Furthermore, with its leader running on a pro-business and anti-social-welfare platform, the Liberals were unable to counter the NDP in many urban ridings, nor to stake out a distinct position within the farming and business community with the ideological right solidly occupied by Walter Weir's repositioned PCs. Throughout its travels the "Bendwagon" (a theme of the campaign and the title of the leader's touring bus) lost, rather than gained, passengers. This was also a good indication of how far the provincial wing was diverging from the federal Liberals and unable to capitalize on the federal party's Trudeaumania of the previous year.

Shortly after the 1969 election defeat, there were those who thought that the PCs and the Liberals might still be able to cobble together a victory. Schreyer's NDP had twenty-eight seats while the others had twenty-nine (twenty-two PC seats, five Liberal, one Social Credit, and one independent). With the newly elected NDP in such a precarious minority situation, a coalition of PCs and Liberals with support from others in the assembly was a possibility. This could take either the form of a new election or the formation of an anti-NDP government.[71] Events, however, unfolded in a manner that surprised many, in that it would be the Liberal representative from the francophone community of St. Boniface, Larry Desjardins, who would come to the NDP's aid.

A discerning observer might have foreseen Desjardins's defection. Up to this time the Liberal vote in St. Boniface had been taken for granted by the party, in spite of growing displeasure within francophone communities over Molgat's resignation and Bend's rural anglophone style. Desjardins had seen his margins of victory (over the NDP) halved in the space of three years; in 1966 it was 3007 and then 1325 in 1969.[72] At least for Desjardins, therefore, it appeared that the Liberals were a sinking ship. Desjardins's decision to support the NDP as a "Liberal Democrat" brought the number of pro-government votes in the house to twenty-nine while reducing the opposition to twenty-eight. It was an excruciatingly tiny majority that could come apart at any time but did not, and it led to the solidification of the province's electoral realignment for years to come.

The biggest loser, of course, was the Liberal Party. One of Schreyer's top advisors recounts that on the day after the votes were counted, and as members of the newly elected NDP were congratulating each other, Schreyer remarked that "the next election will be won by whoever wins the soft Liberal votes."[73] However, in successfully drawing these voters into the NDP fold, Schreyer also cautioned his colleagues that the NDP needed the Liberal Party to survive, so that at least a portion of centre-right voters would be kept out of the PC camp. If the Liberal Party disappeared from the electoral scene, he warned, so too would future chances for the NDP to win government power.[74]

The One-Half Party

The Liberals had dropped like a rock in a pond, from fourteen seats in 1966 to five seats in 1969. Yet even after Desjardins's defection, they were not going down without a fight. The party's new acting leader, Stan Roberts, with support from Molgat and editorials in the *Winnipeg Free Press*, began pushing for a "non-partisan" (a euphemism for "anti-NDP") constituency-level collaboration among Liberals and PCs. Under this proposed arrangement, the party that had the best chance for unseating an NDP candidate would be the only one of the two to field a candidate in an NDP-held constituency. A similar strategy would be used a few years later in British Columbia to defeat Dave Barrett's NDP in 1975 and, to a limited extent, later in Manitoba. However, at the time in Manitoba such Liberal Party overtures were spurned. Among PCs, the Liberals were perceived as mere elitist campaign spoilers. This perspective was articulated by an editorial in the

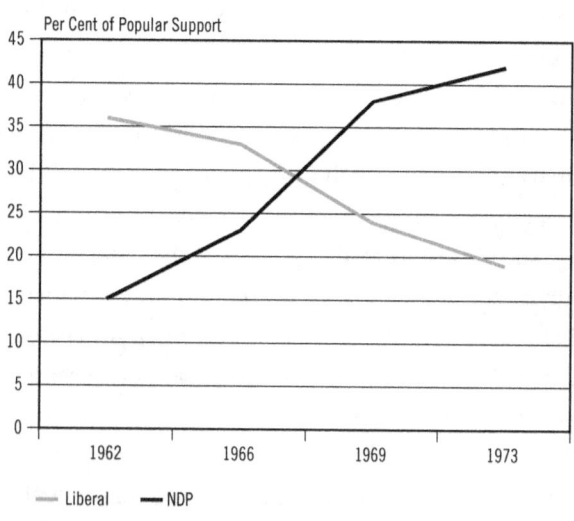

Figure 3.3:
Based on Elections Manitoba, "Historical Summaries"

Winnipeg Tribune: "A significant reason [for the NDP's success] has to be the blind [pro-Liberal] partisan opposition of the *Winnipeg Free Press* and the Liberal big business establishment which has wielded untold power here for years."[75]

A shift to the centre made sense in that the Liberals needed to win back Winnipeg voters from the NDP. However, this also moved the provincial wing closer to that of the national Liberal wing, a party generally disliked by Manitobans. With the exception of what became known as Trudeaumania in the 1968 federal election (in which the new and charismatic leader, Pierre Trudeau, helped the Liberals win five of thirteen federal ridings in Manitoba), in each election from 1957 to 1984 federal Liberal representation only ranged from no seats to two seats. Some years later Lloyd Axworthy would describe the provincial party's dilemma in the following manner: "There is the problem of the eight-hundred-pound gorilla, more fondly known as the federal Liberals, which has been the most successful political machine in the Western world (even taking into account the somewhat spotty record of the past few years). 'The feds,' as they are called in provincial party circles, have caused and will continue to cause no end of trouble for their provincial cousins. They have a record of making unpopular decisions usually at inopportune moments. Asper's 1973 campaign was seriously undermined by a federal budget that raised taxes, for example."[76]

In contrast to its rurally-oriented leaders in the 1950s and 1960s—Campbell, Molgat, and Bend—in the 1970s the party chose a number of leaders from the Winnipeg legal community. The first of many, Israel "Izzy" Asper won the leadership by 720 votes to John Nesbitt's 329 on 31 October 1970 and proceeded to practise what political scientist David Smith terms the "ideological fluidity" of the Prairie Liberals of the time.[77] Asper's aim was "to portray both the NDP and the Conservatives as parties dominated by extremists."[78] Declaring himself as "not a left-wing Liberal ... perhaps just a little more right of centre,"[79] he was elected in Duff Roblin's old urban riding of Wolseley in a 1972 by-election and then narrowly re-elected—by four votes—in the 1973 provincial election.[80] He was an influential public speaker, according to Schreyer's top advisor, Herb Schulz, who regularly watched the debates from public gallery: "The election of Liberal Leader Izzy Asper ... brought new excitement to the legislature. Intellectually agile and swift of tongue, he delighted in keeping the government off balance with oblique assertions disguised as questions: a niggling point here, an implied accusation there; a scholastic argumentation on an obscure issue, sometimes farcical but enough to embarrass the government."[81]

In their first election with Asper as their leader, the Liberals forged a collaborative effort in 1973 to work with the PCs to oust the NDP. Termed the "One Candidate"[82] strategy, in ten ridings voters saw either a Liberal or PC candidate, but not both, running against the NDP (in an eleventh riding, The Pas, both parties held back candidates in deference to an independent candidate). This strategy was used where the NDP had won in 1969, and in St. Boniface (which was, of course, now in the NDP fold).[83] However, it was only in St. Boniface where it met with success, with Desjardins being defeated by a single vote to the Liberal candidate, Paul Marion.[84] The results were later overturned by the courts, with Desjardins regaining his seat in a by-election.

Winning only 19 percent of the popular vote in the 1973 provincial election, and in spite of the best efforts of Asper and his campaign team, the Liberals sank even deeper than they did in 1969. Once the dust had settled, the Liberals held only five seats in the legislature. These were in Portage la Prairie, and the Winnipeg ridings of Wolseley, Fort Rouge, and St. Boniface (which was overturned) as well as the semi-rural riding of Assiniboia. Gone was the party's rural base. Furthermore, the party's electoral fortunes did not improve when Asper's successor, Charles Huband, took over the party's leadership on 22 February 1975. Huband was unable to win the Crescentwood riding in a 1975 by-election and again in the same riding in the 1977 provincial election when, a tight three-way developed. Province-wide, the Liberals slipped even further by winning a mere 12 percent, down from 19 percent, of the popular vote with only one Liberal candidate elected: Lloyd Axworthy in Fort Rouge. Having only a single seat signified that the

Liberals no longer held party status in the legislature. With no place to hang his hat, Huband resigned as leader in 1978 and was appointed by the federal Liberal government to the Court of Appeal, thereby leaving the provincial party leaderless and in complete disarray. This left Axworthy as the sitting Liberal MLA, which made him become, by default, the party leader of the provincial Liberal caucus. Yet he consistently resisted all attempts to make him the formal leader of the party.

Resurgence

The 1980s commenced with a return to power for Trudeau's federal Liberals, yet the provincial ship remained mired in a sea of mud. Axworthy had left provincial politics a year earlier to run in the federal riding of Winnipeg Fort Garry and proceeded to win narrowly over PC candidate Sidney Spivak. With only one sitting MLA (June Westbury replaced Axworthy as the MLA for Fort Rouge in a 1979 by-election), no leader, and a sense of electoral irrelevance, Douglas Lauchlan, a former Axworthy staff worker, beat out Hugh Moran, a Portage la Prairie real-estate agent who represented the rural wing of the party, for the party leadership by a vote of 493 to 300.

The party's continuing frailty was evident in the 1981 provincial election, when only thirty-nine candidates could be found to run in fifty-seven constituencies. Sharon Carstairs recounts her pre-leadership days while working at the ground level: "I became the office manager for Beverly McCaffrey, who was running in the Tuxedo constituency. I recognized that the Liberal campaign in general was in very bad straits. There were neither campaign manuals nor policy manuals. Candidates like Beverly were left on their own to sink or swim ... [and] there was no money. It is not surprising that our popular vote was 6.68 percent."[86] No Liberals were elected in 1981 and the luckless Lauchlan resigned in early 1982. The party remained leaderless until 1984 when Carstairs, originally from Halifax and with prominent Maritime Liberal family ties (including her father, Harold Connolly, who had been premier of Nova Scotia), ran against Bill Ridgeway, a farmer with few contacts among the Winnipeg establishment.[87]

Table 3.3: Liberal Seats from 1969 to 2007 – Winnipeg and Non-Winnipeg[85]

Election	Provincial Popular Vote	Winnipeg Area Seats	Non-Winnipeg Seats
1969	24%	2 Seats: Assiniboia, St. Boniface	3 Seats: La Verendrye, Portage La Prairie, Ste. Rose
1973	19%	4 Seats: Assiniboia, Fort Rouge, Wolseley, St. Boniface (later overturned)	1 Seat: Portage La Prairie
1977	12%	1 Seat: Fort Rouge	0 Seats
1981	7%	0 Seats	0 Seats
1986	14%	1 Seat: River Heights	0 Seats
1988	35%	19 Seats: Assiniboia, Burrows, Ellice, Fort Garry, Fort Rouge, Inkster, Kildonan, Niakwa, Osborne, Radisson, River Heights, St. Boniface, St. James, St. Norbert, St. Vital, Seven Oaks, Sturgeon Creek, Transcona, Wolseley	1 Seat: Selkirk
1990	28%	7 Seats: Crescentwood, Inkster, Osborne, River Heights, St. Boniface, St. James, The Maples	0 Seats
1995	24%	3 Seats: Inkster, St. Boniface, The Maples	0 Seats
1999	13%	1 Seat: River Heights	0 Seats
2003	13%	2 Seats: Inkster, River Heights	0 Seats
2007	12%	2 Seats: Inkster, River Heights	0 Seats

Carstairs won with 307 votes to Ridgeway's 238 votes by marshalling together delegates from both the party's urban and youth wings. She was the first woman to lead a major provincial party in Canada. However, without a seat in the house, office, salary, or support staff, Carstairs's opposition to the government took the form of public meetings, media interviews, and attending each day's legislative session by sitting in the visitors' gallery.[88] She was realistic about the upcoming challenges: "I often became angry in national strategy meetings when officials from Quebec and Ontario would tell us we just didn't campaign properly. Little did they know about the shortage of bodies, the antipathy to the federal leadership, the anti-bilingual, anti-metric and other negative feelings directed towards Liberals."[89]

Table 3.4: Provincial Elections, 1986 to 1990[90]

	1986		1988		1990	
	Popular Vote	Seats	Popular Vote (%)	Seats	Popular Vote (%)	Seats
Liberal	14%	1	35%	20	28%	7
NDP	41%	30	24%	12	29%	20
PC	40%	26	38%	25	42%	30

In the provincial election of 1986, the party was able to double its voter support (from 7 percent to 14 percent) and put its leader into the legislature as the MLA for the affluent riding of River Heights. Then, and as shown in Table 3.4, in 1988 the party enjoyed a rapid upswing by obtaining 35 percent of the vote and twenty seats. A confluence of factors caused this to occur. First, Trudeau was long gone, and it was now the provincial Progressive Conservatives who were paying the price for unpopular decisions made by their national wing. Indeed, disaffection for Mulroney's PCs among western Canadians was sufficiently strong to produce a number of regional right-wing protest parties.[91] Second, the NDP under Howard Pawley had clearly run out of gas. The NDP was facing an unexpected election at the end of a second term in government and was exhausted from dealing with the

French-language rights issue, deficit budgets, higher taxes, and the introduction of sky-rocketing public automobile insurance rates. In contrast to a worn Pawley and an untested new leader named Gary Doer, Carstairs presented a fresh new face to the electorate.[92]

Having pushed the NDP into third place in 1988, many Liberals were now hoping that 1988 could do for the Liberals what 1969 did for the NDP. That is, signal a new era in provincial politics with a new party system in which the NDP would become the province's new one-half party. Yet, as University of Manitoba political scientist Geoffrey Lambert correctly recognized at the time, the results were symptomatic of the NDP's collapse rather than a Liberal resurgence.[93] Neither able to emulate the PCs' centre-right coalition of the rural South with the Winnipeg business class, nor (and even more unlikely) the NDP's alternatively successful North Manitoba-North Winnipeg formula, the Liberal breakthrough was limited to Winnipeg (with the single exception of nearby Selkirk). That is, the Liberals could break neither into the conservatively dominated agricultural areas (where the Liberal "brand" was intensely disliked due to Trudeau) nor the province's North due to a lack of attachment to northern workers and First Nations voters. In another era, Carstairs might have turned to a federal Liberal minister of Indian and Northern Affairs, such as a Jean Chrétien or John Munro, to build bridges between the provincial Liberals and these northern communities. However, with Mulroney's PCs in power in Ottawa, this avenue was not available.

Return to Half-Party

The 1988 election produced a minority government for Gary Filmon and his PCs. With the governing party holding only twenty-five seats to the Liberals' twenty (later to become twenty-one with PC MLA Gilles Roch crossing the floor) and the NDP's twelve seats, the new government could easily have fallen. However, the opportunity slipped away as the PCs held on, with tacit support coming from the NDP. The badly defeated NDP under Gary Doer needed to avoid a quick election so that it could rebuild. The Liberals were the official opposition, and from 1988 to 1990 their leader became enmeshed with the government's deliberations over whether or not Manitoba should ratify the Meech Lake Accord.

In the election of 1990, Carstairs faced what appeared to be a very different Gary Filmon. In contrast to his image in the 1980s as a political neophyte, during the Meech Lake negotiations he appeared to be both capable and competent. In the meantime, Carstairs increasingly appeared as a vulnerable and exhausted leader.[94] Her deterioration was compounded by her poor performance during the televised leadership debate. Yet the party's misfortunes were rooted in something more than the failings of leadership. A second factor was that the political skills among members of her caucus were said to be uneven, with many failing to build up their constituency organizations during their first two years in office.[95] Third, in Ontario, the Liberals unexpectedly lost power to Bob Rae's NDP which, in turn, deflated the Manitoba Liberal campaign and boosted NDP spirits. What ensued was that the Liberals failed on two fronts to build on their 1988 victory. They lost seats to the NDP in Winnipeg and to Filmon's PCs elsewhere. Only seven Liberals were elected, of which two would eventually leave for other opportunities: Reg Alcock to run federally and Jim Carr to return to journalism (and later become the president and CEO of the Business Council of Manitoba). It was cold comfort that this was the first time since 1973 that the Liberals had maintained official party status for more than one term.

Carstairs retired from provincial politics in 1993. On 5 June of the same year Winnipeg lawyer and MLA Paul Edwards beat out fellow caucus member Kevin Lamoureux for the leadership race by a vote of 1087 to 937. Raised in River Heights, Edwards had become known as a young and hardworking MLA who, in contrast to a very young Axworthy in 1966, was able to successfully win St. James for the Liberals in both 1988 and 1990. At first, things looked promising for the young leader. In a September by-election in The Maples, due to the resignation of Liberal MLA Dr. Gulzar Cheema, the Liberals retained the riding with the election of Gary Kowalski.

In the 1995 provincial election, the party slipped further to 24 percent of the popular vote and dropped to three seats in the legislature—Inkster, St.

Boniface, and The Maples. Added to the defeat was that Edwards lost his seat in St. James. A number of factors contributed to the devastating results, including the federal Liberal government's launch of the gun registry, which produced an anti-Liberal backlash not seen since the Trudeau era in rural Manitoba. Added to this was a lacklustre and problematic campaign that began with Edwards inadvertently walking into a group of protesters in front of the Morgentaler abortion clinic. This led to an "ad-libbed" discussion of abortion issues with the media. It was a terrible beginning to what had been thought a promising election for the party. Edwards cites this event as well as the federal Liberal government's gun registry as two factors that contributed to his party's difficulties in the 1995 election.[96] In the following year Edwards resigned the party leadership and returned to the legal profession. Without official party status, the Liberals were once again adrift. Matters became complicated upon the arrival of its new leader. On 19 October 1996, with backing from what the *Winnipeg Free Press* referred to as the party's "South Winnipeg establishment," including Reg Alcock and Lloyd Axworthy, former party president Ginny Hasselfield took over the leadership.[97]

Figure 3.4:
Derived from Elections Manitoba, "Historical Summaries" and *Winnipeg Free Press*, 23 May 2007

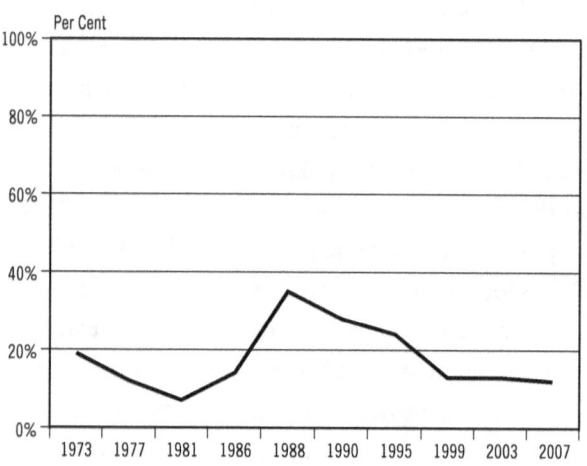

It was a controversial victory in that Kevin Lamoureux, who had support from many new Canadians (primarily from the Philippine and Sikh communities), lost due to a balloting process whereby votes were weighted on a constituency basis rather than having the totals based on raw vote counts. This was to Lamoureux's detriment due to much of his support being concentrated in his home riding. The final vote, with the weights incorporated, was Hasselfield with 958 against Lamoureux's 937. When asked by *Winnipeg Free Press* reporter Paul Samyn what he had learned from this second failed attempt, Lamoureux replied, "I learned not to run for the Liberal leadership."[98] This bitter leadership contest revealed serious rifts in the party. Two of the three sitting members, including Lamoureux, temporarily left the caucus to sit as "Independent Liberals." Facing an untenable situation, and without her own seat in the legislature, Hasselfield stepped down in 1998.[99]

It was an unlikely figure who took over the leadership of this dispirited party. A medical doctor by training and a published author on the topic of bald eagles, Jon Gerrard had been the Liberal MP for Portage-Interlake from 1993 to 1997 while serving in Jean Chrétien's cabinet as Secretary of State for Science, Research and Development.[100] His shift to provincial politics occurred after losing to the Reform Party in 1997, largely due to the unpopular gun registration law. Facing off against Jerry Fontaine, the chief of the Sagkeeng First Nation, for the leadership of the party, Gerrard won by 1336 to 832 votes on 17 October 1998. One can only wonder about the path the party might have taken had the delegates chosen a well-known First Nations leader to lead the party rather than another urban-based professional. Perhaps it would have led the party beyond being, to use Carstairs's words, "primarily an urban party" of South Winnipeg.[101] Alternatively, it might have signalled the party's disappearance as it wandered away from its core supporters.

The NDP and PCs battled for supremacy in the 1999 provincial election. In the rubble was Gerrard's Liberal Party with 13 percent of the popular vote and a single seat in the legislature. Fortunately for the party and its leadership, this seat belonged to Gerrard, who had opted to run for Carstairs's old seat in River Heights.[102] The subsequent 2003 provincial election produced only small gains for the party. Kevin Lamoureux was re-elected alongside Gerrard, which caused the party leader to inform his supporters that "I can have someone to second motions in the legislature."[103] It was a small victory and the *Winnipeg Free Press* reported the next day that the "Liberals take pride in doubling MLAs."[104] Still short of having official party status, and only able to take the same two seats in the 2007 election, it is unclear what the party can do to regain its former stature. Under Gerrard, the party appears united and in better shape financially. However, in large part the Liberals' fortunes will continue to hinge on the performance of the other two parties.

Conclusion

The Manitoba Liberal Party is now essentially an urban party. The party began its decline with its defeat to Duff Roblin's PCs in the late 1950s, a decline which continued into the late 1960s and 1970s as the word "liberal" became a pejorative term. The provincial Liberals were damaged by its association with the national party which, under Trudeau, was identified with economic mismanagement, official bilingualism, ineffective farm policies, and Ottawa-oriented arrogance. The provincial party paid the price by losing all of its rural seats. Secondly, the provincial party's shift following the 1969 provincial election towards urban voters who had drifted to the NDP signalled a further move away from the previously successful Liberal-Progressive rural-urban strategy. At the same time, one could argue that this was compounded by the party's brand becoming strongly tied to Ottawa and federal Liberal cabinet ministers, especially James Richardson and Lloyd Axworthy. Thirdly, the Liberals were unable to capitalize on the temporary euphoria of Carstairs's success in 1988.[105] The party's subsequent dissipation was connected to complications relating to strategy and leadership, failure to create beachheads outside Winnipeg, and an inability to hold down a badly bruised NDP in Winnipeg.

The party's next opportunity came in 1999 in the wake of the PC government's vote-splitting scandal and an NDP, led by Gary Doer, which had lost the three previous elections. However, the Liberals were still recovering from internal divisions and needed time to heal. While those on the ideological right hunkered down in the PC trenches, other voters wanting a change in government opted for the NDP as their best chance of success. In both the 1999 and the 2003 provincial elections, the Liberals won 13 percent of the vote. It obtained 12 percent in 2007. During the last two elections it won only two seats. Unless something of consequence affects either of the two other parties, it is doubtful that the Liberals can soon expand beyond serving as Manitoba's "one-half party."

The construction of the new Legislative Building in 1914, with the old Victorian-style Legislative Building in the foreground, (Provincial Archives of Manitoba)

(above) An election advertisement from the United Grain Growers, 1922. (Provincial Archives of Manitoba)

(right) A delegate's ribbon from the 1914 Liberal party convention, featuring the image of party leader T. C. Norris. (Provincial Archives of Manitoba)

The first United Farmers cabinet after the 1922 election, lead by John Bracken (second from left). (Provincial Archives of Manitoba)

A Gildas Molgat campaign brochure for the 1962 election.
(Allison Molgat)

The televised leaders' debate from the 1962 provincal election, with premier Duff Roblin (far left) and Liberal leader Gil Molgat and NDP leader Russ Paulley to his right. (University of Manitoba Archives & Special Collection Tribune Collection)

These two newspaper advertisements from the 1969 provincial election demonstrate the very different styles of the two party leaders.

(top) Edward Shreyer on election night, 1973. (University of Manitoba Archives & Special Collections Tribune Collection)

(left) Liberal leader Isreal (Izzy) Asper campaigning in a 1973 by-election. (Babs Asper)

(above) Sterling Lyon entering the premier's office after his 1977 election win. (University of Manitoba Archives & Special Collections Tribune Collection)

(above) Howard Pawley with his wife Adele after winning the NDP leadership in 1979. (University of Manitoba Archives & Special Collections Tribune Collection)

(left) Gary Filmon and family after his first election to the legislature in 1979. (University of Manitoba Archives & Special Collections Tribune Collection)

Liberal leader Sharon Carstairs after the 1988 election. (Sharon Carstairs)

Hugh McFadyen on election night, 2007. (Winnipeg Free Press)

Gary Doer enjoys his third consecutive majority win in 2007. (Winnipeg Free Press)

Jon Gerrard holds onto his two Liberal seats in 2007. (Winnipeg Free Press)

Chapter 4

The New Democratic Party

MANITOBA'S LEFT-WING POLITICAL TRADITION IS CHIEFLY ROOTED IN the evolution of urban-based worker politics. This contrasts sharply with its neighbour to the west, where farmers produced a victory for the CCF in the Saskatchewan election of 1944. While Saskatchewan farmers were centrally important to the Saskatchewan CCF and NDP, southern Manitoban farmers have been a predominantly conservative force with their support going to generally anti-labour and pro-business parties with platforms calling for small government and laissez-faire economic policies.[1] It is the City of Winnipeg that served as an incubator for the province's early left-wing political movements.[2] It produced such influential "labourite" leaders as J.S. Woodsworth and Stanley Knowles on the national stage and provided much of the organizational backbone for the national CCF and its successor, the NDP. Yet, it would be a mistake to think of Winnipeg's working class as a cohesive whole.

In the first few decades of the twentieth century, two types of working-class parties came to dominate the local scene. These were hard-core socialist (and communist) parties and labour-reform parties. The socialists looked to the Soviet Union for inspiration and direction while moderate labourites modelled their activities and platforms on the Independent Labour Party in England (the British Labour Party's precursor), with its blend of radicalism and respect for parliamentary democracy, the electoral process, and unions.[3] Of this latter group, there existed a number of Winnipeg-based organizations and parties that were ancestors to the CCF and the currently operating provincial NDP. These included various labour parties formed prior to the 1919 Winnipeg General Strike, the most notable being the Independent Labour Party (ILP).[4] For decades to come, labour-oriented provincial candidates were hampered by the same two factors plaguing Canada's national labour movement: ongoing struggles with socialists on the left and, to the right, a Liberal Party that was often willing to appropriate labour-oriented platforms. The ILP, with successes in both Winnipeg and Brandon,[5] was eventually replaced by the Co-operative Commonwealth Federation in the 1930s, which in turn was reshaped into the NDP in 1961.[6]

Early Labour Politics

The twentieth century began on an optimistic note for the labour movement. In January 1900, Winnipeg Labour Party candidate Arthur Puttee was elected to Parliament in a federal by-election.[7] The results reflected something more than the rise of labour; they revealed a city deeply divided along ethnic and class lines that would continue to define Winnipeg politics throughout the subsequent century and to the present day. Winnipeg's more affluent residents in the South End of the city gave 69 percent of their vote to the Liberals while the working-class North End contributed 66 percent of their vote to Labour, with the downtown area mixing its support between the two parties.[8] As the province's economy underwent massive industrial growth from 1900 to 1910, as indicated by a rise in output from $13 million to $54 million, numbers within Winnipeg's labour force grew correspondingly from 5000 to 17,000 individuals.[9] With such growth it appeared inevitable that a successful provincial labour party would soon develop.

In spite of Puttee's success in 1900, for the most part Winnipeg's North End voters were politically divided along ethnic lines: between workers of British ancestry and the newly arriving immigrants from continental Europe who brought with them different languages and customs. These new labour-market entrants came to be seen as both a threat to job security and good wages. The workers' vote therefore tended to split between British-oriented labourite candidates and European-oriented "scientific socialists." This self-defeating dynamic was demonstrated when the short-lived Manitoba Labour Party's star candidate, Fred Dixon, went down to defeat in 1910 in Winnipeg Centre due largely to a socialist "spoiler" campaign. The result was that a Conservative candidate won the riding.[10]

Divisions continued in the 1914 provincial election, yet this time Fred Dixon was able to win his Winnipeg seat, albeit as an independent with support from both Norris's reformist and urban-oriented Liberal Party and some (but not all) members of the Labour Representation Committee (LRC), which had since replaced the Manitoba Labour Party.[11] However, there remained no MLAs who could be specifically identified as "labour" representatives in the provincial assembly.[12] The situation improved slightly in the 1915 election (which had been called after the downfall of Roblin's Conservative government) with Dixon re-elected as a labour-oriented independent (with Liberal Party support) and LRC-endorsed Richard Rigg winning his seat in North Winnipeg.[13] But for a city with such a large working-class population with grievances regarding working conditions, housing shortages, living wages, and public education, these could only be considered extraordinarily small victories for the labour movement and the LRC.

Winnipeg labour politics cannot be understood without recognizing that a strong push for social reform came from the social gospel movement. With parallels to the controversial Latin American Christian "liberation movement" in the 1970s and 1980s, the social gospel movement in the early years of Winnipeg incorporated Christian teachings with social justice. Christian salvation was obtainable through good works in the current world, not by waiting for an afterworld. Many of those who preached the social gospel would later become important leaders in the ILP and the CCF. In Winnipeg, two early and influential figures were Salem Bland, a Christian minister and professor at Wesley College (which later became the University of Winnipeg), and J.S. Woodworth. Bland's radicalism included prohibitionism, work with the Winnipeg Trade and Labor Council, and preaching at Grain Grower meetings across the Prairies.[14] As did Bland, J.S. Woodsworth blended together his academic background, Christian ministry, and politics. After growing up in Brandon, becoming a circuit minister, and then studying in Toronto and Oxford, Woodsworth returned to Winnipeg to head the All People's Mission and promote social-welfare issues. By the time of the Winnipeg General Strike, he had become heavily involved in labour politics across western Canada, and, in 1921, Winnipeg voters elected him to serve as an ILP MP.[15] He would later work with others to forge a coalition of radical farmers, labourites, and urban intellectuals to form the CCF. The active focus of both Bland and Woodsworth, according to historian Richard Allen, demonstrates that the social gospel movement and the parties it spawned were "first derived from urban rather than agrarian responses to industrialism. Its framework of thought derived from urban universities, urban civil servants, and urban pastors. It could be described as a metropolitan concoction which the hinterland came to share."[16]

As a presage to the 1940s, when Mackenzie King and his Liberal Party wooed CCF voters, T.C. Norris and his Manitoba Liberals worked hard in the 1914 and 1915 provincial elections to attract the labourite vote by pushing forward a platform built upon social and industrial reforms. In 1915, Norris was able to capitalize on a combination of South Winnipeg voters' concerns about the scandal-ridden Conservatives and support from urban workers and social reformers. In that election, the Liberals took forty seats with 55 percent of the popular support. The large-scale victory based on an unusual cross-urban electoral alliance produced immediate benefits for Winnipeg's working class. In his history of the Manitoba labour movement, Doug Smith writes: "The Norris government was a progressive administration for its time and the labour movement had high hopes for it. Previous Conservative administrations had passed a number of shop and factory acts, but little was done to make sure that employers abided by them ... The new premier, Norris, moved quickly to expand the size of the bureau of labour, and the shops and factory acts were amended to increase their scope and plug many of their loopholes."[17] The new government also introduced a workers' compensation program and, in 1916, the vote for women.[18]

Norris's gradual reformism, however, came to a halt with the 1919 Winnipeg General Strike, which was born from many factors that were beyond the premier's control. These included a post-war hangover, in which workers were squeezed between high living costs and low wages, the drifting home of jobless war veterans, the federal government's wartime suppression of existing eastern European worker organizations, the growth of trade union organizations, including the One Big Union (OBU), which was linked to American labour politics, and the growing influence of the International Workers of the World (IWW), and the advent of the Russian Revolution, which inspired many workers to seek their own political destiny and control the economy for themselves.[19]

The strike ended badly for the workers, their representative organizations, and Norris's Liberals. The use of paramilitary forces, growing fears about insecurity and job losses, and the use of strike breakers combined to discredit the government. In the end, for workers in Manitoba and across Canada, the general strike was what McCormack describes as a "revolutionary tactic" which "led the workers to disaster ... workers [subsequently] turned their backs on militant industrial unionism and rejected revolutionary doctrines."[20] It was out of these ashes, and a discredited Norris government, that a new ILP was formed in 1920. In the provincial election of that same year the ILP obtained close to one-fifth (17.7 percent) of the provincial vote and one-third of the city's electorate, bringing it within 1 percent of the Conservative's 18.5 percent figure.[21] The Communist Party of Canada (CPC) was formed shortly after, in 1921, yet became increasingly isolated from the ILP's gradualist agenda and mainstream labour unions.²² Regardless of the strategies used by either party, the electoral system's bias with its over-representation of rural voters strongly dampened both the ILP and CPC's chances for success.

Figure 4.1:
Derived from Elections Manitoba, "Historical Summaries"

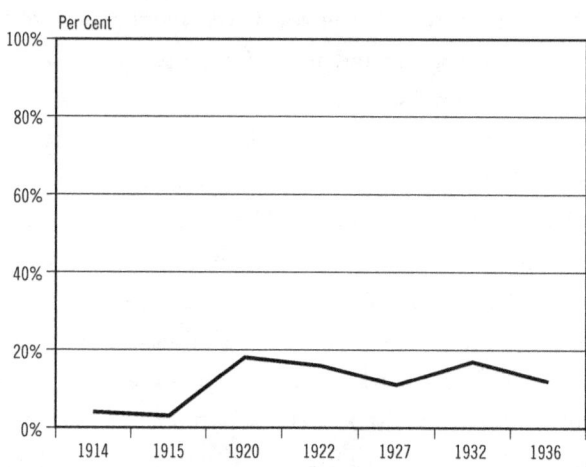

Provincial Labour Party Support 1914 to 1936

By the early 1930s, the ILP had close to 1000 members. It operated with seventeen branches in Manitoba, including Winnipeg, Brandon, and northern Manitoba. The ILP also had twenty-eight elected members serving across three levels of government (provincial, civic, and school board).²³ However, its popular support in the province did not break the 20 percent mark and, by 1932, in spite of the deepening Depression and failed attempts to forge a province-wide alliance with rural voters in a "Farmer-Labour" party,²⁴ the party was stalled at 17 percent. It was in this same year that the national Co-operative Commonwealth Federation was founded in Calgary, with its base of labourites, radical farmers, Ontario-based intellectuals, and social gospel proponents.

The newly formed national party with its strong connection to prairie-oriented agrarianism caused concern for many members in the urban-oriented Manitoba ILP. Therefore, in Manitoba the switch from the ILP to the new CCF identity occurred gradually, as demonstrated in the 1936 provincial election in which candidates ran under the transitional "ILP-CCF" banner.[25] Winnipeg-based resistance to a full merger persisted into the late 1930s, much to the consternation of the national party's leaders. Intra-party divisions became further exacerbated by debates among its national leaders, including the pacifist leader Woodsworth, over Canada's involvement in the war and the possibility of conscription.[26] Despite attempts by some members within the Winnipeg ILP to disaffiliate, the ILP-CCF alliance survived, and the ILP was formally dissolved in 1943.[27] Perhaps if the ILP had won more support in the Manitoba elections of 1932 and 1936 it might not have disappeared as a distinct entity within the larger national party. Instead, the ILP lamely lurched from election to election. Its provincial popular vote declined to 12 percent in the 1936 election, and, in Winnipeg, only one out of every eight votes was cast for ILP-CCF candidates.[28]

The Manitoba CCF

While the CCF was establishing itself as a distinct political entity at the national level under the direction of such notables as J.S. Woodsworth and David Lewis, the provincial CCF, under the leadership of S.J. Farmer, was entering into a new and surreal relationship with Premier Bracken's all-party government coalition of Liberal-Progressives, Conservatives, and Social Credit MLAs. A Welshman by birth, in his early twenties Farmer moved to Canada in 1900. He helped found the Labour Church in Winnipeg, became heavily involved in the 1919 Winnipeg General Strike, helped in the rebirth of the ILP in 1921, and was mayor of Winnipeg from 1922 to 1923.[29] Under different circumstances, therefore, it is probable that Farmer would have refused Bracken's offer to join the all-party coalition. However, in 1940 there was public pressure for parties to work in cooperation with the Liberal-Progressives, signifying that there would be electoral consequences for those who did not.

After much hand-wringing within the provincial and national party by those such as Woodsworth and Stanley Knowles, the MP for Winnipeg North Centre,[30] Farmer was sworn into the cabinet as minister of labour on 4 November 1940. He thereby became the first CCF representative to enter a cabinet minister's post anywhere in Canada.[31] Although part of the governing coalition, CCF members attempted to maintain some semblance of autonomy by sitting together in the legislature to the left of the Speaker rather than mixing with the Liberal-Progressive MLAs.[32] Unfortunately for the CCF, as well as for the Conservatives and Social Credit, the Liberal-Progressives would reap most of the rewards from the "non-partisanship" arrangement. In the 1941 election, the CCF dropped to a mere three seats, with two candidates elected in Winnipeg and one in Gimli.[33]

In December 1942, Farmer resigned from the cabinet, and at the 1943 party's convention the membership passed a motion put forward by Knowles to formally recognize the party's withdrawal from the non-partisan arrangement.[34] It signalled the beginning of a new period for the party. Provincial membership numbers were growing from less than 800 in the early 1940s to 3300 in 1943, and then close to 5000 in 1944 and 1945.[35] In 1943, the CCF won two provincial by-elections, one in The Pas and the other in Brandon, while also winning the Selkirk riding in the federal by-election of that same year. The CCF was gaining support across the country. Next door in Ontario, the CCF took thirty-four out of ninety seats in the 1943 provincial election, and, in the same year, the Gallup Poll was pegging national CCF support at 29 percent, which was a slight lead over both the Liberals and Conservatives.[36] In January 1944, *Maclean's* would report: "There is no gainsaying the fact that the CCF has gripped the imagination and harnessed the hopes of a large number of people."[37] Later in 1944 the CCF would go on to victory in Saskatchewan with the election of Tommy Douglas as premier.

This growth in the CCF's support both within Manitoba and across the country in many ways reflected a growing recognition among Canadians that the state could—and should—be more involved in both the economy and social-welfare programs. A 1943 Gallup Poll reportessd that 71 percent of Canadians supported social-welfare reforms, with large numbers specifically mentioning employment supports, better working conditions, and the redistribution of wealth.[38] This did not go unnoticed by the governing Liberals, and in August 1943 Mackenzie King would reflect in his diaries that this new mood should push Liberals "to realize that labour has to be dealt with in a considerate way. In my heart, I am not sorry to see the mass of the people coming into their own, but I do regret that it is not a Liberal party that is winning that position for them. It should be, and it can still be that our people will learn their lesson in time."[39] Later, and after making a surprise visit to the annual meeting of the Trades and Labour Congress, King privately reflected: "I think in the end, Labour can win the most by returning a Liberal Government, but I know much work will have to be done to effect that end."[40]

Lloyd Stinson, who would later lead the Manitoba CCF in the 1950s, reflected in his memoirs that CCF expectations had been high "prior to the federal election of 1945; in fact there was a mood of over-confidence in CCF ranks in almost every province. It appeared that the CCF was on the verge of taking power in Canada."[41] It was therefore disappointing to party supporters when the federal election produced only twenty-eight seats for the CCF compared to sixty-eight for the PCs and 127 for the Liberals. In Manitoba, the federal CCF obtained 32 percent of the vote, which was more than the PCs' 25 percent (a surprising result when one considers that ex-Manitoba Premier Bracken was the national party's leader at the time) but less than the Liberals' 35 percent.[42]

It is easy to draw parallels between King's Liberals and their ability to sap the national CCF's strength in the 1940s with that of Norris's provincial Liberals and the ILP in 1915. In both cases the left had been outflanked by the Liberal Party's adoption of elements found in the labour platform. In the post-war era, King enacted expanded programs of social-welfare spending, employment support, and post-war economic planning. He effectively inaugurated what political scientists Jane Jenson and Susan Phillips describe as an era in which the "government entered into a relationship with each Canadian via several new social programs. Cheques came from the federal government for family allowances and pensions. Unemployment insurance was a country-wide program ... [and] for the first time, the vision of individual citizens linked by a set of national institutions made everyday sense."[43] Robert Campbell, in his economic history of post-war Canada, further identifies three effects from this new period of state interventionism. The new "Keynesian state" laid the basis for technocratic understandings of policy priorities, promoted gradualism over radical change, and reduced class conflicts.[44] In effect, the Liberal Party was introducing new measures to prevent the same kind of post-war depression that had occurred at the close of World War I, thereby avoiding the same political disturbances of that period.

In contrast to the national Liberals, the Liberal-Progressives exhibited little interest in adopting any part of the CCF's platform. In the 1945 provincial election, Premier Stuart Garson left expansionist social-spending policies to the federal government while continuing to steer the Manitoba government along a path of small-government priorities with its pro-farmer and

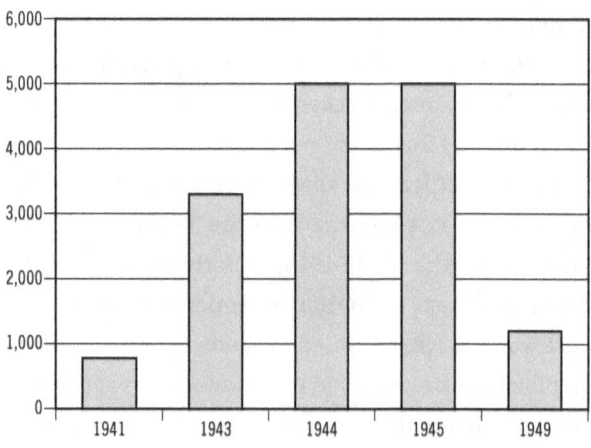

Figure 4.2:
Nelson Wiseman, *Social Democracy in Manitoba*

pro-business orientation. In the meantime, the CCF continued to struggle against the continuing imbalance between urban and rural representation caused by the electoral process itself. The 1945 election was perhaps the most telling instance of the system's bias against urban voters. CCF support grew from 17 percent in 1941 to 34 percent in 1945, which exceeded the popular support for any of the other parties that year. However, the CCF won only nine out of fifty-five seats. In contrast, the Liberal-Progressives with 32 percent of the provincial vote were able to capture twenty-five ridings, of which two were by acclamation. Adding insult to injury, the Conservatives (who were now operating under the "Progressive" Conservative banner) obtained thirteen seats with a mere 16 percent of the vote.[45] Admittedly, the impact of the rural-urban imbalance might be overstated for the 1945 election due to popular support tallies being made only for those ridings in which elections were held. Seven rural ridings were taken by non-CCF candidates by acclamation. Therefore, one can only surmise that if all these ridings were contested, the CCF's popular support would have been proportionately lower.

With Farmer's resignation as provincial party leader in 1947, the CCF began a long exodus into the political wilderness. In 1948, E.A. Hansford, the sitting MLA for St. Boniface, became the CCF's new leader and saw his party's popular vote descend to 26 percent in the election of the following year, with twenty-six ridings going unchallenged and only seven of its candidates being elected.[46] Behind the scenes, the organization had been in trouble, with thousands dropping their party membership since joining in the heydays of 1944 and 1945 (Figure 4.2). Only 1200 members remained on the party's books by 1949. By 1951, twenty-seven of the province's constituencies were without a functioning CCF riding association, and in the following year its newspaper, the *Manitoba Commonwealth*, folded.[47] Conditions would remain unimproved for the 1953 election, in which twenty-eight ridings went without a CCF candidate and the party's popular vote dropped to 16 percent. The result was that only five candidates were elected.⁴⁸ The party's dissipation was further demonstrated that year when Hansford resigned and the CCF went without an annual meeting.⁴⁹

Lloyd Stinson took over the party's helm in 1953 following a very brief leadership of William "Scottie" Bryce, who had left federal politics as the MP for Selkirk to enter the provincial scene.⁵⁰ In addition to having a career as a United Church minister for nine years until 1942, Stinson came to the leadership in 1953 with impeccable credentials. He had campaigned on behalf of the party in the 1930s, was the editor of the *Manitoba Commonwealth* from 1943 to 1946, served as a Winnipeg alderman from 1943 to 1944, was elected as an MLA in 1945, and became party house leader in 1952. But even Stinson was unable to find a path back for the party to electoral popularity and, in the 1953 election, the party was able only to field candidates in nineteen out of forty-seven ridings (including Winnipeg and St. Boniface, which were multiple-seat ridings). After leaving provincial politics, Stinson continued his career by serving as a very active Winnipeg city councillor from 1963 to 1971.⁵¹

Nelson Wiseman identifies two factors that contributed to the party's poor showings in this period. The first was self-inflicted by Stinson and his followers, many of whom cut their political teeth during the Depression and therefore from the 1940s and 1950s erroneously built their campaigns around the idea that a post-war depression was impending. This created the sense among voters that the party was "bad news" and out of touch with the times. Secondly, the CCF was unable to counter Canada's growing Cold War political culture.⁵² This was not due to a lack of effort. In 1949, at the CCF provincial convention, party members distanced themselves further from communism by voting fifty-six to eighteen to expel Berry Richards, the CCF MLA for The Pas, and Wilbert Doneleyko, the CCF MLA for St. Clements, for expressing their opposition to NATO and its activities in Europe.⁵³ In spite of such drastic actions by the party, and due to Winnipeg's large Ukrainian and Polish communities in the North End, news from Russia and eastern Europe continued to affect the provincial scene as anti-Soviet fears became exacerbated regarding all left-wing parties, even the reformist CCF. The message the CCF was trying to send by expelling Richards and Doneleyko during an era of hysteria was that voting for a worker-based party was not a vote for the USSR.

The CCF's fortunes began changing when substantial electoral reform finally arrived in 1957 in the form of the Electoral Divisions Boundaries Commission. Based on its recommendations, Winnipeg was divided into single-member constituencies with the same first-past-the-post process of selection used elsewhere in the province. More importantly, it was the beginning of a long-overdue series of adjustments to the election system. It replaced the two-to-one rural-urban ratio with a seven-to-four rural-urban ratio when revising electoral boundaries.[54] The process of electoral reform would have a larger impact in the 1960s, when more adjustments were introduced to further enhance urban representation in the legislature. In the meantime, the CCF had to contend with an even more potent challenge in the form of Duff Roblin and his Progressive Conservatives. Just as King had used portions of the CCF's platform to move the national Liberals to the ideological centre in the 1940s, Roblin initiated reforms that had previously been put forward by the CCF.[55] These included expanded supports for education, new social-welfare programs, and promotion of northern development.

While Roblin was enjoying the benefits of a smoothly running PC Party machine, all four wheels of the provincial CCF were falling off. The party was in a state of organizational disarray, had problematic finances, appeared ideologically confused, and appeared unable to stem declining voter support. In the words of Stinson, "the CCF was broke, and we needed time to re-organize our forces and gather some election funds."[56] Due to this vulnerability, and to gain time for regrouping, the eleven-member CCF caucus supported Roblin's 1958 minority government. However, this strategy allowed the PCs to introduce their own reformist government agenda. This in turn caused the CCF to be unable to articulate a distinct position in the subsequent campaign. The CCF was therefore lucky to win the ten seats that it did in the 1959 election, as Roblin rolled on to a majority victory.

The New Party

Two events led to the CCF's transformation at both the national and provincial level. First, the Trades and Labour Congress of Canada merged with the Canadian Congress of Labor to produce the Canadian Labour Congress (CLC). In 1958, CLC delegates passed a motion to begin discussions with the CCF and other membership-based organizations with the aim of forming a "political instrument of the Canadian people."[57] Secondly, John Diefenbaker's popularity across the West and his Progressive Conservative landslide of 1958 had direct implications for the CCF. The 1958 election reduced the CCF's parliamentary presence from twenty-five to eight seats. Even the widely respected Stanley Knowles had been defeated in Winnipeg. Left without a role in Parliament, he was subsequently elected to serve as a vice-president of the CLC with a mandate to work towards forming the "New Party."[58]

The New Party idea received strong support among those directing the Manitoba CCF as well as from the Manitoba Federation of Labour and the Winnipeg District Labour Council. In 1960, at its provincial convention, CCF delegates passed a motion in support of creating the New Party. There was some resistance from younger and more radical members, including Howard Pawley (later to become Schreyer's Attorney General and provincial premier). However, and in spite of all the fuss regarding the organization's newly formed affiliation to labour, it appeared as old wine in new bottles. Two political historians in separate studies, James McAllister and Nelson Wiseman, observed that little distinguished the NDP platform from the old CCF, and that NDP meetings were chiefly populated by ex-CCF members. Even those representing the newly affiliated unions were reported to be predominantly from the CCF.[59]

The NDP remained in third place, behind the PCs and Liberals, throughout most of the 1960s, both in its share of popular support and seats in the assembly. Under its leader Russ Paulley, the MLA for Transcona, a Canadian National Railways shops worker, and past mayor of Transcona, the NDP were able to field a partial slate of only thirty-nine candidates in the 1962 provincial election. Support thereby slumped to 15 percent of the vote with only seven candidates elected. In the 1966 election, however, the CCF boosted its fortunes with 23 percent of the popular vote and eleven MLAS elected. Furthermore, 1966 signified that an electoral shift in Winnipeg was occurring to the detriment of the Liberals, with 32 percent of voters supporting the NDP compared to 29 percent for the Liberals.[60] Yet still to develop alongside this urban realignment was change within the province's northern electorate. In 1966, NDP candidates placed third in The Pas (with 6.6 percent of the vote) and Rupertsland (11.3 percent).[61] Both of these ridings would be taken by the NDP in 1969.

The 1969 Election

On the night of the 1969 election, Manitobans discovered that, in the words of the *Winnipeg Free Press*, "Yesterday's Boy Wonder of Manitoba politics is likely to be tomorrow's premier[.] Ed Schreyer and a barnstorming team of New Democrats poleaxed the Progressive Conservative government."[62] A combination of factors produced the NDP victory. The first included the socio-economic impact of a growing service sector and the baby boom. The second was the fact that the NDP was facing off against two parties that were each led by rurally oriented social conservatives who appeared out of step with the times. Third, the growing significance of television on the everyday lives of Manitobans meant that the operational nature of campaigns and how leaders could be presented to the public were changing. The fourth major influence was electoral redistribution, first initiated in the 1950s, which oriented the system further towards the more heavily populated City of Winnipeg.

Looking back on the election of 1969, earlier in the year fortune appeared to be smiling on Premier Weir and his governing PCs. They were high in the polls, were coming off successful by-elections, and were enjoying a springtime provincial budget surplus. Meanwhile, one of the party's two major opponents, the NDP, was operating without a leader. When Weir called the election for 25 June, the NDP was forced to move quickly and change its previously arranged leadership convention to 7 June. The firebrand Sidney Green, a thirty-nine-year-old Winnipeg-based lawyer from the North End, sparred with Edward Schreyer in well-attended and widely televised debates that were held across the province. Schreyer won with 506 votes compared to Green's 177.[63] In his memoirs, Green reflected on the remarkable aura generated by the race. It "seemed to overshadow the election campaign with extensive media coverage of both candidates. There were almost daily reports of the leadership delegates and the positions taken—which were essentially anti-Conservative rather than personal attacks."[64] Even young Liberals who had enjoyed the excitement of Trudeaumania during the 1968 federal election were attracted to the NDP, in part due to leader Robert Bend, who represented the more rurally oriented right-of-centre elements in the provincial Liberal Party. Many of these young Liberals were said to have entered the fray to pick sides in the NDP's leadership race.[65]

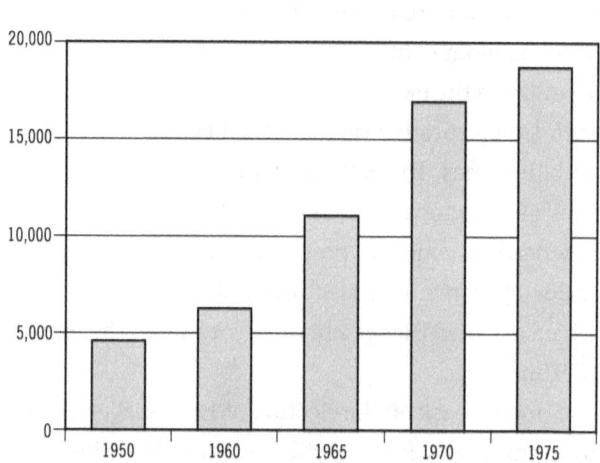

Figure 4.3: Source, M.C. Leacy, ed., *Historical Statistics of Canada*, 2nd Edition Table W340-438

University Fulltime Enrolment, Manitoba 1950 to 1975

A political moderate who appeared comfortable on TV while appealing to a wide range of voters, Schreyer grew up in a Roman Catholic family of German-Austrian extraction. In his young adult days teaching school in his hometown of Beausejour, he served as a campaign manager for the CCF candidate in the federal riding of Springfield. This was Jake Schulz, a founder of the Manitoba Farmers' Union, who would later become Schreyer's father-in-law. With Schreyer's help, Schulz was elected in 1957. He went down to defeat a year later in the Diefenbaker landslide. At the ripe age of twenty-two, Schreyer himself entered politics and won the provincial riding of Brokenhead in 1958, and then subsequently in both the 1959 and 1962 elections. In 1965 he switched to federal politics to successfully win the riding of Springfield. After seeing his riding redistributed out of existence, in 1968 he won the federal riding of Selkirk, which spanned both urban and rural neighbourhoods.[66]

Choosing Schreyer signalled to voters that the party could reach beyond urban working-class neighbourhoods and appeal to rural and urban Manitobans alike, including younger urban middle-class voters who might otherwise have supported the Liberals. Furthermore, it could reach out to the growing "new" middle class comprised of better educated men and women employed in such service-sector areas as health care, social services, and education (Figure 4.3 provides one indication of the changing provincial society by showing that the full-time university population in Manitoba almost doubled between 1960 and 1965 and continued to increase into the 1970s).

A sense of how Schreyer's NDP put forward an image better suited to the new times when compared to the PCs can be found by examining two advertisements that appeared in the *Winnipeg Free Press* on 21 June. In the PC advertisement, Premier Weir has a 1950s haircut and voters are soberly instructed that "With a big lift for industrial growth, Work with Weir to keep Manitoba going ahead."[67] In contrast, the NDP advertisement includes a picture of a smart and relaxed-looking Schreyer accompanied with the following message: "The man for all reasons. Our next Premier must truly represent all Manitobans. He must know and understand the needs of both rural and urban Manitoba ... He must be young—33—and he must have the experience to work effectively on our behalf."[68]

While the PCs held onto much of their traditional support in 1969, Liberal support collapsed and leader Robert Bend lost his own seat. His seemingly out-of-touch party dropped in popular support by 30 percent from the 1966 election. In the end, one out of every six voters was said to have switched his or her vote from another party to the NDP, with the Liberals taking the brunt of the damage.[69]

Schreyer's victory was initially interpreted by some to be a victory for the "ethnic" vote over WASP voters based in the rural southern farm areas and South Winnipeg. Not since John Norquay, who was of mixed Aboriginal and Scottish heritage, had Manitobans elected a non-WASP premier. Others pointed to the fact, as did political scientist Tom Peterson shortly after the election, that "it was the first time in Manitoba history" that "persons of non-British origin comprised a majority" in the legislature.[70] However, in a later and more developed piece, Peterson cautions that this was not a simple "ethnic revolt," but a sign that with each passing decade Manitobans were identifying less with their ancestral countries of origin and more with Canada as well as their own individual socio-economic interests. "The traditional ethnic appeals" as practised by the Liberals and PCs, Peterson writes, "were now less effective" and the "NDP victory appeared to have been made possible by a decline in ethnic consciousness," which has been replaced by class-related interests.[71] Peterson's thesis is supported by John Wilson's polling data from 1973. Wilson's research shows that NDP support tended to be higher among working-class voters compared to middle-class voters, regardless of whether or not they were British Protestant, non-British Protestant, and non-British Roman Catholic.[72]

In Winnipeg, the NDP won victories in the newly created ridings of Crescentwood, Point Douglas, Rossmere, and Transcona, and took seats from the PCs in Osborne, St. James, St. Matthews, and Winnipeg Centre. In rural ridings to the north of Winnipeg, chiefly settled by farmers of non-British heritage, the NDP took from the PCs Lac du Bonnet and Springfield and, from the Liberals, St. George[73] and Selkirk.

Another major breakthrough occurred in the North, one which would have long-term rewards for the party based on support from both labour and Aboriginal voters. Here there was a realignment occurring with the NDP taking—for the first time—three of Manitoba's four most northerly ridings from the PCs: Flin Flon, The Pas, and Rupertsland. The NDP also took the newly formed riding of Thompson.[74] The PCs were able to hold onto Churchill, but were defeated eventually by NDP candidate Jay Cowan in 1977. Following upon his own defeat in The Pas to NDP candidate Ron McBryde, Weir's consumer affairs minister, Jack Carroll, blamed Aboriginal voters. Quoted in the *Winnipeg Free Press*, he asserted that "quite a few IOU's [sic] were put out (to the Indians) by the NDP" and, according to the newspaper report, "he could cite no reason for the decline in popularity of his party."[75] Perhaps a lack of empathy could be mentioned by more astute observers.

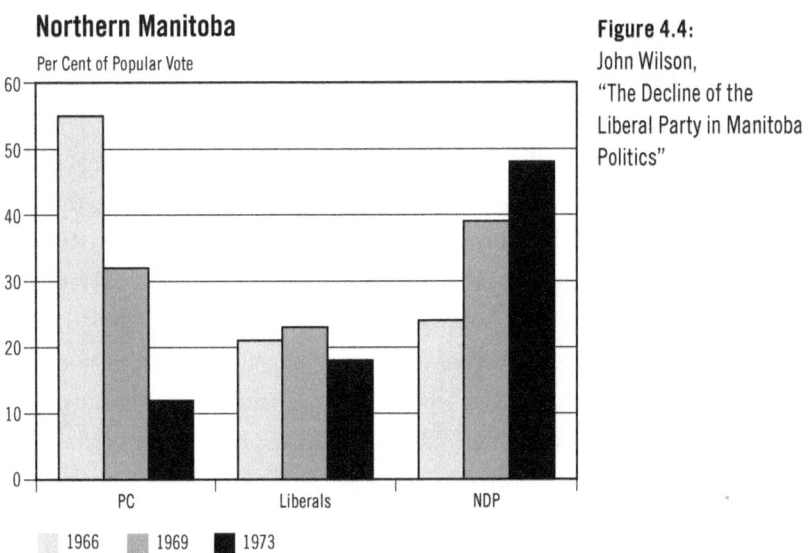

Figure 4.4: John Wilson, "The Decline of the Liberal Party in Manitoba Politics"

It was clear that the North was changing with developments in mining and energy, but also with regard to First Nations communities. In 1952 the right to vote was returned to treaty Indians, thus providing an opportunity for those seeking new electoral opportunities. By the late 1960s, hydro development and northern flooding were emerging as major issues in the North—as well as among Winnipeg residents who were interested in cheap power and the financial rewards from northern development—and concerns were raised about how these would be negotiated with the First Nations.[76] There were many in the NDP, including Schreyer, who felt that they had a better understanding than their Liberal and PC opponents, not only of blue-collar labourers in the northern resource sectors, but also the life of an Aboriginal fisher, trapper, or woodsman. (In their youth, Schreyer and his brothers went "into the bush" after harvest time to work in the pulp industry. He credits this experience for developing his personal sense and interest in northern issues and lifestyles.[77])

Another factor contributing to the NDP's breakthrough was in the electoral system itself, which had been reformed just one year prior to the PC government's downfall. In the 1968 redistribution, the Electoral Divisions Boundaries Commission made a new adjustment to the electoral process by replacing the existing seven-to-four rural-urban formula with a more equitable population-based system. Under the new rules, adjustments to enhance rural representation were restricted to a 25 percent level of tolerance. In other words, the notion that representation by population could be qualified to reflect also the representation of territory (and that adjustments should be made to ensure representation for sparsely populated regions) held less substance in setting boundaries after 1968. The result was that almost half of the province's ridings were now in Winnipeg and its immediate vicinity. Years later, when asked whether or not the NDP could have won in 1969 without the 1968 redistribution, and after a moment of reflection, Schreyer responded with "probably not."[78]

At the time of the 1969 election, few understood that it was signalling a long-term realignment of the province. In this sense, it was what political scientists call a "critical election."[79] At first it looked like a temporary situation. It was only much later that Schreyer was able to convert his fragile minority victory into a majority government. The day after the 1969 election there was uncertainty over who would be forming the next government. The subsequent day-to-day events proved to be some of the most defining moments in Manitoba's modern political history, in that a new winning formula had been created that counteracted the long-standing formula of combining South Winnipeg with the southern rural farm vote. In 1969, the NDP captured seventeen of the twenty-seven Winnipeg seats (with 45 percent of the popular vote in eastern Winnipeg, 47 percent in central Winnipeg, and 63 percent in the northern parts of Winnipeg),[80] one of the two Brandon seats, and 43 percent of the vote across the less prosperous northern and eastern regions of the province.[81] With similarities to Roosevelt's 1932 election in the US in which the Democrats linked together support from the South with voters in the Northeast, the NDP had forged its own Manitoba-oriented formula that would be used with success again by Schreyer in 1973, Howard Pawley in 1981 and 1986, and Gary Doer in 1999, 2003, and 2007.

It was the first time that the NDP had captured government power outside Saskatchewan. In spite of the pronounced fears and Cold War red-baiting by media commentators on radio and in print, including the *Winnipeg Free Press* and the *Winnipeg Tribune*, as well as the business community,[82] the NDP's activities during its first term in office can only be described as pragmatically moderate. In many ways Schreyer's government more closely resembled that of Duff Roblin than the post-war labour-based governments of the UK or western Europe. New policies were developed mostly in the areas of education and social supports rather than economic restructuring or nationalizing industries.[83] No doubt this was partly due to jurisdictional limits placed on the provinces, as was especially demonstrated by the disallowance of Alberta's Social Credit legislation regarding banking and currency by the federal courts in the 1930s.[84]

The NDP's most controversial measure was the introduction of a public automobile insurance program. Throughout the country, automobile insurance rates were rising, and many governments were under pressure by consumer groups to respond. When Schreyer's government put forward legislation for the establishment of a provincially operated program called

Autopac, it was stiffly resisted by the local business community and the national insurance industry. Attacked as a socialist measure, it almost led to the government's downfall. With the visitors' gallery packed on 13 August 1970, it was not until the votes were cast with support given to the government by Larry Desjardins, who had wavered on the issue, that the legislation was passed. More significantly, the government survived, which enabled the NDP to solidify its reputation as a party that was able to govern both responsibly and effectively.[85]

Other government activities in its first term involved carry-overs from the previous government, including the aftermath of the province's entanglement in the Churchill Forestry Industry scandal, in which a total of over $100 million had been given to foreign investors who subsequently vanished. More satisfying to those in the new government was furthering the progress of Manitoba Hydro development that had been initiated previously by the Roblin government. The government also showed strong support for medicare as well as provincially sponsored pharmacare, new social programs including public housing, and labour reforms. Two other measures included the establishment of the Department of Northern Affairs and the creation of "Unicity," which involved a major restructuring of both the government and administration of the greater Winnipeg region.

There is no doubt that the NDP's initial successes were linked to Schreyer's moderate leadership style, which appealed to voters across the political spectrum. His wide appeal as a moderate leader was revealed in a 1973 pre-election poll that showed many Liberals (42 percent) and Conservatives (36 percent) preferring Schreyer over leaders of their own party. Many were reported to feel that Schreyer was "in the wrong party."[86] Shocking is that only 31 percent of PC supporters thought that their own leader, Sidney Spivak, would be the better premier while only 38 percent of Liberals identified Izzy Asper as the best of the three. However, when the vote was cast in June 1973, it appeared that Schreyer's popularity did not necessarily translate into NDP votes. The NDP's success was less than expected, with 42 percent of the provincial vote (up from 38 percent) and thirty-one of the fifty-seven seats in the house going to the NDP. Yet it was a majority government victory that signified that 1969 had been more than an historical aberration.

Some blamed the party's eventual defeat in 1977 on broad international trends including a recession, inflation, and the rise of neo-conservatism. Others blamed the NDP itself, claiming that the party had become uninspired, ideologically adrift, and oriented to maintaining the "status quo" after two terms in office.[87] Cy Gonick in his account of this period writes that after 1973 the government was not as inactive as some thought. It increased the province's commitment to hydro development to the point where in 1977 it constituted 60 percent of the province's total debt. Ongoing and new measures during this period included more public housing, more tax credits, increased education expenditures, guaranteed incomes and pharmacare for seniors, and free legal aid, daycare, and employment training for low-income individuals. It also helped, through the Manitoba Development Corporation (previously called the Manitoba Development Fund), to bail out a number of companies that eventually went into receivership.[88] No doubt this helped the PCs in their claim that the NDP was a tax-and-spend party that had little regard for the middle-class taxpayer. Schreyer and his NDP were defeated in 1977. Its popular support slipped from 42 percent to 38 percent while Sterling Lyon's PCs skyrocketed from 37 percent to a stunning 49 percent. The PCs took thirty-three seats to the NDP's twenty-three.

Shortly thereafter, the party's fortunes took an even more unexpected turn when the forty-three-year-old ex-premier, a person considered to be one of Canada's bright lights on the left, and a potential leader for the national NDP, was enticed by Pierre Trudeau to leave politics to serve as Canada's Governor General in 1979. One has to wonder who was best served by the move, the federal Liberals or Schreyer. It certainly was not the NDP. After retiring from his position as the Queen's representative in Canada, Schreyer served as the Canadian High Commissioner to Australia until 1988. Since the 1977 provincial election, he steadfastly remained outside the electoral fray and, in the manner of a retired political statesman, left his successors free to make their own mark on the provincial scene. Nineteen years later, however, he surprised many again by announcing that he was re-entering politics in the 2006 federal election to win back his old seat of Selkirk. While providing a spark for what was at the time a sagging campaign for Jack Layton and his NDP, Schreyer was unsuccessful. Since his younger days the area had become small-c conservative, and voters appeared more interested in tax reduction, attacking crime, and removing the Liberals from power.[89]

The Post-Schreyer Era

Having unsuccessfully fought in his early days against the CCF becoming the "New Party," it might have seemed a little odd that Howard Pawley would come to succeed Schreyer as leader in 1979. However, it was a natural choice. He was a member of Schreyer's cabinet and proved himself invaluable by handling the province's municipal government portfolio and successfully implementing Manitoba's public automobile insurance program.[90] In 1981, under Pawley's leadership, the party recaptured power from Lyon's PC government with 47 percent of the popular vote. It was the first time in Manitoba that an elected premier had been defeated after serving only one term in office. Unlike the fiery Lyon, who had pulled the leadership from Sydney Spivak and then the premiership from Schreyer, Pawley was seen by many as an uninspiring yet decent leader, and thereby able to position the NDP as a moderate alternative to the right-of-centre PCs, while also appealing to urban-based voters who might otherwise have voted for the Liberal Party. As in 1969, the campaign was assisted by having a well-crafted advertising strategy. This time the party's campaign included the music of well-known local folk performers Heather Bishop and Dan Donoghue and the services of the film company Credo Group (which later became, for a time, the province's biggest film producer).

By once again linking northern and urban working-class areas, the NDP drew 47 percent of the vote to the PCs' 44 percent and the Liberals' 7 percent. It effectively used this support to win thirty-four seats to the PCs' twenty-three seats, while sweeping the forlorn Liberals completely from the legislature. It was a return to the Schreyer era in that the NDP took back most of the ridings that it had lost to the PCs in 1977. This included Dauphin, Gimli, Osborne, Radisson, Springfield, and Thompson. It also took three newly created seats, Concordia, Ellice, and River East. In some ways it signalled a broadening of the party in that the NDP drew into its fold a number of seats that it had not held for two terms, including Brandon West, Riel, and St. James from the PCs, Fort Rouge from the Liberals, and Wolseley, which had been held by both the PCs and the Liberals since 1973.

Five of the newly elected NDP MLAS were women: Mary Beth Dolin (Kildonan), Maureen Hemphill (Logan), Muriel Smith (Osborne), Doreen Dodick (Riel), and Myrna Phillips (Wolseley). This was an improvement to the 1977 election, which produced only one female MLA in the government caucus, Norma Price, who represented Assiniboia for the PCs. The PCs fared poorly in this regard again in 1981, with only one female MLA elected: Charlotte Oleson in Gladstone. The NDP were also able to have elected one of the province's first Asian-Canadians, Conrad Santos in Burrows, and, in Rupertsland, Elijah Harper became the first known elected First Nations MLA.

Although the first term began with great promise, two major issues plagued Pawley's NDP government. The first was the battle over French-language rights which had been dormant since the days of the Greenway and Norris Liberal governments. It surfaced in an unavoidable way with St. Boniface lawyer Roger Bilodeau's court challenge to Manitoba's English-only laws. In May, 1983 the province therefore put forward a proposal to amend the Manitoba Act (Bill 33) that would guarantee to French-speaking citizens the right to communicate in French with head offices of government departments, agencies, and Crown corporations, and in government offices in locations where French-language services might be required. The benefit to the province was that it reduced to 10 percent the burdensome requirement—if the province lost in court—of having all provincial laws passed into French. This proposal was built out of a compromise that was reached with Bilodeau and with the support of both the federal government and the Société Franco-Manitobaine.[91]

Rather than easing tensions, the compromise turned into a political firestorm with the PCs leading the fight in the legislative assembly, including what Frances Russell would later describe as "the longest bell-ringing obstruction in parliamentary history."[92] Also on the attack were organizations such as the Union of Manitoba Municipalities (UMM). Public hearings were held in the autumn of 1983 with long-time NDP MLA for Elmwood, Russell Doern, a political renegade from the NDP caucus, leading much of the opposition. Plebiscites were held in over thirty communities during the October municipal elections. The results could not have been worse for Pawley's government. The government's French-language proposal was rejected by margins of three or four to one in the majority of municipalities where the vote was held.[93] It was an ominous sign in that opposition was not confined to PC voter strongholds. The issue was clearly cutting across regional and class lines, including much of the NDP's traditional base of support, such as working-class voters and those of eastern European ancestry, who were demonstrating little sympathy for special French-language constitutional rights.[94] The impact was felt immediately among civic-level NDP candidates, who in the Winnipeg municipal election won only six of the thirty city council seats. In February 1984, and with PC MLAs refusing to respond to the assembly's call to session, the provincial government's proposal died on the order papers.[95] Without a legislative solution, the issue was thrown back into the courts and continued to evolve after the NDP had left government.

Abortion was the second issue to cause NDP dissension. It exposed deep-rooted and irresolvable value-related differences within the party. This included, on one side, working-class voters with traditional values, especially those who grew up in Roman Catholic, Ukrainian Catholic, and Eastern Orthodox households. And, on the other side, left-wing activists involved in such social issues as human rights, anti-racism, gender equality, and pro-choice campaigns. Therefore, when Montreal activist Dr. Henry Morgentaler announced in 1983 that he was opening an abortion clinic in

Winnipeg, the issue became unavoidable. While pro-life and pro-choice advocates battled each other in the press and in public demonstrations, Health Minister Larry Desjardins and Attorney General Roland Penner represented the two opposing sides within the cabinet. Desjardins refused to allow the clinic to open, and charges were laid. Desjardins then threatened to resign if his party adopted a pro-choice platform at its upcoming policy convention. The party sidestepped the issue by passing a motion to establish "regional reproductive health clinics."[96]

The Fall and Rise of Gary Doer

Howard Pawley's majority was reduced to thirty of fifty-seven seats in the 1986 election. On 10 February 1988, Larry Desjardins resigned his cabinet position as minister of health and sport and announced his retirement from politics. No longer attending sittings in the assembly, Desjardins's retirement left the government with only twenty-eight active MLAS—plus a Speaker—while the Opposition held twenty-seven seats. Hanging by a one-seat thread, the government fell on 8 March 1988 when disgruntled NDP MLA Jim Walding publicly attacked his own government over its handling of new public automobile insurance premium increases and other issues, and voted against his own government's budget.[97] It was an event that should never have happened, especially when one considers that the governing party consisted of veteran politicians and experienced staff. What precipitated the downfall was the premier's inability to placate the MLA who had represented St. Vital for the NDP since being elected in a 1971 by-election and served as Speaker of the House from 1982 to 1986. Leading up to the 1986 election, he was forced to fight for his own riding nomination against one of Pawley's aides and, when re-elected, remained excluded from cabinet. In large part the relationship had soured during Walding's tenure as Speaker when he was accused of doing little to temper the PCs' vitriolic attacks regarding the government's proposed legislation on the French-language issue and refused to call a vote during the PCs' bell-ringing boycott of the assembly.

Pawley announced his own resignation the day following the defeat in the legislature, and by month's end Gary Doer was elected as the new leader, narrowly beating fellow cabinet minister Leonard Harapiak by 835 to 814 votes.[98] With some Manitobans still seething over the French-language issue, an exhausted NDP also presented to voters a politically toxic mix of rising taxes, escalating automobile insurance rates, and a projected budget deficit of $334 million, which, in a province of 1 million people, translated into roughly $334 in additional debt for each person. When the votes were counted, the NDP's popular support had dropped from 41 percent in 1986 to 24 percent. Doer's party suffered mass defections among voters to the Liberals across northern and eastern areas of Winnipeg. Fourteen of the twenty new Liberal seats were taken from the NDP, including such stronghold ridings as Selkirk, Burrows, Ellice, Inkster, and Transcona.

The Winnipeg caucus was reduced to four with victories in Concordia, Elmwood, Logan, and St. Johns. The NDP sidestepped annihilation chiefly by holding on to its northerly base of support. Of its twelve remaining seats, one-third were in Winnipeg, one was in Brandon (Brandon East), and over half located in more northerly farmlands and the North: Dauphin, Churchill, Flin Flon, Interlake, Rupertsland, The Pas, and Thompson. The PCs held power with twenty-five seats and the Liberals with their newly minted twenty seats were able to form the official opposition. It was an ignominious moment for the NDP and its new leader. Yet the NDP was down, but not out. Under Doer, and with a new generation of MLAs, the party successfully re-implemented the tried and true NDP formula of combining support from the North with urban labour and service-sector support. In each subsequent election, it expanded its province-wide base of support by winning 29 percent of the vote in 1990, 33 percent in 1995, and then 44 percent in its breakthrough election of 1999.

Deeply rooted in urban labour after serving for seven years as the president of the Manitoba Government Employees' Union (MGEU) and first elected in the North End Winnipeg riding of Concordia in 1986, Doer proved to be the perfect leader to win back the party's urban vote. The NDP's successful resurrection in urban Manitoba, beginning in 1990, came at great cost to the Liberals. Unlike the 1988 election, Doer had time to prepare for the 1990 election and, unlike Carstairs, performed well in the leadership debate. The NDP also put forward a well-developed platform based on new social programs and maintained a slate of experienced candidates.[99] Under his stewardship, the NDP increased its share of the popular vote, from 24 percent to 29 percent, and in 1990 replaced the Liberals as the official opposition with twenty seats, eleven of which were in Winnipeg.

Table 4. 1: 1999 Party Support — Pre-Election Poll[100]

	Totals (1010) %	Gender		Age			Household Income		
		Men (494) %	Women (516) %	18-34 (339) %	35-54 (370) %	55+ (292) %	<$30K (279) %	$30K-$59K (480) %	$60K+ (250) %
Liberal	13	12	14	18	11	10	15	12	12
PC	42	47	37	35	39	57	32	45	49
NDP	42	38	47	44	49	32	50	42	33
Totals	100	100	100	100	100	100	100	100	100

Source: Probe Research/*Winnipeg Free Press*, "Press Release: The Vote," 16 September 1999

The PC majority victory of 1990 was different from Duff Roblin's success in 1959. Rather than reach across all of the province's major electoral regions, both urban and rural, Filmon achieved power by solidifying voter support in the rural South, South Winnipeg, and many of the rural ridings in the "near North" which had been in the NDP camp for at least a portion of the Pawley years: Gimli, Springfield, Ste. Rose and Lac du Bonnet. Filmon was generally unsuccessful against the NDP in the North End and the North. The 1995 election maintained this pattern, with support for the NDP growing from 29 percent to 33 percent, while the PCs remained dominant at 43 percent (up from 42 percent) and the Liberals declined from 28 percent to 24 percent. The PCs again held onto the rural South and southern parts of Winnipeg, while the NDP won in the North and North Winnipeg.

The NDP's return to power in the 1999 election occurred due to a combination of factors, many of which were rooted in the PCs' inability to adequately address problems relating to the health-care sector and the vote-splitting scandal. However, its success was tied also to the fact that the Liberals were ill-prepared to capitalize on the PCs' vulnerability. The new Liberal Party leader, Jon Gerrard, first had to reunite his provincial Liberal Party caucus before convincing voters they could form a provincial government.

Gary Doer put forward to the electorate an image of practical moderation. This strategy precluded problems faced by the party under Pawley. That is, Doer was convinced that to avoid having the PCs, the media, and the business community define the NDP as radicals who, if elected, would lead a tax-and-spend government, the NDP would shape their own image for the public's consumption. A major step towards this end was to have his caucus vote in support of Premier Filmon's budget and balanced-budget policies leading up to the 1999 election (with the only vote against the budget made by lone Liberal MLA Kevin Lamoureux). Meanwhile, Doer also attacked the PCs for mismanaging the province. After a number of years of PC government cutbacks, fallout from the vote-splitting scandal, and a sense that the PCs were falling out of step with the times, pre-election polling data showed growing support for the NDP among both lower- and middle-class voters, women, and younger-aged voters. Fifty percent of those with household incomes under $30,000 were supporting the party, compared to 32 percent for the PCs and 15 percent for the Liberals. Forty-four percent of those under thirty-five supported the NDP compared to only 35 percent for the PCs, while 49 percent of those in their middle years (thirty-five to fifty-four) supported the NDP compared to 39 percent for the PCs. Among women, 47 percent of women compared to 38 percent of men expressed support for the NDP.

The 1999 election produced thirty-two seats for the NDP, twenty-four seats for the PCs, and one seat for the Liberals. The NDP's popular vote was 44 percent compared to 41 percent for the PCs. With only a three-point difference between the two, the NDP was using its support more efficiently. It did so with the "North-plus-North" formula originally forged under Schreyer and Pawley. The NDP took all of the northern portions of Winnipeg, the mid-North and northern ridings, including the Interlake and Dauphin-Roblin. Significant also was the party's success in four southern Winnipeg ridings: St. Vital, Lord Roberts, Riel, and Fort Rouge. These results signalled what would become a long-term decline for the PCs in Winnipeg, where the party, even when led by Gary Filmon in 1999, could no longer rely on urban middle-class voters.

Once elected, Doer's NDP government put forward a platform similar to that of Tony Blair's re-energized Labour Party and its "Third Way" platform. Rather than promoting the increasingly discredited ideas of post-war state planning, Third Way thinking, which was sweeping across Europe through the vehicle of various social-democratic parties, focussed on "new issues such as economic productivity, participatory policies, community development, and, particularly, ecology."[101] Although Doer avoided using the term, which is viewed by some as a sellout to capitalism among many ardent left-wingers, he put forward a program based on what he claimed to be "a government that works better and costs less."[102] Through this prism, the private sector and financial capital were to be viewed as sources of productivity and innovation rather than forces to be controlled and regulated. For Manitoba, this included nurturing aeronautics, energy, and life sciences. This was demonstrated by the government's 2005 Speech from the Throne, in which it was announced that the province was seeking to help launch a "community-led initiative [Bio-Med City] to establish our province as the Canadian centre for public health research and innovation. The development of a new health industry cluster comes at an opportune time, as many of Manitoba's investments in research, infrastructure and human capital are coming to fruition. Winnipeg is now home to over 120 public health innovation firms, and to a core group of internationally renowned researchers in infectious and chronic diseases. The development of our biomedical sector complements the strong growth of Manitoba's biopharmaceutical industry."[103] Another demonstration of cooperation with the private sector can be seen in how the provincial government launched its provincial "Spirited Energy" branding campaign in 2006 by partnering with a number of business leaders, who in previous decades might have spurned an NDP premier's overtures. These included David Angus of the Winnipeg Chamber of Commerce and the Aspers of CanWest Global. Therefore, few were surprised by the warm reception received by Doer when he spoke at a breakfast meeting of the Manitoba Chambers of Commerce during the 2007 provincial election campaign.

The 2003 and 2007 provincial elections were what some might call "maintaining" elections in that they produced NDP majority victories based on support from the same ridings as before: northern ridings and North Winnipeg. Yet the party was not standing still; it was broadening its base of support, especially in Winnipeg. In 2003, while popular support for the party across the province increased to 49 percent from 45 percent (producing thirty-five seats), the NDP increased its popular support from 47 percent to 53 percent in Winnipeg. Incursions into the city's southern portion continued, with the party holding what it took in 1999 and adding St. Norbert, Seine River, and Fort Garry to its list of newly acquired ridings. In spite of efforts by the PCs to reverse these trends by replacing Stuart Murray with Hugh McFadyen, a new leader who was thought to have more urban appeal, the NDP's urban juggernaut continued into 2007 by again taking 53 percent of the vote in Winnipeg (and 48 percent across the province). In total the party took thirty-six seats, which was an increase of one from 2003, and, in Winnipeg, it pushed back the PCs into the southwest corner ridings of Charleswood, Tuxedo, and Fort Whyte.

Polling data demonstrates that Gary Doer has clearly secured the province's ideological centre, thereby attracting support from a wide range of socio-demographic groupings (see Appendix A). One concern for the party should be what appears to be a "greying effect" on party support, possibly resulting from having held power since 1999. In contrast to the late 1990s, when the NDP appeared attractive to young and middle-aged voters, the party in 2007 appealed more strongly to those who are over fifty-five (51 percent) compared to middle-aged (45 percent) and younger voters (37 percent).[104]

Conclusion

The NDP and its predecessors (the ILP and CCF) have operated in Manitoba for over a hundred years with platforms based on gradual reformism. Not unlike the PCs, whose two most successful leaders in modern times were Duff Roblin and Gary Filmon, the NDP has successfully benefitted from having pragmatically moderate leaders. It has also enjoyed stable leadership by having three consecutively successful leaders guide the party across five different decades: Schreyer, Pawley, and Doer. The provincial NDP's second characteristic is that it has drawn deeply from its urban political roots rather than the prairie agrarianism that is more evident in Saskatchewan. However, and this is its third defining characteristic, its success has been tied to reaching beyond Winnipeg and outwards to comparatively less prosperous farm regions, Aboriginal communities, and northern labourers. In this sense, these characteristics signify that it is a class-based party operating with moderate platforms that appeal across many social segments and important provincial regions.

After winning its third majority victory in a row under Gary Doer, a record unsurpassed by any other previous NDP leader, and even by very few leaders of the other parties, the NDP faces a number of challenges as it moves towards the end of the current decade and beyond. Most critical will be its ability to continue holding the middle-class urban vote from drifting back to the PCs or the Liberals. Furthermore, women voters continue to be important for the party. The NDP also needs to watch that it does not lose more ground among young adults. As must all successful political parties in Western democracies, the NDP must continually refresh itself with young, new supporters as it enters further into the new century.

Conclusion

Understanding Manitoba Party Politics

WHAT SHAPES PARTY POLITICS IN MANITOBA? AFTER EXAMINING each of the major provincial parties it is possible to see that there are three avenues of study by which this question can be answered. The first is through the study of geography. Manitoba is divided into a number of regions that are linked to specific forms of social and economic development. The three most notable regions are the rural southern farmlands, the northern frontier, and Winnipeg. The preceding chapters revealed how each major party is linked in its own unique way to them. The PCs draw much of their support from rural southern ridings and South Winnipeg, and the NDP from the North, North Winnipeg, and marginal farm areas. Meanwhile, the Liberals' support remains focussed in Winnipeg. At least until the late 1960s, those parties that were able to combine support from southern farmers and South Winnipeg business interests were the ones that succeeded. This was demonstrated by Thomas Greenway's Liberals,

Rodmond Roblin's Conservatives, John Bracken's Progressives (and later the Liberal-Progressives), and the Progressive Conservatives under Duff Roblin, Sterling Lyon, and Gary Filmon. A successful counter to this almost unbeatable formula was introduced by Ed Schreyer's NDP in 1969. It was based on winning votes from northern workers, Aboriginal communities, marginal farm areas, and Winnipeg's North End. It was used successfully by Schreyer again in 1973 and then by the NDP under Howard Pawley and Gary Doer.

The second avenue for studying party politics is by examining political culture[1] and ethnicity. Many political historians have noted how Manitoba's political culture has been shaped by settlement patterns. Ontarians of British extraction settled much of the southern fertile farm areas[2] and those who did not move to the farm regions formed much of Winnipeg's commercial class. This had two major effects during the province's formative years. First, these immigrants brought with them values that prized the British Empire, English culture, liberal individualism, property rights, and limited government. Second, loyalties towards the two national parties, the Conservatives and Liberals, were imported into the provincial scene.

Subsequent waves of immigrants, including Scandinavians, Russians, and Ukrainians, had to settle for jobs in mining and manufacturing or for less fertile farmlands that were located closer to the Canadian Shield. Therefore, much of this northern portion of Manitoba's farm belt and North Winnipeg developed a strongly distinct non-British character. In his groundbreaking political study titled "Ethnic and Class Politics in Manitoba," Tom Peterson asserted that many of these immigrants, as well as those who led their local cultural organizations, felt vulnerable in the new society and therefore aligned themselves with those parties that were deemed to have the best chance of winning power (this is what some would term "clientelistic politics": that is, supporting a specific party in exchange for favours). At the same time, others within the working class believed that such tactics were limiting and that socio-economic advancement could be achieved only through more radical measures. Winnipeggers therefore experienced both a growth in ethnic clientelistic politics *and* the rise of European-styled revolutionary socialistic parties. Tempering this working-class radicalism was the fact that many workers had British roots and viewed socialism as something alien to their interests, both culturally and philosophically, and believed that unions and British-style parties would be the best means for furthering their own interests.³ Following the 1919 Winnipeg General Strike, this British Labour Party model dominated working-class electoral politics in Manitoba, an influence that can still be discerned by comparing Gary Doer's NDP government policies to Britain's New Labour and "Third Way" politics that came into vogue during the late 1990s.

One can therefore see that studying ethnicity and political culture in Manitoba leads one to economic class analysis. In fact, over time ethnicity has been replaced by economic self-interest. This is not to say that ethnicity is unimportant but that ethnicity in Manitoba often overlaps with economic class interests. From the end of the 1880s until 1969, Manitoba was ruled by leaders of British extraction, many of whom achieved power for their parties by winning votes from southern farmers and the urban business people whose interest lay in governments that would promote economic expansion and settlement, low taxes, and a complaisant labour force.⁴

Manitoba's politics have changed alongside its evolving economic and social structure. Most notable is the declining importance of the farm vote. In 1941, 34 percent of Manitobans lived on farms, yet by 1971 this figure had declined to 13 percent.⁵ Currently, out of a total of 598,600 employed Manitobans, only 32,500 are employed in the agricultural sector while 559,600 Manitobans are employed in the "services-producing" sector.⁶ The economy is now much more oriented to resource development, manufacturing, telecommunications, transportation, financial services, business consulting, and medical research. Expansion in the public sector has also occurred, especially in such areas as health care and education. The changing nature of "what Manitobans do" has created what sociologists refer to as a "new middle class"⁷ consisting of citizens who tend to be well educated and employed in usually well-paying white-collar jobs. Examples

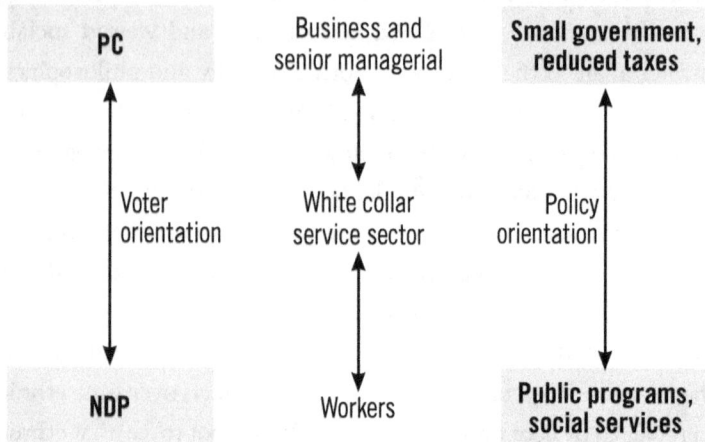

Figure 5.1: Socio-Economic Class and Party Support Schemata

include technicians, accountants, nurses, teachers, computer specialists, and middle-level managers.

The new middle class is conflicted politically in that it is both economically conservative and socially liberal. On the one hand its members share with the business community the same neighbourhoods and lifestyles. Furthermore, they share an interest in seeking policies that promote fiscal prudence, lower taxes, suburban development, crime control, and economic prosperity. It is therefore logical that they would have an interest in supporting a party that leans towards the ideological right, such as the PCs. On the other hand, those in the new middle class also share some of the same concerns as blue-collar workers. They are dependent on wages and salaries rather than income derived by owning a business or capital investments, and their jobs might be vulnerable to downsizing, closures, or organizational restructuring. Of concern also are government policies that may jeopardize public health care, public education, employment equity, and child-care support. Therefore, members of the new middle class have an interest in policies that may be antithetical to the business sector and more closely connected to the NDP. With this push and pull, as depicted in Figure 5.1, one can see how a voter might in a lifetime swing his or her support from Duff Roblin's PCS, to Edward Schreyer's NDP, to Sterling Lyon's PCS, to Howard Pawley's NDP, to Sharon Carstairs's Liberals, to Gary Filmon's PCS, and then to Gary Doer's NDP.

Beyond Provincial Borders

Manitoba party politics are also affected by forces arising from beyond both provincial and national boundaries. International factors have included wars, grain markets and commodity prices, oil prices, inflation, recessions, and stock-market crashes. Greenway's Liberal government benefitted from new waves of immigration as the American West filled up, while T.C. Norris's Liberals were ousted from office in large part due to their inability to cope with labour strife arising from international events and an economic depression. The Lyon and Pawley governments were defeated in part due to their inability to control mounting provincial debts during the international recession of the 1970s and 1980s. In contrast, Duff Roblin's PCS and Gary Doer's NDP enjoyed the luxury of governing during periods in which economic growth was occurring across much of the Western industrial world. In 2006, political scientist Allen Mills referred to this political era as "the perfect calm" and lamented that the Doer government has squandered a rare opportunity for launching new and innovative programs and policies.[8]

National government policies have also influenced Manitoba politics since its birth in 1870. Indeed, the province was created in large part due to Prime Minister Macdonald's interest in pacifying Louis Riel and keeping the region out of the hands of the United States.[9] Ottawa's subsequent influence has included immigration and land-settlement policies, transportation and railway development, federal-provincial fiscal arrangements, constitutional negotiations, and the introduction of medicare and other national programs.[10]

The federal parties have also affected the fortunes of their provincial party wings. This is demonstrated by four powerful examples. The first is how the federal Liberals were able to push the provincial Liberals into fusing with Bracken's Progressives with the aim of keeping the Conservatives from power in the 1930s. The second is the impact that Diefenbaker's Prairie populism had on Duff Roblin's chances at the provincial level in the 1950s. The third is the provincial Liberals' collapse from 1969 onward and its strong connection to western antipathy towards Trudeau and his policies of official bilingualism, the metric system, and agriculture policies, including Crow Rate reform with all of its implications for Prairie farmers. A fourth example is the problematic relationship between Filmon's PCs and that of Mulroney, in which the priorities of the national party were diametrically different from those of the provincial wing, leading many PCs to drift into a newly formed Reform Party. The PCs were fortunate to have the type of provincial leader who could steer the party through the troubled waters of federal-provincial relations and—in contrast to the case of the Manitoba Liberals in the 1970s—successfully distance itself in the voters' eyes from the odium of the national leader.

The Importance of Leadership

In his 1911 classical study of political parties, Roberto Michels wrote: "Leadership is a necessary phenomenon in every form of social life"[11] and demonstrated how democratic organizations—such as political parties—inevitably become hierarchically structured with leaders at the top, organizers in the middle, and supporters and voters at the lower levels. Without this development, democratic organizations easily dissipate into anarchy or dissolution. It is in this sense that Michels refers to "the indispensability of leadership."[12] Manitoba's political parties reveal no exception to this rule. Each provincial party has been strongly marked by its leaders, and one has to wonder what would have happened to the leaderless United Farmers in 1922 had they not invited the somewhat surprised John Bracken to serve as their leader and provincial premier. His subsequent impact on the provincial party system from 1922 to his departure in 1943 cannot be overstated. Bracken successfully steered the party's provincial wing through a number of elections, fused the Progressives with the Liberals, and launched the first of a series of non-partisan coalition governments in the 1940s.[13] Another example is that of Duff Roblin and his ability to turn around the fortunes of the PCs by attracting quality candidates, promoting organizational development, and, upon winning power, launching the province on a path of economic and social-development reform.

Party leaders are windows into their parties. Their selection reveals both the interests and competing factions within the organization. With regard to the PCs, Sanford Evans, Sidney Spivak, and Stuart Murray had strong ties to urban business interests which ill served them when facing the party's rural wing at the end of their political careers. With regards to the Liberal Party, the more rurally oriented Gildas Molgat and Robert Bend[14] were succeeded by Izzy Asper, then by Charles Huband, both Winnipeg-based lawyers. This party continues to be led by well-educated professionals such as Jon Gerrard, who is a medical doctor. Another example can be drawn from the NDP and the choice by its members of the centrist Ed Schreyer over the more strident Sidney Green in 1969. The decision showed that the party was looking for a successful and moderate leader who could draw support from beyond blue-collar neighbourhoods and across all regions in the province. The party membership's continuing link to the labour movement was demonstrated in 1988 by the choice of Gary Doer, who had served for seven years as the president of the Manitoba Government Employees' Union.

In the case of Manitoba, as elsewhere, leaders reflect both the party's past, as indicated by where they draw support from within the organization, but also the party's future, in that new leaders have the potential to take their parties in new directions. In the words of political scientist Leslie Pal, "Leaders are plugged into pre-existing and ongoing political and social processes, and their leadership consists of an ability to harness these various processes in the service of a single vision."[15] Yet at the most basic level leaders need to attract voters to hold onto their leadership. A demonstration of the leader's impact on voter choice, at least at the national level, is consistently found in survey data collected just after each of the federal elections from 1974 to 2004. The results show that the party itself is usually the strongest influence on a voter's decision, followed by the party leader as the second most important factor, and the third being a preference for the local candidate. In a survey that was conducted just after the 2004 federal election, it was found that 50 percent of voters made their choice according to their party preference, while close to one-quarter (24 percent) of Canadian voters reported that the party leader was the most significant factor, and 20 percent stated that they made their choice according to the candidates who were running in their riding.[16] If this is transposed to the provincial scene, one can more easily understand Schreyer's victory over Weir in 1969, Filmon's over Carstairs in 1990, and Doer's over both Murray in 2003 and McFadyen in 2007.

Party Organization

Worth studying also is the impact that organizational factors can have on a party's fortunes. This includes party structure, the health of local associations, attracting and nominating quality candidates, membership, and fundraising. It is no secret that effective campaigns are rooted in having healthy local associations. According to *Globe and Mail* columnist Jeffrey Simpson, "elections are the white-water passages, where political life froths and boils, hurtling the participants at accelerating speeds through a chute of perils towards calm waters at the end."[17] Without campaign workers operating at the local level, candidates are neither able to communicate effectively with the electorate, nor get voters out on election day. There are numerous examples in which a handful of votes determined electoral outcomes in Manitoba. These include the 1973 single-vote defeat of Larry Desjardins by the Liberal Paul Marion in St. Boniface (which was later overturned) and Izzy Asper's success over the NDP's Murdoch MacKay in Wolseley by four votes (which was not overturned).[18]

Organizations themselves help parties weather political storms. The NDP's organizational connection to labour helps explain why the collapse of 1988 did not signal an end to the party itself. Likewise, the PC Party survived the difficult post-Filmon years by continuing to foster local associations and connections to business, and by promoting membership, as demonstrated by the high membership turnout in the selection of Hugh McFadyen as the party's new leader in 2006. In contrast to both the NDP and PCs, since the 1960s the Liberals have failed (sometimes due to causes beyond their control) to build effective local constituency associations or expand into rural and northern Manitoba.[19]

In both Canada and Manitoba, new party financing rules have come into effect that limit the role that businesses, unions, and organizations can play in funding parties and campaigns. At the national level, a 2003 amendment to the Elections Expenses Act bans corporations, organizations, and unions from contributing to parties and candidates, and limits contributions from individuals to a $5000 per annum ceiling.[20] In Manitoba, similar legislation was put forward in 2001 that also banned corporate and union donations while limiting the amount that individuals can contribute to $3000 per year. The impact of these new rules was felt immediately by the PC Party which underwent a drop in funding from $1.28 million in 2000 to $393,674 in 2001. It remains unclear what the long-term effects will be of these new finance rules on each of Manitoba's parties, and more study on this issue in the future will be required.

Media and Communications
In Manitoba, as elsewhere, political campaigns are often battles over visibility, agenda setting, and communicating with the voter. During the province's early years, political information was chiefly imparted through informal networks, including discussions with friends and family, letter writing, church services and events, and public meetings. Newspapers provided the region's first form of mass communication and often served as mouthpieces for a particular party, the most notable being the *Manitoba Free Press* (later the *Winnipeg Free Press*) under its editor, John Dafoe, a strongly partisan and influential Liberal. The *Winnipeg Daily Times*, an early competitor to the *Manitoba Free Press*, even declared itself to be a

creation to serve national Conservative Party interests in Manitoba.[21] In the early 1900s there were also numerous farm-oriented newspapers and magazines such as the Manitoba-based *Grain Growers' Guide,* which by 1920 had a national circulation of 80,000, and 120,000 by 1926 under its new name, *Country Guide.*[22] Such publications were especially useful to the farmer-oriented Progressives in the 1910s and 1920s.

It is no secret, however, that radio and television, which arrived in the province in 1954,[23] became increasingly important in households across the Prairies. Much of Schreyer's popularity was tied to the extensive television coverage of the NDP's highly charged leadership race that occurred in the midst of the 1969 provincial election. Another example is that of Filmon, who won a majority victory in 1990 after performing well on national TV as negotiations unfolded over the Meech Lake Accord, and then against Carstairs in the leaders' debate.

Currently two-thirds of Canadians (63 percent) say that they turn to television for news and information, 13 percent say they turn to radio, and 12 percent say they rely on newspapers.[24] According to political scientist John Meisel, the rise of television in twentieth-century politics has had negative consequences for public debates on political issues: "The problem is, of course, that ... exposure is chosen by the media largely for entertainment value, rather than as a continuous in-depth exploration of the dominant political issues and partisan strategies."[25] It would be a mistake, however, to argue that television has replaced the print media in Manitoba. The *Winnipeg Free Press* remains highly influential and is read by 71 percent of Winnipeggers at least weekly. This is the highest market penetration of any daily in Canada.[26] Coupled with this is the influence of radio. Winnipeggers have for decades provided large audiences for CJOB's morning call-in show, which has been hosted by a series of aggressive interviewers, including Peter Warren, Charles Adler, and, more recently, Richard Cloutier.

It was the CBC and the *Winnipeg Free Press* that were largely responsible for exposing the 1995 vote-splitting scandal. The CBC, CJOB radio, the *Winnipeg Free Press,* and other media outlets regularly devote resources and reporters to cover stories involving the legislature. This has included such ongoing issues as the government's awareness of the Crocus Investment Fund's problems prior to its collapse, as well as regular events, which include provincial budgets, debates, and the introduction of new legislation. The changing nature of the electronic media is, however, creating new challenges to candidates and political parties when seeking to get their message out to prospective voters. In large part this is due to the availability of non-local cable content, satellite TV, and the Internet, which is now used by 72 percent of Manitobans, according to Probe Research survey data.[27] On the other hand, the media's prevalence in the daily lives of Manitobans signifies new opportunities. Independent writers can increasingly sidestep the traditional media gatekeepers by generating their own independent—and sometimes highly partisan—discussions.[28] So far one can only say that the effect of websites and on-line communications on voter preferences has yet to be adequately measured both across Canada and in Manitoba.

Political scientists also need to examine closely the impact that cellular telephones are having on political parties and their ability to communicate with voters. Up until the late 1990s almost every potential voter could be reached via a land-line telephone (with the exception of those living in poverty or in very remote communities). Even those with unlisted telephone numbers could be reached via random dialing techniques.[29] However, this is no longer the case, especially when many young adults and others are opting to have a cellular telephone as their *only* telephone. This signifies that a growing number of voters have unlisted cellular telephone numbers and therefore are beyond the reach of party organizations for "get-out-the-vote" activities, including reminder calls, providing daycare services, and offering transportation to the polling station.[30] Of course, and on the positive side, the Internet is increasingly used by parties to reach out to sympathetic voters and those seeking information about party platforms. It might become used in the future to encourage voter turnout.

The Electoral System

The electoral "rules of the game" have strongly influenced the fortunes of each of the province's parties. Until the late 1960s, the provincial electoral system systematically discriminated against urban voters by assigning more seats per rural voter than in the city. This created an agriculture-oriented bias in the legislature, to the detriment of Winnipeg's working-class, labour-oriented parties, most notably the NDP and its predecessors. Electoral reforms in the 1950s and 1960s rectified this imbalance and thereby contributed to the NDP's 1969 victory. This in turn created a reorientation in the early 1970s by both the PCs and Liberals towards Winnipeg, as signified by the selection of both Spivak and Asper as party leaders. The acrimonious 1975 PC leadership convention in which Spivak was ousted by Lyon revealed that for the PCs this shift was not an easy one. For the Liberals, the shift was less troublesome due to the loss of its rural wing.

The system by which candidates are elected to the legislature, the single-member-plurality vote (SMP), is another factor to consider, especially when one sees that it solidifies the regional nature of Manitoba's political landscape.[31] In other words, in each particular region the SMP system reinforces the support for particular parties while dampening potential support for others. For example, PC supporters in a traditional working-class neighbourhood such as Transcona might be disinclined to vote due to a perception that there is little chance for unseating the NDP.[32] Alternatively, an NDP supporter in the upper-middle-class riding of River Heights might strategically vote Liberal in order to reduce the PCs' chances of winning the riding. Across the province, the system appears to have its most negative impact on the Liberals and the Green Party. As an illustration, Table 5.1 shows the 2003 provincial election results based on popular support for each of the parties, the actual seats won, and the outcome if a system of proportional representation (PR) had been used, with the province treated as one large constituency. Assuming a hypothetical situation[33] in which voters chose the same parties that they did in 2003, with 13 percent of the popular vote the Liberals would have won seven seats rather than two seats, and the Greens

Conclusion: Understanding Manitoba Party Politics

might have gained a presence in the legislature with one seat.[34] The number of seats for the PCs would have increased by one and the NDP's majority would have been cut from thirty-five seats to twenty-eight seats. The result would have been a NDP minority government with the Liberals (or Greens) holding the balance of power. In general, therefore, the SMP system appears to increase the probability that majority governments will be elected and to curtail the fortunes of Manitoba's smaller parties.

Table 5.1: Manitoba 2003 Popular Vote and Hypothetical Proportional Representation Results

	NDP	PC	Liberal	Green
Popular Vote	49%	36%	13%	1%
Actual Seats	35	20	2	0
PR Seats	28	21	7	1
(Difference)	(- 7)	(+1)	(+5)	(+1)

Political Choice: A Schema

This study has used a blend of political science, history, sociology, and even geography to examine party politics in Manitoba. As the reader has seen, multiple factors contribute to the success and failure of the provincial parties, as well as to the structure of the overall party system. The effect that these factors have on whether or not specific parties will win voter support is summarized in Figure 5.2. These can be divided into two groups: (1) longer-term and enduring factors and (2) short-term factors. The first includes regionalism, economic classes, and social groupings. Coupled with these are historically significant events such as the introduction of railways, major economic recessions, and world wars. Together these factors largely shape the values and perceptions within the political culture. The social and economic groupings to which a person belongs (for example, a farmer of eastern European ancestry) will influence the values and perceptions that a voter holds and guide this person towards specific tendencies. Following upon this, short-term factors that influence voter preferences during specific

Politics in Manitoba

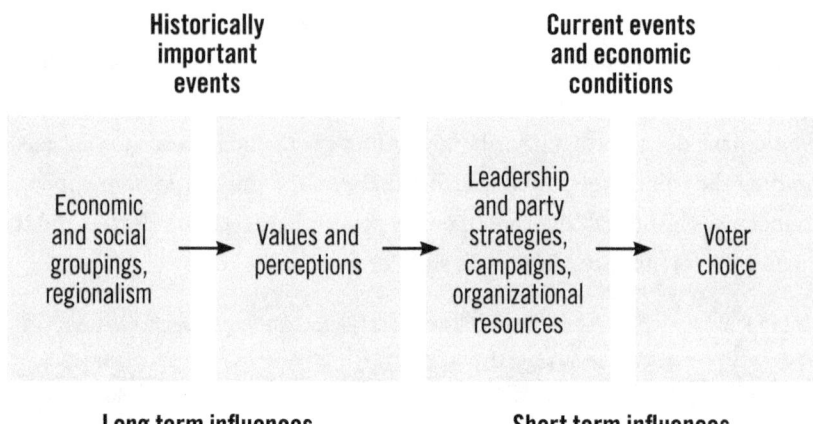

Figure 5.2: Schema for Understanding Party Preferences

elections include news events and media coverage, economic conditions, party leadership, platforms, and campaign strategies. Added to these different types of factors are (1) the electoral process itself, what can be called "the rules of the game," (2) the extent to which the principles of representative democracy are respected (including peaceful changes in government), and (3) whether or not citizens practise their right to vote.

Final Thoughts

Work on this book began shortly following the re-election of Gary Doer and his NDP in 2003. The data analysis and manuscript were finished a few months after his 2007 re-election. During this time it became clear that the NDP's repeated successes were tied to Doer's moderate leadership style and personal charisma. This, coupled with positive economic conditions in the province has allowed the NDP to fend off with what appears to be relative ease the PCs and the Liberals. However, as the NDP moves into a "post-Doer" era, and with an economic downturn in the international economy which, like death and taxes, is always inevitable, the PCs are waiting to replace the NDP. It is probable that the current two-and-a-half-party system will remain in place. However, unforeseen events might unfold to produce either a reversion to a traditional two-party system, or, with electoral reform, a multi-party system with newcomers such as the Green Party finding representation in the Manitoba legislature.

Appendix A

*Party Preferences
and Survey Data*

SO FAR THE FOCUS OF THIS BOOK AS BEEN ON EACH OF MANITOBA'S MAJOR parties and their histories, including changing leadership, ideas and platforms, organizational resources, and electoral fortunes within the context of changing economic conditions. Far less attention has been paid to attitudinal data and the characteristics of those who prefer one party over another. Every three months Probe Research surveys 1000 Manitobans on numerous issues. Included in each survey are questions regarding provincial party preferences. This has generated over 30,000 interviews during the past decade. In addition to this, the firm has provided a number of pre-election polls, including polls for the *Winnipeg Free Press* and Global-TV in 2003 and 2007. Results from these polls were combined into a series of large-scale databases in order that they could be re-examined for this portion of the study.

1. PC Supporters

Throughout much of this book a case was made that to win power, the PCs need to move beyond their traditional base of business and rural voter support. Using polling data, examined in this first section are three questions. First, to what extent can the PCs now be considered a rural-based party? Second, compared to those who support the NDP and Liberals, to what extent can we say that PC supporters show a higher level of concern for such traditional issues as reducing government spending and taxes or crime control? And third, is the common perception that Manitoba's PCs tend to attract higher levels of support among men compared to women, older voters rather than younger voters, and higher-income rather than lower-income groups empirically valid?

The PCs and Their Non-Winnipeg Base

Using survey data collected from 1999 to just prior to the 2007 provincial election (shown in Table 6.1), it is easy to see that the PCs derive consistently higher levels of support outside the province's capital.[1] Outside Winnipeg, the PCs attract support in the 37 percent to 51 percent range. Support drops considerably among Winnipeg residents, where the party's support has been limited to a range of 25 percent and 37 percent. Its highest level of support (37 percent) in Winnipeg occurred during Gary Filmon's tenure in 1999, a level that has not been seen since that time. The chiefly non-urban nature of the PCs' support contrasts sharply with that of the Liberal Party and the NDP, which are both much more strongly oriented to Winnipeg supporters (this is discussed in Sections 2 and 3). However, even with the PCs' non-urban bias, PC supporters far outnumber the Liberals in both Winnipeg and outside Winnipeg.

Table 6.1: Provincial PC Support

	Winnipeg	Non-Winnipeg	Manitoba
1999	37	46	40
2000	31	37	33
2001	27	39	31
2002	27	37	31
2003	25	38	30
2004	27	45	34
2005	30	45	36
2006	34	50	40
2007	31	51	39

Derived from Probe Research press releases, 1999-2007.

Appendix A: Party Preferences and Survey Data

Table 6.2: Party Support and Issues of Concern

	Total Respondents (n=4403) (%)	PC Supporters (n=1059) (%)	NDP Supporters (n=1026) (%)	Liberal Supporters (n=395) (%)
Crime and Violence	26	26	26	24
Infrastructure	22	21	25	23
Health Care	10	11	9	10
The Economy	8	9	7	8
Poverty	7	5	9	7
Jobs and Employment	6	6	5	8
Taxes and Government Spending	4	6	3	4
Education	4	4	4	5
Environment	3	3	3	3
Agriculture	2	2	1	2

Source: Derived from the Probe Research 2006-2007 database

Top-of-Mind Concerns and Issues

The second question raised earlier is to what extent those who prefer the PCs over other parties demonstrate a high level of concern for such traditionally conservative issues as crime control, government restraint, and reduced taxes. Surprisingly to some is that those who support the PCs are similar to those who support the other two main parties when identifying what they consider to be the most important issue facing their local community.[2] This is shown in Table 6.2. With regard to concerns about social violence and crime, this is clearly a major issue regardless of party preference. Twenty-six percent of those who support either the PCs or the NDP identify this issue as a top-of-mind concern. There is some difference between the parties on issues pertaining to taxation, with PC supporters twice as likely to identify taxes and government spending as their top-of-mind concern compared to those who support the NDP (6 percent compared to 3 percent of NDP supporters).

While there are similarities between those who support the PCs and the two other parties, differences do exist when results are examined from the perspective of specific issue areas and the extent to which they might be linked to the support for particular parties. That is, here we flip the analysis around and examine the extent to which those who are concerned about such issues as taxes or crime as their top-of-mind concern are drawn to the PCs over the NDP. The results are shown in Table 6.3. Those who are concerned about crime and violence issues are equally likely to vote for the PCs or the NDP (due to sample sizes, the Liberals are not shown here). However, of those who reported a top-of-mind concern about the economy, employment, or taxes, there is a stronger likelihood to support the PCs over the NDP. This is especially true among those who expressed a concern about taxes.

Table 6.3: Issues and Party Preference

	Crime and Violence (n=653) %	The Economy (n=206) %	Jobs and Employment (n=156) %	Taxes and Government Spending (n=115) %
PC	41	44	43	59
NDP	40	34	31	24

Source: Derived from the Probe Research 2006-2007 database

When the data regarding the different issue areas are broken into regional components other than the issue of taxes and government spending, a number of interesting differences are found between Winnipeg-based PC supporters and those who reside in other parts of the province. In Winnipeg, close to one-third (31 percent) of those who would vote PC identify crime

Appendix A: Party Preferences and Survey Data

and violence issues as their top concern compared to only 16 percent in the non-Winnipeg regions in southern Manitoba.[3] Non-Winnipeg supporters are also more concerned about health-care issues (17 percent) compared to Winnipeg supporters (7 percent). They also show more concern for the economy and employment (20 percent compared to 11 percent). Not surprisingly, PC supporters in southern Manitoba (outside Winnipeg) are more concerned about agriculture and farm issues than are to Winnipeg supporters (4 percent compared to 0 percent).

Social Segments and PC Support

To what extent do PC supporters in Manitoba fit the stereotype of conservatives (of both the capital-C and small-c varieties) in other provinces or countries? That is, do the PCs in Manitoba draw higher levels of support among males, older voters, and those in generally higher-income categories as is usually the case for conservative parties throughout Western democracies? To answer this question, results for each of these three socio-demographic categories (gender, age, and income) were examined and are shown in Table 6.4. These are also broken out for two of Manitoba's major provincial regions (Winnipeg and southern Manitoba excluding Winnipeg).

Table 6.4: PC Support by Gender and Age

Region	Totals % PC Preference	Gender		Age Cohort		
		Male (1428)	Female (1447)	18–34 (899)	35–54 (1062)	55+ (841)
South—Non-Winnipeg (N=994)	52%	55%	49%	49%	54%	55%
Winnipeg (N=1803)	34%	41%	28%	30%	36%	37%
Manitoba (N=2871)	40%	45%	35%	37%	41%	43%

Source: Derived from the Probe Research 2006–2007 database

153

Across the province, 45 percent of males reported a preference for the PCs compared to 35 percent of women.[4] Regardless of whether one looks at Winnipeg or the non-Winnipeg southern region, a gender difference in PC support is discernible. The strongest separation between women and men is in Winnipeg, where only 28 percent of women compared to 41 percent of men showed a preference for the PCs. This difference narrows when looking at non-Winnipeg southerners (with 6 percentage points separating men from women). This gender gap is also consistently evident when examining longitudinal data for PC support across the province from 2000 to 2007.

Table 6.5: PC Support by Age: 2000-2007

	18-34	35-54	55+
2000	29	36	33
2001	27	31	36
2002	22	34	35
2003	23	29	31
2004	32	34	37
2005	33	36	40
2006	40	41	43
2007	44	39	39

Derived from Probe Research data and press releases, 1999-2007.

With regard to the extent to which different age groups are drawn to the PCs, at least until 2005 the old adage "Socialist at twenty, Tory at forty" appeared to fit Manitoba. Those in their middle and older years showed more support for the right-of-centre party compared to those under the age of thirty-five. Yet, perhaps due to the change in leadership (ie., McFayden replacing Murray) and the length of time that the NDP has been in office, and as shown in Table 6.5, this generational difference disappeared in 2006. By 2007, and leading up to the provincial election of that year, a higher percentage of those under thirty-five (44 percent) were willing to vote for the party, compared to 39 percent in the two older age categories. It will be shown later in this chapter that the NDP now tends to draw more strongly from the older population, and the much less strongly supported Liberal Party and Green Party tend to draw more from the under-thirty-five age group compared to older Manitobans.

Socio-Economic Status and PC Party Support

It is logical to expect that the party that has historically represented the interests of the business community will draw higher levels of support among those who reside in higher-income households (as measured by having a household income of at least $60,000 per year). Table 6.6 shows polling data for 2006 and 2007 that illustrate that PC support is higher among the middle- (40 percent) and higher-income (44 percent) categories compared to those who reside in lower-income households (in which only 33 percent support the PCs). This pattern is especially pronounced in Winnipeg, where support drops to the low twenties among those in lower-income households.[5]

Table 6.6: PC Support Among Household Income Categories, 2006 and 2007

Region	Totals % PC Preference	Household Income Category		
		< $30k (510)	$30k to $59k (899)	$60k + (1115)
South—Non-Winnipeg (N=994)	52%	53%	56%	48%
Winnipeg (N=1803)	34%	22%	31%	42%
Manitoba (N=2871)	40%	33%	40%	44%

Source: Derived from the Probe Research 2006-2007 database

Another means by which the link between socio-economic class and party preference can be measured is through studying party support among those with different levels of educational achievement. Examined here is the extent to which there might be an association between having a university degree and choosing the PCs over other parties.

When the 2006 and 2007 polling data are examined according to regional lines (Table 6.7), there appears to be what might be termed a "conditional relationship"[6] between education and PC support. That is, whether or not one resides in Winnipeg (the conditional variable) influences the extent to which a link appears between the two variables of education and party preference. While a university degree appears to have no effect on one's likelihood of supporting the PCs among Winnipeg residents, within the southern Manitoba non-Winnipeg population there is a *negative* association between having an advanced education and likelihood of supporting the PCs. That is, more than half (55 percent) of those in this region who are limited to a high-school degree support the PCs compared to 44 percent of those with a university education (this inverse relationship is statistically significant at the 95 percent confidence level[7]). One possible explanation for this pattern is that many of those who reside outside Winnipeg and have a post-secondary education are employed in the health-care and education sectors, and would therefore be disinclined to support a party that during the 1990s curbed public spending and public-sector jobs.

Table 6.7: PC Support by Education and by Region

Region	Totals % PC Preference	Highest Education Attained Category	
		High School (610)	Completed University (928)
South—Non-Winnipeg (N=471)	52%	55%	44%
Winnipeg (N=1037)	34%	34%	34%
Manitoba (N=1538)	40%	43%	37%

Source: Derived from the Probe Research 2006-2007 database

2. Liberal Supporters

From its heights, nearly a century ago, as Manitoba's governing party under Thomas Greenway and T.C. Norris, the Liberals have been reduced to a non-contender in the province's current political scene. A number of questions arise as they pertain to the depth and ongoing viability of public support for the Liberals. First, to what extent does the provincial party suffer from strategic voting? That is, does the party attract higher levels of support between elections, and do voters then opt to support either the PCs or the NDP when it comes time to choose a government? Second, do those who report a preference for the Liberals also show a higher level of concern for health care compared to such other issues as crime or taxes? When one considers that a medical doctor has led the party for much of its modern history and that the party emphasized health-care issues in the elections of 1999, 2003, and 2007, it is expected that this would be the case. The third question relates to age. As discussed in Chapter 3, a strong antipathy arose among western Canadians towards the national Liberal Party during the 1970s and early 1980s. Is the provincial party still paying for problems created in the Trudeau era? That is, do those who are older exhibit a lower level of support for the party compared to younger people? The fourth question pertains to socio-economic status. As a party that is led by well-educated professionals, including lawyers and doctors, can we expect that it attracts comparatively higher levels of support among wealthier and better-educated voters?

Liberal Party Support Between Elections

Survey results show that the Liberals suffer from the effects of strategic voting. That is, because few consider the Liberals capable of winning a sufficient number of seats during a provincial election, many voters appear to be opting for one of the two larger parties as their second preference. Table 6.8 shows that Liberal support increased during the non-election years of 2000, 2001, and 2002 and then dropped during the 2003 election year. This pattern re-emerges for the non-election years occurring between 2003 and 2007.[8]

The Liberal Party and Health Care

To what extent are those who are concerned about health-care issues attracted to the Liberal Party? When survey results from 2006 and 2007 involving 4000 Manitobans are examined, little difference is found to occur between the three parties. Ten percent of Liberals, compared to 9 percent of those who support the NDP and 11 percent of those who support the PCs, identify health care as their top-of-mind concern (see Table 6.1). When the issue is studied on its own with regards to Manitobans who identified health care as their main concern (n=265), there is no advantage shown for the Liberals. Only 14 percent of those Manitobans who are most concerned about health care report a preference for the Liberals, compared to 42 percent for the PC supporters and 35 percent for the NDP.

Table 6.8: Liberal Party Support: 1999-2007

	Winnipeg	Non-Winnipeg	Manitoba
1999	15	10	13
2000	23	17	21
2001	25	20	23
2002	22	17	20
2003	20	16	18
2004	18	13	16
2005	21	17	19
2006	16	14	15
2007	15	11	14

Compiled from Probe Research press releases and 1999-2007 and *Winnipeg Free Press*, May 23, 2007

The Generational Effect

The Liberals clearly draw higher levels of support among younger voters (those who are under thirty-five) compared to older voters. Within the

Appendix A: Party Preferences and Survey Data

2006-2007 data, the nature of Liberal support is very much marked by youth. Table 6.9 shows the age and gender composition of each party's supporters. Almost one-half (46 percent) of those who report a preference for the Liberals are in the eighteen to thirty-four age range. This is a much higher prevalence when compared to the other two parties. Only 28 percent of NDP supporters and 30 percent of PC supporters are in this age range.

Table 6.9: Composition of Party Support—Age and Gender

	Liberals (446)	PCs (661)	NDP (1125)
18–34	46%	30%	28%
35–54	31%	38%	41%
55+	23%	32%	32%
Men	44%	56%	45%
Women	56%	44%	55%

Source: Derived from the Probe Research 2006–2007 database

Gender

Another characteristic of the Liberal Party is that it attracts more women than men. Table 6.6 shows that among those who report a preference for the Liberals, 56 percent are women compared to 44 percent being men, which is a characteristic that it shares with the NDP, which has 55 percent of its support coming from women. Not shown in the table, but worth noting, is that when older Liberals are examined, the gender gap increases, with 65 percent of those who are over the age of fifty-five being women.

Income

Do voters in higher-income households show more support for the Liberals compared to those in lower-income households? Table 6.10 shows that, contrary to expectations, those in *lower*-income households have generally shown slightly more support for the Liberals than those in the middle- and higher-income categories. While the differences are not strong in each particular year, when the results are compiled for the entire period, the difference between the lowest category and the other two is statistically significant (though differences between the $30,000 to $59,999 and the $60,000 or higher category were not statistically significant).[9] Therefore, it is untrue that Liberal Party support tends to be higher among middle- and upper-income households. In fact, survey results for the seven-year period show that overall socio-economic status may be *inversely* related to Liberal Party support. As a final note, it appears also that differences between the three income levels might be disappearing as the party slides into what may be a general decline. No doubt, new survey data will help confirm whether or not this is a temporary or more permanent pattern.

Table 6.10: Liberal Party Support by Household Income: 2000-2007

	<$30k	$30k-$59k	$60k+
2000	23	20	18
2001	25	22	23
2002	22	20	20
2003	20	17	19
2004	18	15	17
2005	23	19	18
2006	18	14	15
2007	17	13	17

Compiled from Probe Research Press Releases, 2000-2007

3. NDP Supporters

By the mid-1970s, the NDP had become one of the two major provincial parties in the province by drawing together support from urban and northern voters. This support included those in a wide range of social groupings, including those with low incomes, working people, organized labour, educators, environmentalists, feminists, and Aboriginal people. Based on public

Appendix A: Party Preferences and Survey Data

opinion polling data, to what extent can one say that the NDP continues to draw higher levels of support among those residing in lower-income households compared to those in higher-income households? Secondly, do NDP supporters show comparatively higher levels of concern for such traditionally left-wing issues as the environment, job creation, and social welfare? Thirdly, to what extent do women more strongly support the NDP than men? That is, does the party's comparatively stronger record for promoting gender-equality issues and expanded supports for working-class mothers translate into voter support? Finally, does the NDP continue to be the youth-oriented party that it was during the Schreyer breakthrough of 1969?

Table 6.11: NDP Support by Household Income: 2000-2007

	<$30k	$30k-$59k	$60k+
2000	48	44	37
2001	48	42	38
2002	47	44	40
2003	55	52	47
2004	51	43	44
2005	43	43	40
2006	46	39	38
2007	42	44	41

Calculated from Probe Research Press Releases, 2000-2007

The NDP and Lower Income Voters

Based on survey data from 1999 to 2006, the NDP drew higher levels of support from Manitobans who resided in lower-income households (that is, incomes of less than $30,000 per year) when compared to those in higher-income categories (that is, those in the $30,000 to $59,000 household-income range and those in households with incomes of $60,000 or over). Furthermore, those in the middle household-income category tended to show stronger levels of support for the party when compared to those with household incomes of $60,000 or higher.[10] However, as shown in Table 6.11, in the period leading up to the 2007 election, support among lower-income respondents dipped while it increased among the two other groups. This made the gaps between the three different household-income segments insignificant.[11]

Table 6.12: NDP Support by Education and by Region

Region	Totals % NDP Preference	Highest Education Attained	
		High School (610)	Completed University (928)
South—Non-Winnipeg (N=471)	28%	24%	40%
Winnipeg (N=1037)	44%	50%	43%
Manitoba (N=1538)	39%	38%	42%

Source: Derived from the Probe Research 2006–2007 database

A study of the data within the context of Manitoba's urban-rural dimension helps to account for the peculiar manner by which education is linked to NDP support. Results from interviews conducted in 2006 and 2007 show that 43 percent of those with university degrees compared to 50 percent of those with only a high-school degree say they prefer the NDP over other parties. However, as Table 6.12 shows, this pattern is reversed outside the city's limits in southern Manitoba, where 40 percent of those with university degrees compared to only 24 percent of those with only a high-school degree supported the NDP. The link here is probably rooted in education. Professionals, health-care workers, and teachers residing outside Winnipeg would be more likely to prefer the NDP due to the party's stronger record for supporting the public sector. Therefore, one can say that unlike household income, which usually has been inversely related to NDP support across the province, the higher the level of education that a respondent has, at least in the non-urban southern portion of the province, the more chance there is that the individual will support the NDP.[12] In summary, the NDP can be classified as the party of lesser-educated Winnipeg voters and of better-educated voters outside Winnipeg.

Top-of-Mind Concerns of NDP Supporters

So far the discussion in this section has focussed on questions regarding the socio-demographic characteristics of NDP support. Turning now to an identification of issues that NDP supporters say are their top-of-mind concern, and the extent to which these concerns may differ from those who support other parties, some interesting results are discovered, with the results from surveys conducted in 2006 and 2007 broken out according to province-wide totals, Winnipeg, and southern Manitoba (excluding Winnipeg). Unfortunately, due to small sample sizes, northern Manitoba is excluded here as a specific region of focus (however, the region is included in the province-wide data).[13] Shown earlier in Table 6.2 is a breakdown of responses that fall into the following issue categories: "crime and violence," "health care," "the economy and jobs," "education," and "the environment." The top-of-mind concerns that are most often mentioned by NDP supporters related to crime and violence (26 percent of respondents), the economy and jobs (12 percent), health care (9 percent), and poverty (9 percent).

When comparing these results to those for the PCs and Liberals, differences appear to be surprisingly small.[14] For example, NDP supporters are just as likely as PC supporters to identify crime and violence as a top-of-mind concern (26 percent among both groups, while the Liberals have 24 percent of their supporters identifying this issue). NDP supporters are also similar to PCs and Liberals in their likelihood of identifying health as an area of concern (9 percent of NDP reported this issue area as their top of concern, while 11 percent of PCs and 10 percent of Liberals reported a concern in this area).

Women and NDP Support

According to University of Winnipeg political scientist Joan Grace, "by all accounts ... the NDP is an important party to women." Which leads her to ask: "Has the NDP been good to women?"[15] Using public-opinion polling data, here the question is switched around: "Have women been good to the NDP?" The answer is yes. Province-wide survey data from 2000 to 2007 (Table 6.13) reveal that women have consistently shown higher levels of support for the NDP,[16] contrasting sharply with male voters, who show higher levels of support for the PCs. This generally supports the views of those such as Brenda O'Neill, who argues that women tend to be more concerned than men with community-related concerns such as health, education, and social services: "Canadian evidence on the gender gap in opinion suggests that women and men, based on their differing political values, have different political priorities and policy preferences. The issues on which gaps appear include nuclear weapons and defence, government spending, welfare policies, and the welfare system in general. Across a number of issues, women are more 'liberal' in their political outlook."[17]

Table 6.13: NDP Support by Gender and Age: 2000-2007

	Males	Females	18-34	35-54	55+
2000	38	47	41	43	45
2001	36	47	39	45	41
2002	43	45	41	46	44
2003	49	52	47	52	53
2004	42	48	40	46	48
2005	39	41	38	43	41
2006	35	42	33	41	41
2007	38	47	37	43	46

Data compiled from Probe Research press releases 2000-2007

Appendix A: Party Preferences and Survey Data

Generational Change and the NDP

To what extent is the NDP still a youth-oriented party? As discussed in Chapter 4, Schreyer's 1969 breakthrough was, in part, due to his ability to attract young voters. Fifteen years later, in the 1980s, this continued to be one of the NDP's strengths, as demonstrated by a 1984 University of Manitoba poll, which revealed that 38 percent of adults under the age of twenty-five preferred the NDP to other parties compared to 25 percent of those aged twenty-five to forty-four, and 19 percent of those aged forty-five to sixty-four, and 20 percent among those aged sixty-five or older.[18] However, another two decades later it appears that the party has undergone a greying revolution. Survey results collected from 2000 to 2007 show that the party drew consistently heavier support from older and middle-aged voters compared to younger voters (those under thirty-five).[19] In 2007, 43 percent of those in their middle years (defined as being in the range of thirty-five to fifty-four years old) and 46 percent of older adults (aged fifty-five or over) reported supporting the NDP. Only 37 percent of those under the age of thirty-five reported support for the NDP (these differences between young adults and the other two age groups are statistically significant at the 95 percent confidence level for both the 2000 to 2007 longitudinal data shown in Table 6.13 as well as for 2007 survey data).

4. But, What About the Greens?

The Manitoba Green Party has run candidates in three provincial elections. It has yet to make an electoral breakthrough, either in popular support or in the legislature. The first appearance in Manitoba for the Greens was during the 1989 Winnipeg civic election, in which a slate of candidates was put forward under the direction of long-time fringe candidate Nick Ternette. None of the candidates were elected and the party quickly disappeared. The provincial Green Party was founded in 1998 largely through the efforts of urban-based environmentalists and its first leader, Markus Buchart, an "apple cheeked" economist and lawyer with a graduate economics degree from McGill and a penchant for quoting the classical economist Thomas Malthus.[20]

In 1999, Buchart ran against Premier Filmon in the affluent riding of Tuxedo and, unsurprisingly, won only 126 votes. Across the six ridings in which the party fielded candidates, support ranged from eighty-seven votes to 356 votes, and provincially the party drew 0.2 percent of the vote. In the subsequent election of 2003 the Greens expanded their reach by running in fourteen ridings but scored less than 1 percent (0.95 percent) of the provincial vote. The range in support within ridings with Green candidates did increase: from a low of 102 votes to 1193 votes. Its strongest showing occurred in the eclectic urban riding of Wolseley (represented decades earlier by such notables as Duff Roblin and Izzy Asper), where supporters were greatly heartened to see Buchart receive almost 20 percent of the total votes cast.[21]

Internal party dissension later led to Buchart's resignation in February 2005 (and afterwards he and other Green supporters announced the launching of a municipal Green Party, which ran six candidates for city council—all unsuccessful—in the 2006 Winnipeg election[22]). Holly Nelson took over the party's leadership in 2005 and was succeeded in 2006 by Andrew Basham, a University of Winnipeg student, who led the party with fifteen candidates into the 2007 election. Voter support ranged from a low of 177 votes (3 percent) for party leader Basham in Concordia (which was Gary Doer's riding) to 714 in Wolseley for Ardythe Basham (who is Basham's mother) with 12 percent of the vote.[23]

Unfortunately there is little hard data regarding those who prefer the Green Party over the other provincial parties. Yet some results can be drawn from 4000 surveys conducted with the general population during 2004 and another 4000 between May 2006 and March 2007. A total of 2938 out of 4000 individuals interviewed were able to identify a provincial party that they would be willing support in a provincial election. Of these, 4.3 percent identified themselves as either voting for, or leaning towards, the Green Party. From these, a total of 199 completed telephone interviews with

Appendix A: Party Preferences and Survey Data

Green Party supporters were extracted from the database. An examination of this small group should give the reader an inkling of where the party derives its support as it seeks to grow in the coming years. Indeed, what stands out from the results that are provided in Table 6.8 is that those who would vote for the Green Party are much more likely to be younger than those who prefer the NDP, with 48 percent of Green supporters being under the age of thirty-five compared to only 28 percent of NDP supporters.

Perhaps due to their age, Green supporters are slightly more likely to be renters rather than owners and have lower incomes. The Greens also draw less of their support from Winnipeg compared to the NDP. This may reflect the fact that environmental concerns, such as global warming, the condition of Lake Winnipeg, and the impact of hog farming, are raised in both rural and urban parts of the province. While environmental issues have moved beyond the well-educated "new middle class," growing public concern does not appear to always translate well into the electoral arena.[24]

Table 6.14: Demographic Comparison of NDP and Green Party Supporters

	NDP (N=1,316)	Green Party (N=199)	Difference
% Women	55%	51%	-4
% Under 35	28%	48%	+20
% Living in Rental Property	27%	31%	+4
% Completed Post-Secondary	48%	44%	-4
% Household Income <$30,000	23%	26%	+3
% Living in Winnipeg	72%	63%	-9%

Source: Probe Research 2004 and 2006–2007 databases

5. Summary of Survey Findings

With regard to the PCs, the results show that many of the factors that have contributed to the party's problems since 1999 remain unresolved. Its support tends to come from men, non-urban residents, and, in Winnipeg, from those in upper-income households. The PCs also continue to be supported by those who are concerned with economic issues and keeping taxes low, two areas that were not at the top of the general population's agenda in the elections of 2003 and 2007. Furthermore, and contrary to what one might expect for a right-of-centre party, the 2006 and 2007 data show that the PCs have been unable to marshal higher levels of support than the NDP among those concerned with crime and violence. In the meantime, the NDP continues to draw support from among lower-income voters, women, northerners, and middle-class voters. However, it can no longer be considered the youth-oriented party that it was in previous decades, or a party that occupies a left-of-centre position in the minds of the electorate.

The Liberals tend to draw more strongly from urban areas, women, and younger voters. However, the party appears unable to mark out its own distinct place among the mainstream electorate, especially with both the PCs and NDP actively courting middle-class voters. To illustrate this, results regarding those who identified health care as their top-of-mind concern revealed no clear sign that they were opting for the Liberals on this issue. More distant from political power is the Green Party; however, it is doubtful that the Greens will soon fade from the public's eye, due largely to its support among youth and the issues to which it speaks.

Appendix B

Manitoba Election Results, 1870 to 2007

Table A: Provincial Elections in Manitoba, 1870 to 1915

Election Year	Political Party	Seats	% Total Votes	Party and Premier
1870	Government	18	56%	Alfred Boyd (1870–71)
	Opposition	4	23%	Marc Girard (1871–72, 1874) – Cons.
	Other*	2	21%	Henry Clarke (1872–74) .
1874	Government	9	19%	Robert Davis – n.a.
	Opposition	6	18%	
	Other*	9	63%	
1878	Government	7	9%	John Norquay – Cons.
	Other*	17	91%	
1879	Conservative	14	34%	John Norquay – Cons.
	Liberal	2	7%	
	Other*	8	59%	
1883	Conservative	20	55%	John Norquay – Cons.
	Liberal	10	45%	
1886	Liberal	14	48%	John Norquay – Cons. David Harrison (1887) – Cons.
	Conservative	21**	51%	
	Other*	0	1%	

Politics in Manitoba

Election Year	Political Party	Seats	% Total Votes	Party and Premier
1888	Liberal	32	57%	Thomas Greenway – Lib.
	Conservative	5	34%	
	Other*	1	10%	
1892	Liberal	24	50%	Thomas Greenway – Lib.
	Conservative	9	41%	
	Other*	7	9%	
1896	Liberal	32	50%	Thomas Greenway – Lib.
	Conservative	5	40%	
	Patrons of Industry	2	8%	
	Independent	1	2%	
1899	Liberal	17	50%	Hugh John Macdonald – Cons.
	Conservative	18	44%	Rodmond Roblin – Cons.
	Other/Independent	5	7%	
1903	Liberal	9	45%	Rodmond Roblin – Cons.
	Conservative	29	48%	
	Other/Independent	2	8%	
1907	Liberal	13	48%	Rodmond Roblin – Cons.
	Conservative	28	51%	
	Labour	0	2%	
1910	Liberal	13	44%	Rodmond Roblin – Cons.
	Conservative	28	51%	
	Socialist/Labour	0	4%	
	Independent	0	1%	

Appendix B: Manitoba Election Results, 1870 to 2007

Election Year	Political Party	Seats	% Total Votes	Party and Premier
1914***	Liberal	20	43%	Rodmond Roblin – Cons.
	Conservative	28	47%	
	Labour	0	5%	
	Independent	1	6%	
1915***	Liberal	40	55%	T.C. (Tobias) Norris – Lib.
	Conservative	5	33%	
	Labour2	0	3%	
	Independent	2	9%	

* Candidate was undeclared or affiliation is unknown. For 1879 results, this includes such designations as Independent-Conservative, National Party, and Independent Liberal.
** This includes David Glass who ran as an independent but then became Speaker in the Norquay Government (Hilts, 1974, p. 98).
*** The 1914 provincial election gave Winnipeg voters two ballots each in order to vote for candidates for an "A" riding and a "B" riding. Percentage figures provided here are based on Elections Manitoba figures that have been adjusted to equalize the Winnipeg number of votes cast within the provincial voting population.

Table B: Provincial Elections in Manitoba, 1920 to 1949

Election Year	Political Party	Seats	% Total Votes	Party and Premier
1920	Liberal	21	35%	T.C. Norris – Lib.
	Conservative	9	19%	
	Farmers	9	14%	
	Labour	10	18%	
	Independent	4	12%	
	Socialist	2	3%	

Politics in Manitoba

Election Year	Political Party	Seats	% Total Votes	Party and Premier
1922	Liberal	8	23%	John Bracken – UFM
	Conservative	7	16%	
	UFM	28	33%	
	Labour	6	16%	
	Independent	6	13%	
1927	Liberal	7	21%	John Bracken – Progressive
	Conservative	15	27%	
	Progressive	29	32%	
	Farmer-Labour	3	11%	
	Independent	1	9%	
1932	Liberal-Progressive	38	40%	John Bracken – Lib.-Progressive
	Conservative	10	35%	
	Farmer-Labour	6	17%	
	Independent	1	7%	
	Liberal (non-fusion candidates)	0	2%	
1936	Liberal-Progressive	23	35%	John Bracken – Lib-Progressive
	Conservative	16	28%	
	Ind. Labour/CCF	7	12%	
	Social Credit	5	9%	
	Independent	3	12%	
	Communist	1	2%	

Appendix B: Manitoba Election Results, 1870 to 2007

Election Year	Political Party	Seats	% Total Votes	Party and Premier
1941	Govt. Coalition:			John Bracken
	- Liberal-Progressive	27	35%	- Lib.-Progressive S.S. Garson (1943–)
	- Conservative	12	16%	- Lib.-Progressive
	- CCF	3	17%	
	- Social Credit	3	2%	
	- Independent	5	11%	
	Anti-Coalition:			
	- Conservative	3	4%	
	- Social Credit	0	6%	
	- Independent	1	5%	
	- Communist	1	3	
1945***	Govt. Coalition:			S.S. Garson
	- Liberal-Progressive	25	32%	- Lib.-Progressive D.L. Campbell (1948–)
	- Progressive Conservative	13	16%	- Lib.-Progressive
	- Social Credit	2	1%	
	- Independent	3	5%	
	Anti-Coalition:			
	- CCF	9	34%	
	- Social Credit	0	1%	
	- Labour-Progressive	1	5%	
	- Independent/Ind. CCF	2	6%	

Politics in Manitoba

Election Year	Political Party	Seats	% Total Votes	Party and Premier
1949	Govt. Coalition:			D.L. Campbell - Lib.-Progressive
	- Liberal-Progressive	30	38%	
	- Progressive Conservative	9	12%	
	- Ind. Lib/Lib. Prog.	1	4%	
	- Independent	4	4%	
	Anti-Coalition:			
	- CCF	7	26%	
	- Cons & Ind. PC	4	7%	
	- Ind. Lib/Lib. Prog.	1	3%	
	- Others	1	6%	

Table C: Provincial Elections in Manitoba, 1953 to 1966

Election Year	Political Party	Seats	% Total Votes	Party and Premier
1953	Liberal-Progressive	33	39%	D.L. Campbell - Lib.-Progressive
	Progressive Conservative	12	21%	
	CCF	5	16%	
	Independent Lib.-Progressive	3	5%	
	Social Credit	1	13%	
	Independent	2	4%	
	Communist	1	1%	
	Labour-Progressive	0	1%	

Appendix B: Manitoba Election Results, 1870 to 2007

Election Year	Political Party	Seats	% Total Votes	Party and Premier
1958	Liberal-Progressive	19	35%	Duff Roblin – PC
	Progressive Conservative	26	40%	
	CCF	11	20%	
	Independent	1	2%	
	Other	0	2%	
1959	Liberal	11	30%	Duff Roblin – PC
	Progressive Conservative	36	46%	
	CCF	10	22%	
	Independent and Other	0	1%	
1962	Liberal	13	36%	Duff Roblin – PC
	Progressive Conservative	36	45%	
	NDP	7	15%	
	Social Credit	1	3%	
1966	Progressive Conservative	31	40%	Duff Roblin – PC Walter Weir (1967–) – PC
	Liberal	14	33%	
	NDP	11	23%	
	Social Credit	1	4%	

Politics in Manitoba

Table D: Provincial Elections in Manitoba, 1969 to 2007

Election Year	Political Party	Seats	% Total Votes	Party and Premier
1969	Progressive Conservative	22	35%	Edward Schreyer – NDP
	NDP	28	38%	
	Liberal	5	24%	
	Social Credit	1	1%	
	Independent	1	1%	
1973	Progressive Conservative	21	37%	Edward Schreyer – NDP
	NDP	31	42%	
	Liberal	5	19%	
1977	Progressive Conservative	33	49%	Sterling Lyon – PC
	NDP	23	38%	
	Liberal	1	12%	
1981	Progressive Conservative	23	44%	Howard Pawley – NDP
	NDP	34	47%	
	Liberal	0	7%	
1986	Progressive Conservative	26	40%	Howard Pawley – NDP
	NDP	30	41%	
	Liberal	1	14%	
1988	Progressive Conservative	25	38%	Gary Filmon – PC
	NDP	12	24%	
	Liberal	20	35%	
1990	Progressive Conservative	30	42%	Gary Filmon – PC
	NDP	20	29%	
	Liberal	7	28%	

Appendix B: Manitoba Election Results, 1870 to 2007

Election Year	Political Party	Seats	% Total Votes	Party and Premier
1995	Progressive Conservative	31	43%	Gary Filmon – PC
	NDP	23	33%	
	Liberal	3	24%	
1999	Progressive Conservative	24	41%	Gary Doer – NDP
	NDP	32	44%	
	Liberal	1	13%	
2003	Progressive Conservative	20	36%	Gary Doer – NDP
	NDP	35	49%	
	Liberal	2	13%	
	Green Party	0	1%	
2007	Progressive Conservative	19	38%	Gary Doer – NDP
	NDP	36	48%	
	Liberal	2	12%	
	Green Party	0	1%	

Notes

For Further Reading

There exist numerous works regarding specific aspects of Manitoba politics. For an overview, see W.L. Morton's *Manitoba: A History* (Toronto: University of Toronto Press, 1957) and Gerald Friesen's *The Canadian Prairies: A History* (Toronto: University of Toronto Press, 1984). Regarding the province's northern region, the reader is referred to Jim Mochoruk's excellent *Formidable Heritage: Manitoba's North and the Cost of Development 1870 to 1930* (Winnipeg: University of Manitoba Press, 2004). Among chapters and articles specifically concerning Manitoba politics that appear in various collections, the most interesting is written by Tom Peterso n in his examination of how provincial politics has moved from ethnic-based patterns to those of social class. See Tom Peterson, "Ethnic and Class Politics in Manitoba," in Martin Robin, ed., *Canadian Provincial Politics: The Party Systems in the Ten Provinces* (Scarborough: Prentice-Hall, 1972). Other interesting and well-written articles appearing in collected works about the Canadian provinces include Andy Anstett and Paul Thomas, "Manitoba: The Role of the Legislature in a Polarized Political System," in Gary Levy and Graham White, eds., *Provincial and Territorial Legislatures in Canada* (Toronto: University of Toronto Press, 1989); and Alex Netherton, "Paradigm Shift: A Sketch of Manitoba Politics," in Keith Brownsey and Michael Howlett, eds., *The Provincial State in Canada: Politics in Provinces and Territories* (Toronto: Broadview Press, 2001). For works regarding specific political parties, the two best works deal with the NDP. They are Nelson Wiseman, *Social Democracy in Manitoba: A History of the CCF/NDP* (Winnipeg: University of Manitoba Press, 1983) and James McAllister, *The Government of Edward Schreyer: Democratic Socialism in Manitoba* (Montreal: McGill-Queen's University Press, 1984). The reader might also wish to read Jon Gerrard's *Battling for a Better Manitoba: A History of the Provincial Liberal Party* (Winnipeg: Heartland, 2006). Unfortunately there are no books written about the history of the PCs in Manitoba. Among published accounts written by government insiders are Ben Levin, *Governing Education* (Toronto: University of Toronto Press, 2005); Russell Doern, *Wednesdays are Cabinet Days: A Personal Account of the Schreyer Administration* (Winnipeg: Queenston House, 1981); and Herb Schulz, *A View from the Ledge: An Insider's Look at the Schreyer Years* (Winnipeg: Heartland, 2005). There are of course numerous political biographies and autobiographies worth consulting.

Notes

See, for example, Kenneth McNaught, *A Prophet in Politics: A Biography of J.S. Woodsworth* (Toronto: University of Toronto Press, 1959); and John Kendle, *John Bracken: A Political Biography* (Toronto: University of Toronto Press, 1979). See also Sharon Carstairs, *Not One of the Boys* (Toronto: Macmillan, 1993); and Duff Roblin, *Speaking for Myself: Politics and Other Pursuits* (Winnipeg: Great Plains, 1999). For a full range of biographical descriptions of Manitoba's political figures see also J.M. Bumsted, *Dictionary of Manitoba Biography* (Winnipeg: University of Manitoba Press, 1999); Ken Coates and Fred McGuinness, *Manitoba: The Province and The People* (Edmonton: Hurtig Publishers, 1987); and *The Encyclopedia of Manitoba* (Winnipeg: Great Plains Publications, 2007).

Introduction

1. See Christopher Adams, *Interest Groups in the Canadian Grain Sector: Twentieth Century Developments at the National Level* (PhD diss., Carleton University, 1995). See also my research on the Confederation of Regions Party and the Reform Party, including Christopher Adams, "The COR and Reform Parties: Locations of Canadian Protest Party Support" (paper presented to the Canadian Political Science Association, Kingston, ON, 1991); Christopher Adams, "The Reform Party and Roots of Western protest," *Parliamentary Government*, Fall 1989.

2. An historical analysis of the Communist Party of Canada is not provided here, nor for that matter are analyses for other parties that have since disappeared, such as the Patrons of Industry in the late 1800s and Social Credit, which made electoral inroads in the province during the 1930s and 1940s. Regarding the Communist Party and its rise and fall within the Canadian labour movement, see Ivan Avakumovic, *The Communist Party in Canada: A History* (Toronto: McLelland and Stewart, 1975); Ross McCormack, *Reformers, Rebels, and Revolutionaries: The Western Canadian Radical Movement, 1899–1919* (Toronto: University of Toronto Press, 1977), chaps. 4 and 5; and M. Janine Brodie and Jane Jenson, *Crisis, Challenge and Change: Party and Class in Canada* (Toronto: Methuen, 1980), chaps. 1 and 2.

Chapter 1

1. Usage of the term "system" should not imply that I will be using Giovanni Sartori's Downsian "systems theory" approach to studying party politics. See Giovanni Sartori, *Parties and Party Systems: A Framework for Analysis*, Vol. 1 (Cambridge: Cambridge University Press, 1976). Rather, the term "system" is used throughout this book to refer to patterns of competition among political parties as they seek voter support and government power. This is similar to how it is used by James Bickerton, Alain Gagnon, and Patrick Smith in *Ties that Bind: Parties and Voters in Canada* (Don Mills, ON: Oxford University Press, 1999).

2   This term is borrowed from C.B. Macpherson's *Democracy in Alberta: The Theory and Practice of a Quasi-Party System* (Toronto: University of Toronto Press, 1953).

3   See William Nisbet Chambers, "Party Development and Party Action: The American Origins," *History and Theory* 3, 1: 90–120. With regard to ministerialism as a predecessor to the rise of party politics in Canada, see Escott Reid, "The Rise of National Parties in Canada," *Papers and Proceedings of the Canadian Political Science Association*, 1932, repr. in Hugh Thorburn, ed., *Party Politics in Canada*, 5th ed. (Scarborough: Prentice-Hall, 1985).

4   For example, Murray Donnelly refers to the Norquay government of 1878 as "Conservative" and its opposition as being "Liberal." Murray Donnelly, *The Government of Manitoba* (Toronto: University of Toronto Press, 1963), 46. Tom Peterson writes that a provincial "Conservative ministry was formed in 1878." Tom Peterson, "Ethnic and Class Politics in Canada," in Martin Robin, ed., *Canadian Provincial Politics: The Party Systems in the Ten Provinces* (Scarborough: Prentice-Hall, 1972), 71.

5   "The Winnipeg Election," *Manitoba Daily Free Press*, 16 December 1879.

6   "Provincial Politics and Press," *Manitoba Daily Free Press*, 29 December 1879, p. 3.

7   "The Campaign, Getting Ready for Nomination of Candidates To-day," *Manitoba Daily Free Press*, 16 January 1883, p. 8.

8   Maurice Duverger, *Political Parties: Their Organization and Activity in the Modern State* (London: Methuen, 1964), 214–215.

9   C.B. Macpherson, *Democracy in Alberta: Social Credit and the Party System*, 2nd ed. (Toronto: University of Toronto Press, 1962); Russell Hann, *The Farmers Confront Industrialism: Some Historical Perspectives on Ontario Agrarian Movements* (Toronto: New Hogtown Press, 1975); Kerry Badgely, *Ringing in the Common Love of the Good: The United Farmers of Ontario, 1914–1926* (Montreal: McGill-Queen's University Press, 2003).

10 The "Progressive" label was used by United Farmers of Manitoba candidates in Winnipeg as demonstrated by references to the Winnipeg Progressive Association in "Progressives Accept Challenge to Debate," *Manitoba Free Press*, 4 July 1922, p. 4.

11 Gerald Friesen, *The Canadian Prairies: A History* (Toronto: University of Toronto Press, 1984), 402.

12 See, for example, Russell Dalton, *Citizen Politics: Public Opinion and Political Parties in Advanced Industrial Democracies*, 2nd ed. (New Jersey: Chatham House, 1996), 146.

13 Otto Kirchheimer, "The Transformation of the Western European Party System," in Frederic Burin and Kurt Shell, eds., *Political Law and Social Change: Selected Essays* (New York: Columbia University Press, 1969), 354.

14 Christine McCall-Newman, *Grits: An Intimate Portrait of the Liberal Party* (Toronto: Mcmillan, 1982). See also Reginald Whitaker, *The Government Party: Organiziang and Financing The Liberal Party of Canada 1930–58* (Toronto: University of Toronto Press, 1977); and Joseph Wearing, *The L-Shaped Party: The Liberal Party of Canada, 1958–1980* (Toronto: McGill-Ryerson, 1980).
15 Based on 2006 Census of Canada figures available at http://www.statcan.ca.
16 In the 1960s, in his major analysis of Canadian society, sociologist John Porter showed how Canada is not a "melting pot" but a mosaic of distinct ethnic tiles that are arranged vertically according to social class. See John Porter, *The Vertical Mosaic* (Toronto: University of Toronto Press, 1965).
17 For a discussion of early immigration patterns in Winnipeg, see Ken Coates and Fred McGuinness, *Manitoba: The Province and The People* (Edmonton: Hurtig Publishers, 1987), 65, 77, and 108.
18 For a discussion of the impact that Ontario settlers have had on Manitoba's political culture, see Nelson Wiseman, "The Pattern of Prairie Politics," in Hugh G. Thorburn, ed., *Party Politics in Canada*, 5th ed. (Scarborough: Prentice-Hall, 1985).
19 With regard to where Winnipeggers went for their cottage country activities, one can compare the working-class orientation of Winnipeg Beach to that of Victoria Beach, which was an Anglo-Saxon Protestant enclave. For example, Jim Blanchard writes that Sandy Hook property was sold in 1912 with advertisements in the *Winnipeg Telegram* highlighting ethnic restrictions. See Jim Blanchard, *Winnipeg 1912* (Winnipeg: University of Manitoba Press, 2005), 162. However, it would be a mistake to see this as Manitoba-specific; it was a broadly Canadian phenomenon. On racism and the exclusive nature of beach communities, see Lita-Rose Betcherman, *The Swastika and the Maple Leaf: Fascist Movements in Canada in the Thirties* (Toronto: Fitzhenry and Whiteside, 1975), 53.
20 Wiseman, "The Pattern of Prairie Politics," 245 and 247.
21 Bill Redekop, "The New Settlers," *Winnipeg Free Press*, 12 March 2005.
22 Jim Mochoruk, *A Formidable Heritage: Manitoba's North and the Cost of Development, 1870–1930* (Winnipeg: University of Manitoba Press, 2004), xiii.
23 For a discussion of Manitoba's economy, agriculture, and resource production, see Paul Phillips, "Manitoba in the Agrarian Era: 1870–1940," in Jim Silver and Jeremy Hall, eds., *The Political Economy of Manitoba* (Regina: Canadian Plains Research Centre, 1990).
24 Seymour Martin Lipset and Stein Rokkan, "Cleavage Structures, Party Systems, and Voter Alignments," in Seymour Martin Lipset and Stein Rokkan, eds., *Party Systems and Voter Alignments: Cross-National Perspectives* (New York: Free Press, 1967).
25 Tom Peterson, "Ethnic and Class Politics in Manitoba," 69. Geoffrey Lambert also makes this point in his article "Voting Patterns, Canada," in David J.

Wishart, ed., *Encyclopedia of the Great Plains* (Lincoln: Nebraska University Press, 2004) p. 692. See also Meir Serfaty, "Electoral Behaviour in Manitoba: The Convergence of Geography and Politics," in John Welsted et al., eds., *The Geography of Manitoba: Its Land and Its People* (Winnipeg: University of Manitoba Press, 1996).

26 See Gordon H.A. Mackintosh, "The Parliamentary Tradition in Manitoba," *Canadian Parliamentary Review* 6, 2 (1983), 2–3.

27 Elections Manitoba, "Historical Summaries," in *Statement of Votes for the 38th Provincial General Election* (Winnipeg: Government of Manitoba, 2003), 194.

28 Gordon H.A. Mackintosh, "Parliamentary Tradition," 2. Mackintosh describes this first meeting as being held in a "rented log cabin" and W.L. Morton reports that this first meeting was "in the house of A.G.B. Bannatyne, no public building being available." W.L. Morton, *Manitoba: A History* (Toronto: University of Toronto Press, 1957), 146. The original mace was used for thirteen years and remains on display in the Speaker's office at the Manitoba legislature. Government of Manitoba, *Manitoba Legislative Building Guide* [pamphlet], c. 2000, 7.

29 Friesen, *Canadian Prairies*, 200.

30 Andy Anstett and Paul G. Thomas, "Manitoba: The Role of the Legislature in a Polarized Political System," in Gary Levy and Graham White, eds., *Provincial and Territorial Legislatures in Canada* (Toronto: University of Toronto Press, 1989).

31 Morton, *Manitoba: A History*, 146.

32 For a biographical description of these early government leaders see J.M. Bumsted, *Dictionary of Manitoba Biography* (Winnipeg: University of Manitoba Press, 1999), 31, 51, 65, and 92. See also Coates and McGuinness, *Manitoba: The Province and The People* (Edmonton: Hurtig Publishers, 1987), 9, 31, 35, and 36.

33 Anstett and Thomas, "Manitoba: The Role of the Legislature," 91. At the time the provincial government was dependent on funds from Ottawa. Federal transfers were increased in 1875 on condition that the province disband the Legislative Council. Morton, *Manitoba: A History*, 149.

34 In his 1902 work on the rise of modern political parties, Moisei Ostrogorski identified two main functions: to register voters and educate citizens. M. Ostrogorski, *Democracy and the Organization of Political Parties, Vol. 1: England*, S.M. Lipset, ed. (Chicago: Quadrangle Books, 1964), 188.

35 Anstett and Thomas, "Manitoba: The Role of the Legislature." There are numerous authors who identify this influence. See, for example, Nelson Wiseman, "The Pattern of Prairie Politics" and Tom Peterson, "Ethnic and Class Politics in Canada."

36 Based on figures as presented in Hugh Thorburn, "Federal Election Results, 1878–1984," in Hugh G. Thorburn, ed., *Party Politics in Canada*, 5th ed. (Scarborough: Prentice-Hall Canada, 1985), 344.

37 See for example the Conservative Party advertisement placed in the *Manitoba Free Press*, 9 July 1914, p. 11 and the pro-Liberal list of candidates provided in *Manitoba Free Press*, 10 July 1914, pp. 1 and 20.
38 Mackintosh, "Parliamentary Tradition," 6.
39 Elections Manitoba, "Historical Summaries," 194–195.
40 "Dixon Heads Polls in City by Thousands," *Manitoba Free Press*, 30 June 1920, p. 6; "P.R. Not Responsible," *Manitoba Free Press*, 30 June 1920, p. 15; "Tabulating Ballots at Science Building," *Manitoba Free Press*, 19 July 1922, p. 7.
41 Elections Manitoba, "Historical Summaries," 195.
42 Donnelly, *The Government of Manitoba*, 79.
43 Lloyd Stinson, *Political Warriors: Recollections of a Social Democrat* (Winnipeg: Queenston House, 1975), 158.
44 For a background understanding of how these reforms were put forward by the Campbell government see Stinson, *Political Warriors*, 160–161. For an historical chronology of reforms regarding electoral redistribution in Manitoba see Donnelly, *The Government of Manitoba*, 78–80; and Elections Manitoba, "Historical Summaries," 195.
45 James McAllister, *The Government of Edward Schreyer: Democratic Socialism in Manitoba* (Montreal: McGill-Queen's University Press, 1984), 116. See also Wiseman, "Pattern of Prairie Politics," 121. It is a remarkable oversight that Elections Manitoba makes no reference in its historical summary of events to this important change that occurred in the province's redistribution formula in 1968. Elections Manitoba, "Historical Summaries," 194–196.
46 Anstett and Thomas, "Manitoba: The Role of the Legislature," 93.
47 Nelson Wiseman, *Social Democracy in Manitoba: A History of the CCF/NDP* (Winnipeg: University of Manitoba Press, 1983), 12.
48 See Richard Dawson and James Robinson, "Inter-Party Competition, Economic Variables, and Welfare Policies in the American States," *Journal of Politics* 25 (1963): 265–289.
49 Duff Roblin, *Speaking for Myself: Politics and Other Pursuits* (Winnipeg: Great Plains Publications, 1999), 52.
50 Robert Bend who ran as an Independent Conservative in 1949 is incorrectly identified in Elections Manitoba, "Historical Summaries," as a Liberal-Progressive candidate. This chart is adjusted to reflect a change in tallies.
51 Roblin, *Speaking for Myself*, 89–90. Chapter 2 provides further insights into the machinations to keep Roblin's PCs from power.
52 Ed Schreyer asserts that Desjardins's action was not a simple act of disloyalty to the Liberals. It was done only after the MLA had consulted with his local party association and obtained their approval. Ed Schreyer, interview with author, 7 September 2006.
53 Russell Dalton et al., "Electoral Change in Advanced Industrial Democracies," in R. Dalton et al., eds., *Electoral Change in Advanced Industrial Democracies:*

Realignment or Dealignment? (Princeton: Princeton University Press, 1984), 13.

54 It might be said that the system had really become a two-party system with the Liberals playing an insignificant role after 1969 (with the exception of 1988). The Liberals throughout the 1970s and onwards have fielded candidates in both rural and urban ridings, maintained a media presence in each election, operated with a head office and organizational base, and participated in the televised leadership debates. In part this might be attributed to the federal party's continued presence in Manitoba, which has included such powerful regional ministers as James Richardson, Lloyd Axworthy, and Reg Alcock.

55 "The Popular Vote," *Winnipeg Free Press*, 23 May 2007, p. 1.

Chapter 2

1 The term "Conservative" will be used when discussing the party during periods in which it operated under this name. The "Progressive Conservative" label will be used when discussing the party in its more recent form as well as when discussing the party in general (i.e., across all historical periods).

2 Regarding the national Conservative Party in Canada see James Bickerton, Alain Gagnon, and Patrick Smith, "The Progressive Conservatives: Broken Ties, Broken Dreams," in James Bickerton, Alain Gagnon, and Patrick Smith, *Ties that Bind: Parties and Voters in Canada* (Don Mills, ON: Oxford University Press, 1999).

3 For more on the Conservatives' National Policy, see Robert MacGregor Dawson, *The Government of Canada* (Toronto: University of Toronto Press, 1958), 497–498. See also Edgar McInnis, *Canada: A Political and Social History*, 3rd ed. (Toronto: Holt, Rinehart and Winston, 1969), 383–388; Kenneth Norrie and Douglas Owram, *A History of the Canadian Economy* (Toronto: Harcourt Brace Jovanovich, 1991), 301–316.

4 Premier Marc-Amble Girard was elected as a Conservative and was premier of Manitoba from 1871 to 1872 and 1874; however, the government did not operate according to party lines. Norquay is identified as a Conservative according to Elections Manitoba results from 1878 onward, yet being identified as a Conservative in that period simply signified that one supported the policies of Macdonald's national party. For a discussion of the nature of Canadian political parties in the 1870s and 1880s, see Escott Reid, "The Rise of National Parties in Canada."

5 Coates and McGuinness, *Manitoba: The Province and The People*, 45.

6 Peterson, "Ethnic and Class Politics in Manitoba," 71. It should be said, however, that some would say that Peterson uses the term "Métis" in a loose manner. According to J.M. Bumsted, Norquay would have been considered at the time as "mixed-blood" due to his British-Aboriginal ancestry. Those deemed Métis were those who had a combination of French and Aboriginal ancestry, usually

tied to the fur trade. For distinctions on how the Red River community's population was differentiated according to ethnic lines, see J.M. Bumsted, *The Red River Rebellion* (Winnipeg: Watson and Dwyer, 1996), 18–25.

7   Coates and McGuinness, *Manitoba: The Province and The People*.
8   Gerald Friesen, "John Norquay," *Dictionary of Canadian Biography*, http:// www.biogaphi.ca, accessed 29 July 2006.
9   Friesen, *The Canadian Prairies: A History*, 212–213; Coates and McGuinness, *Manitoba: The Province and The People*, 45.
10 Friesen, *The Canadian Prairies*, 201.
11 Gerald Friesen, *River Road: Essays on Manitoba and Prairie History* (Winnipeg: University of Manitoba Press, 1996), 11.
12 Friesen, *River Road*. A further example of this perspective can be found in Grant MacEwan's biography of John Norquay, *Fifty Mighty Men*, which was first published in 1958. MacEwan provides much detail about the premier's Orkney heritage and nothing regarding his Aboriginal heritage aside from Norquay's knowledge of local languages and an opaque reference to the opposition referring to him as an "Indian" in the Legislature. Grant MacEwan, *Fifty Mighty Men* (Saskatoon: Modern Press, 1958), chap. 40 passim.
13 Macdonald became the party leader in 1897 while Roblin remained the opposition leader in the legislature. PC Party, "Our Leaders," unpublished document provided to the author, 2006. See also Allan Levine, "Chicago of the North," *Manitoba 125: Volume 2, Gateway to the West*, Gregg Shilliday, ed. (Winnipeg: Great Plains Publications, 1994), 72. Regarding the year in which the provincial party was officially formed, see Frances Russell, *The Canadian Crucible: Manitoba's Role in Canada's Great Divide* (Winnipeg: Heartland, 2003), 150.
14 Dafoe provides a detailed and colourful account of how the riding was lost due to strategic blundering by the Conservatives and a significant debate that turned the course of the Brandon election. John W. Dafoe, *Clifford Sifton in Relation to His Times* (Toronto: Macmillan Company, 1931), 203–210.
15 See Keith Wilson, *Manitobans in Profile: Hugh John Macdonald* (Winnipeg: Peguis Publishers, 1980). See also Coates and McGuinness, *Manitoba: The Province and The People*, 69. Regarding his childhood and differences with his father, see Patricia Phenix, *Private Demons: The Tragic Personal Life of John A. Macdonald* (Toronto: McClelland and Stewart, 2006), chap. 9 and passim.
16 This influential leader of the provincial Conservatives first ran as a Liberal in 1886 in Dufferin North, and lost by five votes to Conservative cabinet minister David Wilson. He was subsequently elected as a Liberal on 12 May 1888 in a by-election. In the July 1888 provincial election he was elected in the southern rural riding of Dufferin by acclamation, again as a Liberal candidate. Believing that Greenway was not doing enough to reduce transportation costs in the region, Roblin crossed the floor to sit with the Conservatives in 1889. Elections Manitoba, "Historical Summaries," 210; Allan Levine, "Chicago of the North,"

in Gregg Shilliday, ed., *Manitoba 125: Volume 2, Gateway to the West* (Winnipeg: Great Plains Publications, 1994), 75.
17 Donnelly, *The Government of Manitoba*, 48.
18 Census of Canada, 1901 and 1911, cited in Alan Artibise, *Winnipeg: An Illustrated History* (Toronto: James Lorimer, 1977), 204. General population figures are also cited in Jim Blanchard, *Winnipeg 1912* (Winnipeg: University of Manitoba Press, 2005), 9. Blanchard also points out that the correct population figure for 1911 is 166,533 if seasonal workers are included.
19 Peterson, "Ethnic and Class Politics in Manitoba," 74–75. For an overview of Tammany Hall see William Safire, *Safire's Political Dictionary*, updated ed. (New York: Random House, 1978), 712–713; Michael Tomasky, "The Boss," *The New York Review*, 1 December 2005, pp. 52–55.
20 Levine, "Chicago of the North," 72.
21 W. Leland Clark, *Brandon's Politics and Politicians* (Altona, MB: Brandon Sun, 1981), 77–78. Morton, *Manitoba: A History*, 347. As discussed in Chapter 3, many were not convinced of the new leader's sincerity regarding the female vote.
22 This account based on Morton, *Manitoba: A History*, 341–346. See also Donnelly, *The Government of Manitoba*, 48–51.
23 Morton, *Manitoba: A History*, 346.
24 Russell, *The Canadian Crucible*, 192–194.
25 John Kendle, *John Bracken: A Political Biography* (Toronto: University of Toronto Press, 1979), 47.
26 Stinson, *Political Warriors*, 130–131. Prefontaine's son, Edmond, later served in Premier Douglas Campbell's Liberal-Progressive cabinet in the 1950s.
27 PC Party, "Our Leaders"; Morton, *Manitoba: A History*, 375.
28 Kendle, *John Bracken*, 41.
29 Kendle, *John Bracken*, 40; PC Party of Manitoba, "Our Leaders."
30 Kendle, *John Bracken*, 66 and 85–86.
31 Allan Levine writes that Evans, along with others among the city's commercial elite, "socialized together at the Manitoba and Carleton Clubs, played golf together at the exclusive St. Charles Country Club, and holidayed with their families at Victoria Beach and Lake of the Woods." Levine, "Chicago of the North," 71. For a biographical account see Artibise, *Winnipeg: An Illustrated History*, 98–99; Bumsted, *Dictionary of Manitoba Biography*, 78.
32 Kendle, *John Bracken*, 142.
33 Kendle, *John Bracken*, 142. Willis's age and occupation are taken from PC Manitoba, "Our History," http://www.pcmanitoba.com/, accessed 27 July 2006. Further details about Willis's political career can be found in Stinson, *Political Warriors*, 143–145.
34 Kendle, *John Bracken*, 144–145.

35 Morton, *Manitoba: A History*, 427; Kendle, *John Bracken*, 152.
36 Letter to Willis, 25 October 1940, cited in Kendle, *John Bracken*, 175–176. The same letter to the CCF's leader (S.J. Farmer) is quoted in Stinson, who personally had the letter in his possession at the time of writing his memoirs. See Stinson, *Political Warriors*, 95–96.
37 Donnelly, *The Government of Manitoba*, 66.
38 J.L. Granatstein, *The Politics of Survival: The Conservative Party of Canada, 1939–1945* (Toronto: University of Toronto Press, 1967), 68.
39 Letter from Alice Bracken, 13 December 1942. Quoted in Granatstein, *Politics of Survival*, 147.
40 PC Party of Manitoba, "Our History."
41 Donnelly, *The Government of Manitoba*, 66.
42 Michael Best, "Prog Con Stalwarts Gather for Showdown on Leadership," *Winnipeg Free Press*, 16 June 1954, p. 1.
43 Roblin, *Speaking for Myself*, 62. According to Lloyd Stinson, the CCF leader at the time, Stinson would converse on occasion with Willis during the 1953 session due to their proximate seating arrangements. Stinson reports that the veteran Conservative leader told him on one occasion that he preferred to see MLA Gurney Evans (the son of Sanford Evans) as his successor rather than Roblin. Furthermore, "his dislike and fear of Roblin was intense." Stinson, *Political Warriors*, 144–145.
44 In its convention coverage, the *Winnipeg Free Press* reported a rumour that Roblin and Ross had agreed to support each other if one dropped off prior to a second ballot (Michael Best, "Convention," *Winnipeg Free Press*, 16 June 1954, p. 9.). The outcome supports the strong possibility that this deal existed. The vote tallies are based on Roblin, *Speaking for Myself*, 63, and the *Winnipeg Free Press* (Michael Best, "Roblin Topples Willis as Manitoba PC Chief," *Winnipeg Free Press*, 18 June 1954, pp. 1 and 4). Lloyd Stinson gives a slightly different tally in his memoirs: Roblin 161 and Willis 123. Stinson, *Political Warriors*, 145.
45 Roblin, *Speaking for Myself*, 69.
46 Roblin, *Speaking for Myself*, 68–69, 73.
47 Donnelly, *The Government of Manitoba*, 67.
48 In his memoirs, Diefenbaker wrote that Roblin "might not have become Premier had we not won the 1957 election. We formed a government which gave incentive and enthusiasm to our supporters throughout Canada. The hopelessness and the defeatism of Conservatives everywhere was supplanted by the hope that what had been done nationally could be done provincially. In the 1958 election, we swept Manitoba's fourteen seats. Immediately thereafter Roblin was able to elect a minority government. The following year he went to the people and achieved a majority." John Diefenbaker, *One Canada: Volume Two, The Years of Achievement* (Toronto: Macmillan, 1976), 294.

49 Christopher Adams, "Elections in Manitoba," Ingeborg Boyens, ed., *The Encyclopedia of Manitoba* (Winnipeg: Great Plains Publications, 2007).
50 As reported by Cy Gonick, "Manitoba Economy," 29
51 William Neville, "Climate of Change," Gregg Shilliday, ed., *Manitoba 125: Volume 3, Decades of Diversity* (Winnipeg: Great Plains Publications, 1995), 103.
52 Figures are derived from Manitoba Department of Education Annual Report, reports for 1958–59 to 1966–67, and reported in Shaun McCaffrey, *A Study of Policy Continuity Between the Progressive Conservative and the New Democratic Party Governments of Manitoba, 1958–1977* (MA thesis, University of Manitoba, 1986), 12.
53 Cy Gonick, "The Manitoba Economy Since World War II," James Silver and Jeremy Hull, eds., *The Political Economy of Manitoba* (Regina: Canadian Plains Research Center, 1990), 29–30.
54 This account is provided by Roblin, *Speaking for Myself*, 170–173.
55 Calculations derived from figures as presented in Elections Manitoba, "Historical Summaries," 250–253.
56 Roblin, *Speaking for Myself*, 181.
57 McCaffrey, *A Study of Policy Continuity*, 33–34.
58 *Winnipeg Free Press*, 8 March 1968, quoted by Tom Peterson, "Ethnic and Class Politics in Manitoba," 104.
59 Quoted in Tom Peterson, "Manitoba," in John Saywell, ed., *Canadian Annual Review for 1969* (Toronto: University of Toronto Press, 1970), 128–129.
60 Roblin, *Speaking for Myself*, 106.
61 Peterson, "Manitoba," 133.
62 "Mapping byelection strategy major task for new PC leader, *Winnipeg Tribune*, 1 March 1971, p. 1. See also J.M. Bumsted, "The Socialist Experiment," Gregg Shilliday, ed., *Manitoba 125: Volume 3, Decades of Diversity* (Winnipeg: Great Plains Publications, 1995), 118.
63 Spivak's platform included a range of innovations including an "annual minimum wage" and his strategies were created with the polling work of Toronto's well respected consultant Peter Regenstreif. See "Mapping byelection strategy major task for new PC leader, *Winnipeg Tribune*, 1 March 1971, p. 1 and "PC poll finds Schreyer's popularity down a little," *Winnipeg Tribune*, 1 March 1971, p. 1.
64 Elections Manitoba, "Historical Summaries," 256–257.
65 "Schreyer Has Cake, But Not the Icing," *Winnipeg Tribune*, 29 June 1973. Quoted in Herb Schulz, *A View from the Ledge: An Insider's Look at the Schreyer Years* (Winnipeg: Heartland Associates, 2005), 211.
66 Inflation also had a strong impact in rural Manitoba as farmers had to contend with a growing gap between ROI and increasing capital and operating expenses. Christopher Adams, *Interest Groups in the Canadian Grain Sector: Twentieth Century Developments at the National Level* (PhD diss., Carleton

University, 1995), 187. Regarding general issues facing the Canadian economy during this period, see Kenneth Norrie and Douglas Owram, *A History of the Canadian Economy* (Toronto: Harcourt, Brace Jovanovich, 1991), chap. 22. Regarding economic issues throughout the industrial West, see Michael Piore and Charles Sabel, *The Second Industrial Divide* (New York: Basic Books, 1984), chap. 7.

67 There were some in the Spivak camp who complained that Lyon's forces were anti-Semitic. See Vic Grant, "Tories 'ruined' the PC party, not me," *Winnipeg Tribune*, 2 December 1975, p. 2.

68 "Tory race enters last lap," *Winnipeg Tribune*, 4 December 1975, p. 1. "Lyon victory ends grim campaign," *Winnipeg Tribune*, 8 December 1975, pp. 1 and 5. See also Coates and McGuinness, *Manitoba: The Province and The People*, 171; Bumsted, *Dictionary of Manitoba Biography*, 131. The battles that ensued at the local constituency level were personally witnessed by this author during the months leading up to the convention.

69 "Liberal party's collapse was key to Tory victory," *Winnipeg Tribune*, 12 October 1977, p. 1.

70 Murray Donnelly, "Manitoba," in John Saywell, ed., *Canadian Annual Review of Politics and Public Affairs, 1977* (Toronto: University of Toronto Press, 1979), 182.

71 Vic Grant, "Tories win a blow for free enterprise," *Winnipeg Tribune*, 12 October 1977, p. 2.

72 Donnelly, "Manitoba," 185.

73 "Many Tories felt campaign was faltering," *Winnipeg Free Press*, 18 November 1981, p. 4.

74 This account of the 1981 election is derived from Geoffrey Lambert, "Manitoba," in R.B. Byers, ed., *Canadian Annual Review of Politics and Public Affairs, 1981* (Toronto: University of Toronto Press, 1984), 396–403.

75 "Victory for the NDP," *Winnipeg Free Press*, 18 November 1981, p. 6.

76 This is discussed in Chapter 4.

77 Manitoba, Legislative Assembly, *Debates and Proceedings* (6 June 1983), cited in Raymond Hébert, *Manitoba's French-Language Crisis* (Montreal: McGill-Queen's University Press, 2004), 81.

78 Paul Adams, "Manitoba," in R.B. Byers, ed., *Canadian Annual Review of Politics and Public Affairs, 1983* (Toronto: University of Toronto Press, 1985), 268. The vote numbers are reported in "Filmon faces first test as Tory leader," *Winnipeg Free Press*, 12 December 1983, p. 1.

79 Quoted in "Filmon faces first test as Tory leader," *Winnipeg Free Press*, 12 December 1983, p. 4.

80 Frances Russell, "Tories opt for change," *Winnipeg Free Press*, 12 December 1983, p. 7.

81 Christopher Adams et al., "PC Leadership Candidate Support Among Delegates, 1983," unpublished report, 1983. Mary Ann Fitzgerald, "Filmon faces first test as Tory leader," *Winnipeg Free Press*, 12 December 1983, p. 4.
82 Frances Russell, *Winnipeg Free Press*, 11 January 1984. Quoted in Hébert, *Manitoba's French-Language Crisis*, 156.
83 John Laschinger and Geoffrey Stevens, *Leaders and Lesser Mortals: Backroom Politics in Canada* (Toronto: Key Porter Books, 1992), 99–100. Schulz, *A View From the Ledge*, 500.
84 This account of the 1988 provincial election is drawn from Geoffrey Lambert, "Manitoba," in David Leyton-Brown, ed., *Canadian Annual Review of Politics and Public Affairs, 1988* (Toronto: University of Toronto Press, 1995), 256.
85 Manitoba, Legislative Assembly, *Debates and Proceedings* (21 July 1988), 1. Rocan's political career ended two decades later on a more negative note when he lost a nomination battle with Blaine Pedersen. He subsequently left the PC caucus to sit briefly as an independent. The attack on his nomination was said to be largely orchestrated by former Health Minister Don Orchard, who had retired from the politics in 1995. Dan Lett, "Veteran Tory fights for nomination," *Winnipeg Free Press*, 10 October 2006, p. A4; "Tories give Rocan the boot," *Winnipeg Free Press*, 17 November 2006, p. A4.
86 Lambert, "Manitoba," 256–259.
87 Quoted from a government brochure in Hébert, *Manitoba's French-Language Crisis*, 196.
88 Hébert, *Manitoba's French-Language Crisis*, 196.
89 Ingeborg Boyens, "A Decade of Discontent," Gregg Shilliday, ed., *Manitoba 125: Volume 3, Decades of Diversity* (Winnipeg: Great Plains Publications, 1995), 173–174.
90 Boyens, "A Decade of Discontent," 175.
91 The author wishes to thank Paul Thomas for providing input regarding this period.
92 Lloyd Fridfinnson, "Preparing for a New Century," Gregg Shilliday, ed., *Manitoba 125: Volume 3, Decades of Diversity* (Winnipeg: Great Plains Publications, 1995), 179.
93 Geoffrey Lambert, "Manitoba," in David Leyton-Brown, ed., *Canadian Annual Review of Politics and Public Affairs, 1990* (Toronto: University of Toronto Press, 1997), 188.
94 Rand Dyck, *Provincial Politics in Canada*, 2nd ed. (Scarborough: Prentice-Hall, 1991), 404.
95 John Sawatsky, *Mulroney: The Politics of Ambition* (Toronto: Macfarlane, Walter and Ross, 1991), 515–516.
96 Regarding the impact that the CF-18 contract had on the national PCs and the formation of the Reform Party, see James Bickerton, Alain Gagnon, and Patrick Smith, *Ties that Bind*, 137, and Bob Plamondon, *Full Circle: Death and Resur-*

rection in Canadian Conservative Politics (Toronto: Key Porter Books, 2006), 78–82.

97 Murray Dobbin, *Preston Manning and the Reform Party* (Toronto: James Lorimer, 1991), 74.

98 "1,000 Rake Tax at Anti-GST Rally," *Winnipeg Free Press*, 13 March 1990, p. A1. This opposition was not restricted to the West. Across the country 74 percent opposed the new tax and 71 percent across the Prairies reported the same feelings. Gallup press release, 18 September 1989. There are many studies regarding the of rise of Canadian regional protest parties in the 1980s. Three examples are Christopher Adams, "The COR and Reform Parties: Locations of Canadian Protest Party Support," David Laycock, "Reforming Canadian Democracy? Institutions and Ideology in the Reform Party Project," *Canadian Journal of Political Science* 27, 2 (1994): 213–248; and Richard Sigurdson, "Preston Manning and the Politics of Postmodernism in Canada," *Canadian Journal of Political Science* 27, 2 (1994): 249–276.

99 Dyck, *Provincial Politics*, 404; also Lambert, "Manitoba," *Canadian Annual Review of Politics and Public Affairs, 1990*.

100 "CBC, "On the campaign trail with 'Team Filmon,'" 11 April 1995, http://archives.cbc.ca/politics/elections/clips/13653/, accessed 15 August 2006.

101 Christopher Adams, "The Provincial Political Scene," *Manitoba Reid Report*, Winter 1998, 45.

102 Originally the three candidates ran under the "Independent Native Voice" banner. CBC, "Vote-rigging scandal emerges," broadcasted 29 March 1999; see also additional information provided with same story under "Did You Know," http://archives.cbc.ca/politics/elections/clips/13656/, accessed 15 August 2006.

103 See for example Len Kruzenga, "Aboriginal people used in vote-splitting scheme," *Windspeaker*, March 1999.

104 See Geoffrey Lambert, "Manitoba," in David Mutimer, ed., *Canadian Annual Review of Politics and Public Affairs, 1999* (Toronto: University of Toronto Press, 2005), 169–170; CBC, "Vote-rigging scandal emerges."

105 CBC, "Vote-rigging scandal emerges."

106 Quoted in CBC, "Vote-rigging scandal emerges." See also Alfred Monnin, *Report of the Commission of Inquiry into Allegations of Infractions of The Elections Act and The Elections Finances Act during the 1995 Manitoba General Election* (Winnipeg: Manitoba Queen's Printer, 1999). For more background detail on the scandal, see Doug Smith, *As Many Liars: The Story of the 1995 Manitoba Vote-Splitting Scandal* (Winnipeg: Arbeiter Ring, 2003).

107 See James Rice and Michael Prince, "Martin's Moment: The Social Policy Agenda of a New Prime Minister," in G. Bruce Doern, ed., *How Ottawa Spends: 2004–2005* (Montreal: McGill-Queen's University Press, 2004), 118. For an historical overview of federal cash transfers from 1983 to 2003, see Allan Maslove, "Health and Federal-Provincial Financial Arrangements: Lost Opportunity,"

in G. Bruce Doern, ed., *How Ottawa Spends: 2005-2006* (Montreal: McGill-Queen's University Press, 2005), 27-28.
108 Probe Research, "Winnipeg Public Issues Agenda," press release, 8 March 1999.
109 "Filmon's ride in power long, rocky," *Winnipeg Free Press*, 22 September 1999, p. A2. "Mr. Doer's challenge," *Winnipeg Free Press*, 22 September 1999, p. A12. In a second piece the newspaper's editor stated that the "NDP inherits a strong provincial economy and a slimmed-down public sector."
110 This organizer's perspective appears to be somewhat naïve about how politics works, especially battles over leadership. However, it does indicate a perspective within the party that Murray was the preferred candidate by much of the caucus and party supporters. The quote is from Dan Lett, "Dashed Hopes," *Winnipeg Free Press*, 16 April 2006, p. B3.
111 The details regarding Stuart Murray's background and leadership are derived from the following sources: PC Manitoba, "Stuart Murray: MLA Kirkfield Park," http://www.pcmanitoba.com, accessed 27 July 2006; Dan Lett, "Dashed Hopes," *Winnipeg Free Press*, 16 April 2006, p. B3.
112 Interview with author, 6 July 2007.
113 In fairness to Murray, his inability to recuperate from this self-inflicted wound was partly due to *Winnipeg Free Press* political writer Dan Lett's persistence in raising this matter whenever covering the leader's activities from 2002 to 2006. It was even included in Lett's article regarding Murray's resignation as an MLA. Dan Lett, "Stuart Murray resigns seat, takes hospital job," *Winnipeg Free Press*, 8 September 2006, p. B2.
114 Mia Rabson, "Law will squeeze party fundraising," *Winnipeg Free Press*, 10 April 2006, p. A4.
115 In a 2007 interview with the author, Stuart Murray blamed the new finance laws for his party's weak 2003 campaign. Murray asserted that Randy Moffat's donation of media time averted a campaign disaster by allowing the PCs to obtain a minimal amount of visibility in lieu of a small advertising budget.
116 Mia Rabson, "Murray vows to fight on as Tories hold 20 seats," *Winnipeg Free Press*, 4 June 2003, p. A2. Dan Lett et al., "NDP Captures 49% of smaller vote," *Winnipeg Free Press*, 4 June 2003, p. A1. See also the pre-election coverage regarding the polling results (in which the NDP were at 57%) in Dan Lett, "NDP heads for landslide," *Winnipeg Free Press*, 29 May 2003, p. A1.
117 See, for example, Tom Brodbeck's post-election column titled "No excuses— dump Stu," *Winnipeg Sun*, 4 June 2003, p. 5.
118 1974 and 1976 figures are cited in Herb Schulz, *A View From the Ledge*; other figures are from "PC membership swells," *Winnipeg Free Press*, 2 April 2006, p. A2. Due to conflicting figures given for the 1980s these are not reported here. For a demonstration of this confusion see Mia Rabson, "Murray plans to skip meeting," *Winnipeg Free Press*, 27 April 2006, p. A3 and the editorial "McFadyen's moment," *Winnipeg Free Press*, 1 May 2006, p. A10.

119 Mary Ann Fitzgerald, "Filmon faces first test as Tory leader."
120 "D before y except on leadership ballot," *Winnipeg Free Press*, 28 April 2006, p. A5.
121 Mia Rabson, "Tory hopefuls warm up spotty crowd," *Winnipeg Free Press*, 29 April 2006, p. A3.
122 Mia Rabson, "Tory 1, Tory 2, or Tory 3?" *Winnipeg Free Press*, 17 April 2006, p. A4.
123 Mia Rabson, "Tory hopefuls warm up spotty crowd"; Mia Rabson and Martin Cash, "Tories crown McFadyen chief," *Winnipeg Free Press*, 30 April 2006, p. A3. According to Andrew Enns, a senior-level party activist, in an interview with this author, there were some concerns that some voters might not have met the cut-off date for joining the party to qualify to vote. However, due to the large margin of victory it became a non-issue and not worth pursuing by those concerned.
124 Probe Research, "Winnipeg Free Press/Probe Research News Release," June 2006 and March 2005. See also Chris Adams, "The Image Problem, The Tories Need a Pragmatic, Moderate Platform," *Winnipeg Free Press*, p. A15.
125 This account is based on this author's own study of events leading up to the 2006 election while serving as CanWest Global's federal election analyst during 2005 and 2006.
126 Mia Rabson, "Conservatives top NDP in 2006 fundraising," *Winnipeg Free Press*, 20 August 2007, p. A4.
127 *Winnipeg Free Press*, Global TV, and Probe Research, "News Release: 2007 Manitoba Election Survey," 17 May 2007, p. 4.
128 *Winnipeg Free Press*, Global TV, and Probe Research, "News Release: 2007 Manitoba Election Survey."
129 Dan Lett, "Anatomy of an election: How the NDP talked its way to a third term," *Winnipeg Free Press*, 17 June 2007, p. B5.
130 E-mail correspondence between Kildonan's defeated PC candidate Brent Olynik and the author, 24 May 2007; personal interviews with defeated PC candidate for Fort Garry, Shawn McAffrey, 23 August 2007, and PC candidate for Riel, Trudy Turner, 26 October 2007.
131 *Winnipeg Free Press*, Global TV, and Probe Research, "News Release: 2007 Manitoba Election Survey," p. 4. The reader should note, however, that the differences between the two parties for this age segment are within the margin of error.

Chapter 3

1   As noted in Chapter 2, the official name at the time for the Conservatives was "Liberal-Conservative." However, the common term used to label the party was "Conservative."

2   Due to the often loose connection between candidates and party affiliation at the time, there are differences in the calculated tallies of the size of each party's slate in the 1883 election. A review of Elections Manitoba historical data (Elections Manitoba, "Historical Summaries"), newspaper reports from the period, and the work of Joseph Hilts, which is based on a meticulous treatment of newspaper and primary materials from this period (Joseph Alfred Hilts, *The Political Career of Thomas Greenway* [PhD diss., University of Manitoba, 1974], 72), the probable number of Liberal and Provincial Rights candidates in 1883 was twenty-four. Worth mentioning is that there were also two Liberal candidates running in support of John Norquay's government. These were C.P. Brown in Westbourne and J.A. Davidson in Dauphin, who were both acclaimed. Elections Manitoba lists these two individuals as "Conservative," no doubt due to the individuals' support for the Norquay government. Another correction is needed with regards to Hilts's work where he mistakenly identifies Brown's constituency as Russell, which was not created until 1886. Regarding the party identification of Brown and Davidson, see Hilts, 72.

3   Hilts, *The Political Career of Thomas Greenway*, 41 and passim; Coates and McGuinness, *Manitoba: The Province and The People*, 48.

4   Hilts, *The Political Career of Thomas Greenway*, 72.

5   The use of the "Liberal" label is demonstrated in the following statement: "The meeting broke up with cheers for the *Liberal* candidates and chairman" [emphasis added]. "The Campaign," *Manitoba Daily Free Press*, 26 November 1886, p. 1. With regard to the use of the label "Provincial Rights," see "Provincial Rights," *Manitoba Daily Free Press*, 9 December 1886, p. 1; "The Elections," *Manitoba Daily Free Press*, 10 December 1886, p. 1; and "The Elections," *Manitoba Daily Free Press*, 11 December 1886, p. 2.

6   Elections Manitoba, "Historical Summaries," 208. The tally for the Conservatives is adjusted down by one seat due to the mislabelling of David Glass.

7   Hilts, *The Political Career of Thomas Greenway*, 102; see also J.E. Rea, "Thomas Greenway," *The Dictionary of Canadian Biography Online*, http://www.biographi.ca, accessed 29 July 2006.

8   Some argue that the impact of this wave of immigration established a particular and permanent stamp on the province's political culture. See, for example, Nelson Wiseman, "The Pattern of Prairie Politics."

9   "The Victory," *The Manitoba Daily Free Press*, 12 July 1888, p. 1.

10 Hilts, *The Political Career of Thomas Greenway*, 91–93 and 103a–105.

11 Regarding settlement patterns, see Wiseman, "The Pattern of Prairie Politics."

12 Artibise, *Winnipeg: An Illustrated History*, 30. See also John Lehr, "Settlement: The Making of a Landscape," in John Welsted et al., eds., *The Geography of Manitoba: Its Land and Its People* (Winnipeg: University of Manitoba Press, 1996).

13 For a summary of Greenway's activities see Jon Gerrard, *Battling for a Better Manitoba: A History of the Provincial Liberal Party* (Winnipeg: Heartland,

2006), 35–45; also, Coates and McGuinness, *Manitoba: The Province and The People*, 44–50.

14 These were the main population categories in the negotiations. There were also First Nations and Americans in the area. However, their representatives were not significant players in the deliberations regarding the settlement's entrance into Canada. See Morton, *Manitoba: A History*, chap. 7.

15 A Brandon-based lawyer, Sifton won the riding of North Brandon in the 1888, 1892, and 1896 provincial elections and served as minister of education from 1891 to 1896 before being pulled into federal politics by Wilfrid Laurier. Sifton went on to become an influential minister in Laurier's government and minister of the interior where he promoted aggressive immigration and settlement policies. See John W. Dafoe, *Clifford Sifton in Relation to His Times* (Toronto: Macmillan, 1931), chaps. 2 and 3; Bumsted, *Dictionary of Manitoba Biography*, 227; and David Hall, *Clifford Sifton: Volume 1* (Vancouver: University of British Columbia Press, 1981).

16 Peterson, "Ethnic and Class Politics in Manitoba," 72.

17 These facts are derived from Dafoe, *Clifford Sifton*, 45–46; Bumsted, *The Dictionary of Manitoba Biography, op. cit*, 201; Morton, *Manitoba: A History*, 248.

18 See Donald Creighton, *Canada's First Century: 1867–1967* (Toronto: MacMillan, 1970), 71–74.

19 For a discussion of this compromise see Hébert, *Manitoba's French-Language Crisis*, 12–13; Dafoe, *Clifford Sifton*, 97–98.

20 Hébert, *Manitoba's French-Language Crisis*, 13–14. See also Frances Russell, *The Canadian Crucible*, chap. 5; Alan Artibise, *Winnipeg: An Illustrated History*, 46–55.

21 The author's mother, a francophone from St. Boniface, later described her childhood days in the 1920s and 1930s and how, in preparation for the provincial school inspector's inevitable visit, the nuns would have the children practise hiding their French instructional materials. This practice continued into the 1960s, as reported by a resident of the Métis community of St. Laurent to this author.

22 See Dafoe, *Clifford Sifton*, 56.

23 See Donnelly, *The Government of Manitoba*, 51–52.

24 See James Chace, *1912: Wilson, Roosevelt, Taft and Debs—The Election that Changed the Country* (New York: Simon and Schuster, 2004).

25 Elections Manitoba, "Historical Summaries," 194–195. This is less than Morton's incorrect tally, which has the election producing forty-two elected Liberals (Morton, *Manitoba: A History*, 348).

26 "Giving the News to Cheery Throng at the *Free Press*," *Manitoba Daily Free Press*, 7 August 1915, p. 5.

27 V.O. Key, *Politics, Parties, and Pressure Groups*, 5th ed. (New York: Thomas Y. Crowell Company, 1964), 522.

28 Elections Manitoba, "Historical Summaries," 226–231. The reader should note that this includes results pertaining to "deferred" elections in specific ridings deemed to be part of the general election by Elections Manitoba.
29 The Norris government was blamed by both farmers and labour for mismanaging the strike. Peterson, "Ethnic and Class Politics in Manitoba," 82–83.
30 These were Cypress, Manitou, and St. Boniface.
31 These were Assiniboia, Brandon City, Dauphin, Kildonan and St. Andrews (which was one seat), and St. George.
32 These were Beautiful Plains, Emerson, Gimli, Killarney, and Rockwood.
33 The independent candidate was in La Verendrye where MLA Philippe Talbot had left the Liberals and ran as an independent.
34 "Manitoba Politics," *Manitoba Free Press*, 3 July 1922, p. 1.
35 Gerald Friesen, *The Canadian Prairies*, 367–371; Morton, *Manitoba: A History*, 362.
36 Morton, *Manitoba: A History*, 367. See also, Christopher Adams, "Early Manifestations of Globalization: Pre-1930s Farm Policy and Farmer Politics," *Prairie Forum*, Fall 1997.
37 This also included senior managers from the Hudson's Bay Company and Eaton's. See Donnelly, *The Government of Manitoba*, 59; Peterson, "Ethnic and Class Politics in Manitoba," 84. There are many biographical accounts of Ashdown and his importance to the Winnipeg business community. Among these are Artibise, *Winnipeg: An Illustrated History*, 18; Coates and McGuinness, *Manitoba: The Province and The People*, 18 and Bumsted, *Dictionary of Manitoba Biography*, 10.
38 John Kendle, *John Bracken*, 28–29. Kendle's account is based on interviews he conducted with Douglas Campbell, who had attended the 20 July meeting, and archival research in the Dafoe papers at the University of Manitoba (John Kendle, *John Bracken*, 255n3).
39 There was strong support for Crerar to become the new premier, yet on principle he opposed the idea of governments being based on occupational groups such as the United Farmers of Ontario and elsewhere (known as "group government"). J.E. Rea, *T.A. Crerar: A Political Life* (Montreal: McGill-Queen's University Press, 1997), 91–92.
40 Rea, *T.A. Crerar*, 30.
41 Elections Manitoba, "Historical Summaries," 231.
42 The UFM withdrew from electoral politics. This was part of a national trend among farm organizations to disconnect themselves from agrarian parties. The aim was to become more effective in articulating the concerns of farmers to government in a non-partisan fashion. Christopher Adams, *Interest Groups in the Canadian Grain Sector: Twentieth Century Developments at the National Level*, chap. 2.

43 Hugh Thorburn, "Federal Election Results 1878–1984," 344; also, W.L. Morton, *The Progressive Party in Canada* (1950; repr. Toronto: University of Toronto Press, 1971), 264. There were differences in attitude regarding the federal Liberals among different provincial groupings of the federal Progressives, with Manitobans having the strongest affinity to merging. On this point and with regard to events leading up to the 1926 federal election, see Morton, *Progressive Party*, chap. 8.
44 Kendle, *John Bracken*, 64.
45 Quoted in Kendle, *John Bracken*, 95.
46 John Bracken, letter to Robson, 6 March 1929, quoted in Kendle, *John Bracken*, 96.
47 This table excludes special armed forces seats and is based on figures from Elections Manitoba, "Historical Summaries," 238–241 with corrections (see following note). Percentages may not add to 100 due to rounding.
48 One correction is made here from the Elections Manitoba data. Robert Bend is reported as a Liberal-Progressive in 1949; however, he officially ran as an Independent Progressive Conservative (as reported by Lloyd Stinson, *Political Warriors*, 135). Therefore, one seat is moved from the Elections Manitoba Liberal-Progressive tally to the independent pro-coalition number. The popular vote is also recalculated to reflect this correction. Bend strongly supported Douglas Campbell, and then proceeded to serve in his cabinet and function under the Liberal banner (including as leader of the party in 1969), which explains how this initial error was made.
49 Kendle, *John Bracken*, 156.
50 J.W. Pickersgill, address given at St. John's College, Winnipeg, 8 February 1974, cited in Gerrard, *Battling for a Better Manitoba*, 77.
51 Morton, *Progressive Party*, 461.
52 Kendle, *John Bracken*, 190–191.
53 There is confusion regarding the date upon which Garson was sworn to office. For example, Coates and McGuinness, *Manitoba: The Province and The People*, 133, gives the date of 8 January 1943. Wikipedia has 14 January 1943 ("Stuart Garson," http://en.wikipedia.org/wiki/Stuart_Garson, accessed 13 November 2006), and Jon Gerrard, *Battling for a Better Manitoba*, 96, has it as 15 January 1943. Of these three, Gerrard is correct. According to the *Winnipeg Tribune* coverage on 15 January 2006, Bracken formally resigned on January 15, 1943, and Garson was sworn into office on the same day.
54 See Dyck, *Provincial Politics in Canada*, 386–387; Friesen, *The Canadian Prairies*, 420.
55 He took the seat away from the Conservatives with a margin of 400 votes. Elections Manitoba, "Historical Summaries," 230. For a biographical account of Campbell see Coates and McGuinness, *Manitoba: The Province and The People*, 161.

56 Friesen, *The Canadian Prairies*, 420.
57 See Alex Netherton, "Paradigm and Shift: A Sketch of Manitoba Politics," in Keith Brownsey and Michael Howlett, eds., *The Provincial State in Canada: Politics in the Provinces and Territories* (Peterborough: Broadview, 2001), 214.
58 See, for example, Bumsted, *Dictionary of Manitoba Biography*, 44; and Coates and McGuinness, *Manitoba: The Province and The People*, 161. One cannot help but wonder if rural electrification was something that was inevitable, regardless of the party in power. It is somewhat akin to a parent boasting about a child being toilet trained.
59 For a discussion of the evolution of policy relating to hydro development, see Morton, *Progressive Party*, 458–460 and Alex Netherton, *From Rentiership to Continental Modernization: Shifting Paradigms of State Intervention in Hydro in Manitoba, 1922–1927* (PhD diss., Carleton University, 1993).
60 Stinson, *Political Warriors*, 172–173.
61 Roblin, *Speaking for Myself*, 90.
62 Roberts's unsuccessful bid was just one stage in his eclectic political career which included serving as a bilingual MLA for the La Verendrye riding from 1958 to 1962, two unsuccessful attempts to win the federal riding of Provencher in 1962 and 1963, working as an advisor to Lester Pearson, serving as acting leader of the provincial party after Bobby Bend's 1969 defeat, and then, after working in the grain industry with National Grain, becoming the first president of the Canada West Foundation in 1976. After moving into British Columbia politics, he helped found the Reform Party and ran unsuccessfully in the party's first leadership campaign, against Preston Manning. Very little is written on this individual. For an undocumented but very detailed source see "Stan Roberts," http://en.wikipedia.org/wiki/Stan_Roberts, accessed 5 September 2005); A more reliable source for portions of his biography as they pertain to his activities in the Reform Party is Murray Dobbin, *Preston Manning and the Reform Party* (Toronto: James Lorimer, 1991), 76 and 79.
63 Elizabeth Lumley, ed., *Canadian Who's Who: 1995* (Toronto: University of Toronto Press, 1995), 843.
64 Interview with Allison Molgat, 25 October 2007.
65 "Ginger Group Member Blames Leadership," *Winnipeg Free Press*, 24 June 1966, p. 1.
66 For a breakdown of results for each candidate in the Winnipeg area see "Here's How Candidates Fared at the Polls," *Winnipeg Free Press*, 24 June 1966, p. 10.
67 "NDP Really Hurt Liberals, Says Molgat," *Winnipeg Free Press*, 24 June 1966, p.1
68 Contrary to Gerrard's erroneous claim that Molgat "decided not to run for re-election in 1969" (Gerrard, *Battling for a Better Manitoba*, 131), he did run and was re-elected in the riding of Ste. Rose by a margin of 1049 (Elections Manitoba, "Historical Summaries," 230). It was following this election that he

left provincial politics. He was appointed to the Senate in 1970 and served as Speaker of the Senate from 1994 to 2001.
69 Gerrard, *Battling for a Better Manitoba*, 132. For details about Bend's political career see Stinson, *Political Warriors*, 135–136.
70 Tom Peterson, "Manitoba," in John Saywell, ed., *Canadian Annual Review for 1969* (Toronto: University of Toronto Press, 1970), 128.
71 Alderman Peter Moss, the defeated Liberal candidate for St. James-Assiniboia, according to the *Winnipeg Free Press* in its post-election coverage, believed that "a coalition government would be formed against the New Democratic Party and that Manitobans would go to the polls again 'within a year.'" "Message Didn't Get Across—Liberal," *Winnipeg Free Press*, 26 June 1969, p. 9.
72 Elections Manitoba, "Historical Summaries," 252–255. In light of what transpired, it is ironic that Tom Peterson would report that it was only because of the francophone vote that the Liberals' provincial vote did not suffer a complete collapse. Peterson, "Manitoba," 129.
73 Schulz, *A View from the Ledge*, 95.
74 Ibid.
75 As quoted in Peterson, "Ethnic and Class Politics in Manitoba," 112.
76 Lloyd Axworthy, "Preface," in Gerrard, *Battling for a Better Manitoba*, 8.
77 David Smith, *The Regional Decline of a National Party: Liberals on the Prairies* (Toronto: University of Toronto Press, 1981), 69.78 *The Manitoba Liberal*, January 1971. Cited in Peterson, "Ethnic and Class Politics in Manitoba," 113.
79 Quoted in Smith, *The Regional Decline of a National Party*.
80 Elections Manitoba, "Historical Summaries," 257.
81 Schulz, *A View from the Ledge*, 306.
82 Schulz, *A View from the Ledge*, 214.
83 A review of the results from 1973 shows that the Liberals held back their candidates in the following ridings: Gimli, Roblin, Rossmere, Selkirk, The Pas, Transcona, and Wellington. The PCs held back their candidates in Lac du Bonnet, Point Douglas, St. Boniface, St. George, and The Pas (both parties held back in The Pas to allow an independent to serve as the NDP challenger). Compiled from Elections Manitoba, "Historical Summaries," 256–257.
84 Elections Manitoba, "Historical Summaries," 257. Herb Schulz, an NDP strategist and Premier Schreyer's assistant, gives the following fascinating account: "In St. Boniface, a county court recount tied the two candidates at 4,293 votes each. In the Court of Appeal two judges disagreed, one giving Marion a majority of three (4,301 to 4,298) and the other a majority of one (4,301 to 4,300). The counting was over and Desjardins had lost. But a voter had left us a gift. He had been a patient in St. Boniface Hospital on election day and had voted on a hospital ballot. On these, instead of marking an X, the voter writes the name of the candidate he is voting for. Paul 'Laville' had inadvertently written his own name on the ballot, then stroked out 'Laville' and written Marion over it. But

'Laville' was still visible. All those who had counted and recounted the ballots had accepted this one. We did not. We challenged it on the grounds it identified the voter, a No-No in any election. Paul Laville had died on October 18, 1973, and we had to identify his headstone in the cemetery. The election was controverted. In the subsequent by-election, on December 20, 1974, Desjardins won decisively with 3,711 to 3,092." Schulz, *A View from the Ledge*, 217.

85 Figures are based on Elections Manitoba, *Report of the Chief Electoral Officer*, Winnipeg: Government of Manitoba, 2003) 8–14, "Historical Summaries," 254–271.
86 Sharon Carstairs, *Not One of the Boys* (Toronto: Macmillan, 1993), 60.
87 For an example of how one can show a lack of grace when writing a political memoir, see Carstairs's comments regarding Ridgeway's farm background, inability to raise funds, and questionable commitment to the party. Carstairs, *Not One of the Boys*, 61.
88 While working as a policy analyst in the Executive Council on a summer contract in 1984, this author and others on staff were encouraged to attend question period in the visitors' gallery. On each occasion I recall seeing an unaccompanied Carstairs quietly taking notes in the darkened and sparsely occupied gallery. It was a lesson on how a politician's dedication can easily be overlooked or unappreciated.
89 Carstairs, *Not One of the Boys*, 64.
90 Elections Manitoba, "Historical Summaries," 262–267.
91 See Christopher Adams, "The COR and Reform Parties: Locations of Canadian Protest Party Support."
92 For an overview of the 1988 election, see Geoffrey Lambert, "Manitoba," in David Leyton-Brown, ed., *Canadian Annual Review of Politics and Public Affairs, 1988* (Toronto: University of Toronto Press, 1995).
93 Lambert, "Manitoba," 256 and passim.
94 This included admitting that she resorted to tranquillizers to help her sleep when overly stressed. Geoffrey Lambert, "Manitoba," in David Leyton-Brown, ed., *Canadian Annual Review of Politics and Public Affairs, 1990* (Toronto: University of Toronto Press, 1997), 186. As someone who abstains from alcohol, Carstairs does make a valid point that she was the victim of a double standard. "I suppose if I had said I had had a few stiff drinks no one would have looked askance. But somehow or other my use of tranquillizers, coupled with the fact that I was a woman, had a negative impact the likes of which I could not possibly have imagined." Carstairs, *Not One of the Boys*, 165.
95 Carstairs, *Not One of the Boys*, 133.
96 Author interview with Paul Edwards, 20 October 2006.
97 Hasselfield had served as the chairperson for Reg Alcock's 1993 campaign. Accusations were made during the leadership campaign by members of Lamoureux's team that Hasselfield had won untendered consulting contracts with

the federal Liberal government and Axworthy's department (HRDC). "Mud flies in Liberal contest," *Winnipeg Free Press*, 15 October 1996, pp. A1 and A3; "Close vote expected in Liberal race," *Winnipeg Free Press*, 18 October 1996, p. 11. For an overview of the support each candidate received, see Paul Samyn, "Grits crown new leader," *Winnipeg Free Press*, 20 October 1996, pp. A1–A2.

98 Paul Samyn, "Grits crown new leader."
99 Gerrard, *Battling for a Better Manitoba*, 162–164.
100 In addition to holding an MD from McGill, he holds a PhD from the University of Minnesota in pediatrics and pharmacology. See Gary Girard, "The Building Continues: Jon Gerrard," in Gerrard, *Battling for a Better Manitoba*.
101 Carstairs, *Not One of the Boys*, 178.
102 It was logical that Gerrard picked this riding to run in. It has a high concentration of well-educated professionals, including lawyers, doctors, and professors. Indeed, a review of results done previously by the author of the federal elections of 1979, 1980, and 1984 revealed that even during the dark days of anti-Trudeau feelings across the West and battles over bilingualism in Manitoba, River Heights continued to provide pockets of pro-Liberal votes.
103 "And then there were two," *Winnipeg Sun*, 4 June 2003, p. 8.
104 *Winnipeg Free Press*, 4 June 2003, p. 2.
105 V.O. Key would term this a "deviating election" in that it produced results that were unusual but of a short duration. V.O. Key, "A Theory of Critical Elections," *The Journal of Politics* 17 (1955): 3–18. For its application to the 1988 provincial election see Meir Serfaty, "Electoral Behaviour in Manitoba," 178.

Chapter 4

1   For a discussion on how the Saskatchewan NDP has come to resemble closely the Manitoba NDP, especially with regard to urban-based support, see Chris Adams, "Diverging Paths? Why Manitoba Still Likes the NDP, and Saskatchewan Doesn't," *Inroads: The Canadian Journal of Opinion*, Summer/Fall 2008.
2   This does not mean that the CCF/NDP's growth occurred solely in Winnipeg. Brandon, the North, and less-prosperous farm areas were also sources of support and eventually facilitated Schreyer's 1969 victory. Regarding the history of labour politics in Brandon, see Errol Black and Tom Mitchell, eds., *A Square Deal for all and No Railroading: Historical Essays on Labour in Brandon* (St. John's: Canadian Committee on Labour History, 2000).
3   Regarding the ILP in England see Bob Holton, *British Syndicalism: 1900–1914* (London: Pluto Press, 1976), 47–50 and Samuel Beer, *Modern British Politics* (London: Norton, 1982), 113–116.
4   The word "Labour" in the party's title is given the American spelling (i.e., "Labor") by some authors (Nelson Wisemen, Doug Smith, and Ross McCormack) and the Canadian-British spelling (with the "u") by others (W.L. Morton and Walter Young). For consistency purposes, used here is the Canadian-British

spelling which is also used by Elections Manitoba, "Historical Summaries," 202 and passim.

5   Regarding the ILP in Brandon, see W. Leland Clark, *Brandon's Politics and Politicians* (Brandon: Brandon Sun, 1981), chap. 5.

6   The decision was made at the annual provincial CCF convention in 1960 to create the Manitoba NDP in 1961. Wiseman, *Social Democracy in Manitoba*.

7   A. Ross McCormack, *Reformers, Rebels, and Revolutionaries*, 79. For an in-depth study of this early Canadian labourite, Arthur Puttee, see Bryan Dewalt, *Arthur W. Puttee: Labourism and Working-Class Politics in Winnipeg, 1894–1918* (MA thesis, University of Manitoba, 1985).

8   Smith, *Let Us Rise! An Illustrated History of the Manitoba Labour Movement* (Vancouver, New Star Books, 1985), 28; McCormack, *Reformers, Rebels, and Revolutionaries*, 81.

9   Morton, *Manitoba: A History*, 304.

10 McCormack, *Reformers, Rebels, and Revolutionaries*, 90–92; Smith, *Let Us Rise*, 29.

11 Worth noting is that the "LRC" label appears drawn from Britain where it was in use at the same time. See Beer, *Modern British Politics*, 113. Unfortunately a study of materials in which Dixon's connection to the LRC is identified provides more confusion than enlightenment. Doug Smith reports in his history of Manitoba's labour movement (Smith, *Let Us Rise*, 30) that Dixon was an LRC-endorsed candidate, but provides no direct source for this information. Elections Manitoba ("Historical Summaries," 225) identifies Dixon as an independent. McCormack reports that Dixon was not formally associated with the LRC and that only some of the LRC members supported Dixon's campaign. McCormack also claims that the predominant view held both among LRC members and socialists was that Dixon was more closely associated to the Liberal Party in the 1914 campaign (McCormack, *Reformers, Rebels, and Revolutionaries*, 95). What helps clear these muddy waters is the fact that Dixon appeared as one of the "Candidates Supporting the Liberal Policy" in a 1914 Liberal Party campaign poster (N10135, Manitoba Archives).

12 Murray Donnelly in his *Government of Manitoba* claims that in the 1914 election "Labour got three seats" yet provides no sources for his information (Donnelly, *Government of Manitoba*, 47). A review of Elections Manitoba data reveals no evidence that any seats other than the Dixon independent seat were won by candidates representing either a labour party or socialist party. See Elections Manitoba "Historical Summaries," 224–225.

13 Donnelly appears to be in error when stating that seven seats were won by labour in the 1915 election and compounds the error by observing that after this election the "number of [labour] members in the legislature fell off sharply." Donnelly, *Government of Manitoba*. It is possible that Donnelly might have been identifying a number of Liberal MLAs as being labour representatives, due to the coalition of urban reform forces that Norris was able to pull togeth-

er under the Liberal banner (Donnelly, *Government of Manitoba*, 51–52; also Chapter 3 in this book).

14 Richard Allen, "Social Gospel as the Religion of the Agrarian Revolt," in R. Douglas Francis and Howard Palmer, eds., *The Prairie West: Historical Readings* (Edmonton: Pica Pica, 1985), 441–442.

15 Allen Mills, *Fool for Christ: The Political Thought of J. S. Woodsworth* (Toronto: University of Toronto Press, 1991); Kenneth McNaught, *A Prophet in Politics: A Biography of J.S. Woodsworth* (Toronto: University of Toronto Press, 1959), chap. 4 and passim.

16 Allen, *Fools for Christ*, 447.

17 Smith, *Let us Rise*, 40.

18 Manitoba was the first of the provinces to expand the franchise to women. Alberta and Saskatchewan quickly followed in the same year. See Jane Errington, "Pioneers and Suffragists," in Sandra Burt et al., eds., *Changing Patterns: Women in Canada*, 2nd ed. (Toronto: <cClelland and Stewart, 1993), 79.

19 For a more detailed discussion regarding these international influences and Winnipeg's labour politics see McCormack, *Reformers, Rebels, and Revolutionaries*, 16–17 and 156–159, and Gerald Friesen, "Bob Russell's Political Thought: Socialism and Industrial Unionism in Winnipeg, 1914 to 1919," in Gerald Friesen, *River Road: Essays on Manitoba and Prairie History* (Winnipeg: University of Manitoba Press, 1996).

20 McCormack, *Reformers, Rebels, and Revolutionaries*, 169.

21 15,695 out of 47,427 votes were cast for candidates who identified themselves as "Labour." Elections Manitoba, "Historical Summaries," 229.

22 See Errol Black "Labour in Manitoba: A Refuge in Social Democracy," in James Silver and Jeremy Hull, eds., *The Political Economy of Manitoba* (Regina: Canadian Plains Research Center, 1990), 100–102.

23 Wiseman, *Social Democracy in Manitoba*, 11.

24 This alliance had been inspired by the ILP's activities in Saskatchewan, where the Farmers' Political Association had linked up with the ILP to put forward Farmer-Labour candidates. There were informal links between the two provincial ILP organizations as demonstrated by Woodsworth being invited to speak at a Saskatchewan ILP meeting in 1929; two other Winnipeg labourites, John Queen and Abraham Heaps, spoke at the ILP AGM in Regina later that year. See Walter Young, *Anatomy of a Party: The National CCF, 1932–61* (Toronto: University of Toronto Press, 1969), 20–22.

25 Wiseman, *Social Democracy in Manitoba*, 21 and confirmed in Elections Manitoba, "Historical Summaries," 236–237.

26 Susan Mann Trofimenkoff, *Stanley Knowles: The Man from Winnipeg North Centre* (Saskatoon: Western Producer Prairie Books, 1982), 50–51.

27 Stinson, *Political Warriors*, 88.

28 Calculated from figures as presented in Elections Manitoba, "Historical Summaries," 237.
29 J. M. Bumsted, *Dictionary of Manitoba Biography*, 80. Further details about Farmer's life can be found in Stinson, *Political Warriors*, 83–110.
30 Trofimenkoff, *Stanley Knowles*, 55–56.
31 James McAllister, *The Government of Edward Schreyer: Democratic Socialism in Manitoba* (Montreal: McGill-Queen's University Press, 1984), 100. Regarding the internal party debates that swirled within the national CCF organization and the wisdom of having a provincial wing joining the coalition, see Nelson Wiseman, *Social Democracy in Manitoba*, chap. 2. Details regarding this period are also provided in Stinson, *Political Warriors*, 96–98.
32 Trofimenkoff, *Stanley Knowles*, 56.
33 Elections Manitoba, "Historical Summaries," 238–239.
34 Wiseman, *Social Democracy in Manitoba*, 34, 38, and 55.
35 Wiseman, *Social Democracy in Manitoba*, 38.
36 For a summary table of Gallup Polls and federal party standings during this era see Young, *Anatomy of a Party*, 320.
37 "News Comment," *Maclean's*, cited in Young, *Anatomy of a Party*, 109.
38 Cited in Seymour Martin Lipset, *Agrarian Socialism: The Cooperative Commonwealth Federation in Saskatchewan*, updated ed. (New York: Anchor Books, 1968), 152.
39 Quoted in Jack Pickersgill, *The Mackenzie King Record: Volume 1, 1939–1944* (Toronto: 1960), 571.
40 Jack Pickersgill, *The Mackenzie King Record*, 572.
41 Stinson, *Political Warriors*, 34.
42 Figures are derived from Table B.6 in Bickerton, Gagnon, and Smith, *Ties that Bind*, 224.
43 Jane Jenson and Susan Phillips, "Regime Shift: New Citizenship Practices in Canada," *International Journal of Canadian Studies* 14 (1996): 116.
44 Robert Campbell, *Grand Illusions: The Politics of the Keynesian Experience in Canada, 1945–1975* (Peterborough: Broadview Press, 1987), 59.
45 Elections Manitoba, "Historical Summaries," 240–241.
46 Elections Manitoba, "Historical Summaries," 242–243.
47 Wiseman, *Social Democracy in Manitoba*, 65.
48 Elections Manitoba, "Historical Summaries," 244–245.
49 Wiseman, *Social Democracy in Manitoba*, 65.
50 His successor, Lloyd Stinson, along with others, recruited Bryce to run for the CCF in the 1943 Selkirk by-election. Stinson reports that Bryce knew little about CCF policy at the time but had successfully won the federal campaign (and then in 1945) by talking "to farmers, fishermen, small businessmen, teachers and housewives, including people of Icelandic, Ukrainian, Polish, Indian

and Anglo-Saxon origin in all parts of that far-flung riding." Stinson, *Political Warriors*, 24–25. Nelson Wiseman reports that Bryce left federal politics because he believed, erroneously, that his riding would disappear due to redistribution (Wiseman, *Social Democracy in Manitoba*, 69).

51 Stinson, *Political Warriors*, 2–3 and 118.
52 Wiseman, *Social Democracy in Manitoba*, 51 and 74.
53 Wiseman, *Social Democracy in Manitoba*, 57–60.
54 McAllister, *The Government of Edward Schreyer*, 116. McAllister also reports that this ratio was subsequently abolished in 1968 and a "25 per cent population tolerance between ridings" would be permitted and "nearly half of the seats in the legislature would be held by MLAs from metropolitan Winnipeg."
55 Wiseman, *Social Democracy in Manitoba*, 69.
56 Stinson, *Political Warriors*, 179.
57 McAllister, *The Government of Edward Schreyer*, 103.
58 McAllister, *The Government of Edward Schreyer*, 103. For a sense of the optimistic mood regarding the "New Party" within the CCF and the CLC at this time see Stinson, *Political Warriors*, 53–54. For a detailed biographical description of Stanley Knowles, see Stinson, *Political Warriors*, chap. 4 and Trofimenkoff, *Stanley Knowles*.
59 McAllister, *The Government of Edward Schreyer*, 103 and Wiseman, *Social Democracy in Manitoba*, 104 and 107.
60 Winnipeg area figures for 1966 are from John Wilson, "The Decline of the Liberal Party in Manitoba Politics," *Journal of Canadian Studies*, 10 Feb. 1975, 31.
61 Calculated from figures in Elections Manitoba, "Historical Summaries," 254–255.
62 "NDP Registers Stunning Upset," *Winnipeg Free Press*, 26 June 1969 (final edition), p.1.
63 Peterson, "Manitoba," 128.
64 Sidney Green, *The Rise and Fall of a Political Animal: A Memoir* (Winnipeg: Great Plains Publications, 2003), 66.
65 Ibid.
66 This biographical overview is drawn chiefly from McAllister, *The Government of Edward Schreyer*, 15–19.
67 Advertisement, *Winnipeg Free Press*, 21 June 1969, p. 9.
68 Advertisement, *Winnipeg Free Press*, 21 June 1969, p. 5.
69 McAllister, *The Government of Edward Schreyer*, 15.
70 Peterson, "Manitoba," 132.
71 Peterson, "Ethnic and Class Politics in Manitoba," 110.
72 Wilson, "The Decline of the Liberal Party in Manitoba Politics," 39.
73 St. George, eliminated in 1981, was located in the Interlake region of Manitoba.

74 Elections Manitoba, "Historical Summaries," 252–255.
75 "Carroll Says Indian Vote Defeated Him," *Winnipeg Free Press*, 26 June 1969, p. 10.
76 For a discussion of the development of hydroelectricity and its implications in Manitoba see John Welsted, "Manitoba's Water Resources," in John Welsted et al., eds., *The Geography of Manitoba: Its Land and its People* (Winnipeg: University of Manitoba Press, 1996).
77 Ed Schreyer interview with author, 7 September 2006.
78 Ed Schreyer interview with author, 7 September 2006.
79 V.O. Key, "A Theory of Critical Elections," *The Journal of Politics* 17 (1955): 3–18, repr. in Peter Woll, ed., *American Government: Readings and Cases*, 8th ed. (Boston: Little, Brown, 1984), 207.
80 Tom Peterson, "Manitoba Voting Patterns," *Winnipeg Free Press*, 14 July 1973.
81 Peterson, "Ethnic and Class Politics in Manitoba," 110.
82 For example, see references to Harry Mardon, the associate editor of the *Winnipeg Tribune*, who consistently attacked the new government. Schulz, *A View from the Ledge*, 45 and passim.
83 For a detailed comparison of policies during the Roblin and Schreyer administrations see Shaun McCaffrey, *A Study of Policy Continuity*.
84 See Alvin Finkel, *The Social Credit Phenomenon in Alberta* (Toronto: University of Toronto Press, 1989), 42.
85 Regarding events and interest group politics surrounding the legislation see Schulz, *A View from the Ledge*, 50–51 and Joy Cooper, "The Politics of Automobile Insurance: A Case Study" (MA thesis, University of Manitoba, 1978).
86 Wiseman, *Social Democracy in Manitoba*, 127.
87 Ed Schreyer interview with author, 7 September 2006. Schreyer himself identified this as the main cause of his defeat, whereas the second category of reasoning is given by McAllister, *The Government of Edward Schreyer*.
88 Gonick, "The Manitoba Economy Since World War II," 33–35.
89 This was evident in a joint Global News/*Winnipeg Free Press* constituency poll conducted by Probe Research and released in December 2005.
90 See Schulz, *A View from the Ledge*, chap. 6.
91 Paul Adams, "Manitoba," in R.B. Byers, ed., *Canadian Annual Review of Politics and Public Affairs, 1983* (Toronto: University of Toronto Press, 1985), 263; Paul Adams, "Manitoba," in R.B. Byers, ed., *Canadian Annual Review of Politics and Public Affairs, 1984* (Toronto: University of Toronto Press, 1987), 257.
92 Frances Russell, "Tories barely conceal their contempt for the Charter," *Winnipeg Free Press*, 25 April 2007, p. A13.
93 Adams, "Manitoba," in *Canadian Annual Review of Politics and Public Affairs, 1983*, 264 and 268–269.

94 However, partly in fear of the bigotry that had been unleashed over the issue of French-language rights, support for the SFM and the government's compromise did arise among leaders of organizations representing various ethnic groups. See Hébert, *Manitoba's French-Language Crisis*, 102–103.
95 Adams, "Manitoba," in *Canadian Annual Review of Politics and Public Affairs, 1983*, 264 and 269.
96 Adams, "Manitoba," in *Canadian Annual Review of Politics and Public Affairs, 1983*, 264 and 268.
97 Geoffrey Lambert, "Manitoba," in *Canadian Annual Review of Politics and Public Affairs, 1988*, 253.
98 Geoffrey Lambert, "Manitoba," in *Canadian Annual Review of Politics and Public Affairs, 1988*, 254.
99 Geoffrey Lambert, "Manitoba," in D. Leyton-Brown, ed., *Canadian Annual Review of Politics and Public Affairs, 1990* (Toronto: University of Toronto Press, 1997), 189.
100 The interviews were conducted by Probe Research between 9 September and 15 September 1999 among 1010 Manitobans. The question reads as follows: "Which party's candidate are you most likely to support in this provincial election?"
101 Anthony Giddens, *The Third Way: A Renewal of Social Democracy* (London: Polity Press, 1998), 17–18. See also Tony Blair, *The Third Way: New Politics for the New Century* (London: Fabian Society, 1998). I would like to thank Catherine Gates, a graduate student in the Master's in Public Administration program at the University of Winnipeg for carefully articulating this connection. Catherine Gates, "The Influence of *Third Way* Thinking on Manitoba's Social Policy Agenda," unpublished research paper, 2005.
102 The author would like to thank Paul Thomas for drawing attention to this distinction between Doer and Blair's use of terminologies when discussing their government policies. Regarding concerns raised about Third Way politics and its tie to liberal ideologies, Adam Przeworski comments wryly: "What is it that is being renewed by seeking inspiration in Thatcher and Reagan?" Adam Przeworksi, "How Many Ways Can Be Third?" in Andrew Glyn, ed., *Social Democracy in Neoliberal Times: The Left and Economic Policy Since 1980* (Oxford: Oxford University Press, 2001), 320.
103 Manitoba, Legislative Assembly, *Debates and Proceedings*, "Speech from the Throne," 27 October 2005.
104 The age ranges are eighteen to thirty-four, thirty-five to fifty-four, and those who are fifty-five or over. The results are from Probe Research/*Winnipeg Free Press*, Press Release: 2007 Manitoba Election Survey," 17 May 2007, p. 4.

Conclusion

1. The term "political culture" can be understood as the shared set of values and beliefs held by citizens as they pertain to political values and the practice of politics. Or, in the words of Robert and Doreen Jackson, "The broad patterns of values, beliefs, and attitudes in a society towards political objects are often referred to as political culture." Robert Jackson and Doreen Jackson, *Canadian Government in Transition*, 4th ed. (Toronto: Pearson, 2006), 21.

2. The Mennonites were another group that was part of this early wave of settlement. However, they generally remained outside provincial party politics. Years later they would contribute to the traditionalism in the PC's rural wing. For a discussion of early settlement patterns see John Friesen, "Expansion of Settlement in Manitoba, 1870–1900," in Donald Swainson, ed., *Historical Essays on the Prairie Provinces* (Toronto: McClelland and Stewart, 1970).

3. This is discussed in Chapter 4. See also, Alan Artibise, *Winnipeg: A Social History of Urban Growth, 1874 – 1914* (Montreal: McGill-Queen's University Press, 1975), 37–38.

4. Or, in the words of the philosopher Rousseau regarding property and civil society: "Those among them who were best qualified to foresee abuses were precisely those who expected to benefit by them." Jean-Jacques Rousseau, *The Social Contract and Discourse on the Origin of Inequality* (New York: Pocket Books, 1967), 228.

5. Roger Gibbins, *Prairie Politics and Society: Regionalism in Decline* (Toronto: Butterworths, 1980), 78. According to Canadian and US census data, this was also part of a broad trend occurring across Canada and the United States. In 1931 close to one-third of Canadians (31 percent) lived on farms and by 1951 this declined to one in four (21 percent). In the United States the farm population figures declined from 25 percent in 1930 to 15 percent in 1950. Cited in Christopher Adams, *Interest Groups in the Canadian Grain Sector*, 137 and 174n2.

6. Statistics Canada data for 2003 as cited in the *Canadian Global Almanac: 2005* (Toronto: Wiley, 2005), 241.

7. Ronald Inglehart, *The Silent Revolution: Changing Values and Political Styles Among Western Publics* (Princeton: Princeton University Press, 1977). For a discussion on how Inglehart's "post-materialist" thesis can be applied to understanding environmentalism in Canada see Christopher Adams, "Canadian Public Opinion and the Environment," *Inroads: The Canadian Journal of Opinion*, Summer/Fall 2006.

8. Murray McNeill, "Manitoba economy enjoys strongest year since 2000," *Winnipeg Free Press*, 27 April 2006, p. B1.

9. See Donald Creighton, "John A. Macdonald, Confederation, and the Canadian West," in Donald Swainson, ed., *Historical Essays on the Prairie Provinces* (Toronto: McClelland and Stewart, 1970). Others have attacked strongly this

perspective as being too limited in its perspective and dismissive of the nation building character of the act. See Russell, *The Canadian Crucible*, 218–220.

10 For further discussion, see Richard Simeon, "Federalism and Intergovernmental Relations," in Christopher Dunn, ed., *The Handbook of Canadian Public Administration* (Toronto: Oxford University Press, 2002); and J.C. Strick, *Canadian Public Finance*, 4th ed. (Toronto: Holt Rinehart and Winston, 1992), chap. 7.

11 Roberto Michels, *Political Parties: A Sociological Study of the Oligarchical Tendencies of Modern Democracy*, trans. Edan and Cedar Paul (New York: Collier, 1962), 364.

12 Michels, *Political Parties*, 364.

13 The successful example of Bracken and the UFM/Progressive's ability to hold power during the first decade in office strongly contrasts with the national Progressives who were unable to harness strong voter support in 1922. The federal Progressives rejected the idea of party discipline as it applies to democratically elected Members of Parliament (and hence the power of leadership). Morton, *The Progressive Party in Canada*, 290 and passim. Another contrasting example is the case of the United Farmers of Alberta's attempt to implement "group government" rather than government organized around political parties, which, according to Macpherson, led to its inability to govern effectively. The UFA was replaced in the 1930s by a much more leader-oriented party, the Social Credit Party. C.B. Macpherson, *Democracy in Alberta: Social Credit and the Party System*.

14 Molgat's replacement by Bend was a continuance of the party's rural orientation but also an indication that party members were looking to distance themselves from the federal Liberals and their position on official bilingualism. It was a shift back towards the party's WASPish roots. The author is grateful to Ed Schreyer for highlighting this fact. Ed Schreyer, interview with the author, 7 September 2006.

15 Leslie A. Pal, "The Cauldron of Leadership: Prime Ministers and Their Parties," in R.K. Carty, ed., *Canadian Political Party Systems: A Reader* (Toronto: Broadview Press, 1992), 413.

16 The 1974 to 2004 data is from the Canadian National Election Studies, Insight Canada survey data, and POLLARA. The 2004 results are from POLLARA. Cited by André Turcotte, "Canadians Speak Out," in Jon Pammett and Christopher Dunn, eds., *The Canadian General Election of 2004* (Toronto: Dundurn, 2004), 322.

17 Jeffrey Simpson, *Discipline of Power: The Conservative Interlude and the Liberal Restoration* (Toronto: Personal Library, 1980), xiii.

18 Elections Manitoba, "Historical Summaries," 256–257.

19 Much more research needs to be done on this topic and this author plans to pursue this in future studies. James McAllister and Nelson Wiseman do provide excellent insights into the inner workings of the NDP's organization; how-

ever, because both studies were done in the 1970s, they are now largely out of date. Jon Gerrard's book regarding the Liberal Party's history is generally leader-focussed and provides few insights into the organizational structure of the party.

20 Jackson and Jackson, *Canadian Government in Transition*, 254.
21 "Our Defense. The Conservative Party," *Winnipeg Daily Times*, 16 December 1879, p. 1.
22 Christopher Adams, "Early Manifestations of Globalization: Pre-1930s Farm Policy and Farmer Politics," *Prairie Forum*, Fall 1997, 273.
23 RCA through an advertisement in the *Winnipeg Free Press* announced the opening of the local CBC studio (CBWT) on 2 June 1954. *Winnipeg Free Press*, 2 June 1954, p. 56. I would like to thank my colleague Kevin McDougald for bringing this fact to my attention.
24 Darrell Bricker and John Wright, *What Canadians Think* (Toronto: Doubleday, 2005), 100.
25 John Meisel, "The Decline of Party in Canada," in Hugh Thorburn, ed., *Party Politics in Canada*, 5th ed. (Scarborough: Prentice-Hall, 1985), 105.
26 Geoff Kirbyson, "Free Press Well Read," *Winnipeg Free Press*, 24 March 2007.
27 This figure is based on non-released results from a February 2005 province-wide survey of 1000 Manitobans by Probe Research. The question was worded as follows: "Have you used the Internet for any reason within the past thirty days?" This is an increase from the 50 percent figure that resulted from the same question in late 2000 (*Winnipeg Free Press*/Probe Research, "Online Manitoba," press release, 22 December 2000). While usage is widespread across the province, a study of Aboriginal people in Manitoba conducted by Probe Research reveals that it remains uneven across different segments of the population. This is indicated by the fact that only 41 percent of those residing on First Nations communities are users of the Internet. Probe Research, *Indigenous Voices: Aboriginal People in Manitoba* [syndicated study], November 2005.
28 For a discussion on how the Internet was used by party supporters as well as independent commentators during the 2004 Canadian federal election, see Tamara Small, "parties@canada: The Internet and the 2004 Cyber-Campaign," in Jon Pammett and Christopher Dunn, eds., *The Canadian General Election of 2004* (Toronto: Dundurn, 2004). One set of online political commentators in Manitoba is "The Black Rod," which is operated by individuals under a secret identity who refer to themselves as "citizen journalists." This site regularly provides inside stories and commentary on matters less candidly discussed in the mainstream media. See http:// www.blackrod.blogspot.com. Traditional media outlets are now countering this by offering their own blogs such as that put forward by the *Winnipeg Free Press* during the 2006 Winnipeg election. "Free Press launches civic election citizen blog," *Winnipeg Free Press*, 16 September 2006, p. B1. This was also provided during the 2007 provincial election (http://www.winnipegfreepress.com).

29 One typical approach has been to extract samples from telephone listings and then assign a different final digit to the number pulled. Because telephone exchange numbers (that is, the first three digits such as 942 or 222) were based on locality, a campaign office knew that the newly created telephone number (that is, the one with the final digit altered) still pertained to the same area. Cell phone numbers are not assigned on this basis. Furthermore, residents can now move to different neighbourhoods in Winnipeg and take their old phone numbers with them, thus making the exchange identifier less reliable as an indicator of the person's location.

30 On election day, each party will work to identify—through their volunteers at the voting stations (i.e., scrutineers)—those who have voted and those who have not voted. Updates are collected and examined at campaign headquarters and then cross referenced with party membership lists, donor names, and voter-preference information previously gathered during the campaign. This process serves to identify those supporters who have not yet voted. Volunteers then make telephone calls to the candidate's supporters who have not voted. In a close election such measures can win or lose an election for the candidate. Conservative candidate Joy Smith won a very close election against Liberal candidate Terry Duguid in the Winnipeg riding of East Kildonan during the 2004 federal election by effectively getting PC supporters out to the advanced polls and (for those not having voted) to the election-day polls.

31 In his comparative study of electoral system, Douglas Rae writes, "Under the test of proportionality, plurality systems come off very badly; they produce greater disproportions than majority or P.R. systems under almost any circumstances. Indeed, it is generally believed that single-member plurality elections produce disproportions of cubic proportions." Douglas Rae, *The Political Consequences of Electoral Laws* (New Haven: Yale University Press, 1971), 27. For a discussion on how the SMP system reinforces regionalism in Canadian party politics see Alan Cairns, "The Electoral System and the Party System in Canada, 1921–1965," *Canadian Journal of Political Science* 1 (1968). For a more recent discussion see Donley Studlar, "Consequences of the Unreformed Canadian Electoral System," *American Review of Canadian Studies* 33 (2003).

32 For a discussion on how the SMP system and regional party systems might be contributing to declining turnouts at the national level, see Jon Pammett, "Behind the Turnout Decline," in Jon Pammett and Christopher Dunn, eds., *The Canadian General Election of 2004* (Toronto: Dundurn, 2004).

33 It is recognized that voters might have voted in a different manner if they knew that casting their vote under a different set of rules would produce different outcomes. Therefore, these hypothetical PR results are speculative only. Many articles and books have been written on this subject, see for example, Donley Studlar, "Consequences of the Unreformed Canadian Electoral System."

34 The Greens won 0.95 percent of the vote in 2003. This figure has been rounded up for this discussion to 1 percent.

Appendix A

1. For each year, results from Probe Research quarterly polls are added up and then divided to provide a mean score for the year. Figures for 1999 are based on two sources: An October 1999 poll and the September election results. Results for 2007 are derived from the averages of the March and May 2007 polls.
2. The question was asked in an open-ended fashion: "I would like you to tell me what you consider to be the most important issue or concern facing your community today." The open-ended responses were captured by using a "soft-coding" procedure by which interviewers would see (but not read to the respondent) and tick off the answer from a list of approximately twenty possible responses. These categories were subsequently collapsed into a fewer number of categories during the data-analysis stage. For example, complaints about sales taxes and income taxes would be combined into one category called "spending and taxes" while youth gangs and crime would be combined into a concern about crime. Because the question wording pertains to "issues and concerns" and does not include any specific reference to the government, it is possible that issues such as government spending and taxes are under-reported in the data.
3. Due to small sample sizes in the North (N=74 PC supporters), this region is excluded here.
4. Based on standard chi square calculations, these differences are statistically significant at the 95 percent confidence level. For an explanation of chi square and how this is calculated see Earl Babbie, *The Practice of Social Research*, 10th ed. (Belmont: Thomson Wadsworth, 2004), 464–467 and A20–A21.
5. The basic variable of household income sometimes masks other variables that can affect a person's financial well-being, such as location of residence and the number of people residing in the household (i.e., a large number of people in a home signifies fewer resources per person). For a discussion on this matter see National Council of Welfare, *Poverty Profile 1995* (Ottawa: Supply and Services Canada, 1997), 5–8.
6. For a discussion on conditional variables in associational analysis see David Nachmias and Chava Nachmias, *Research Methods in the Social Sciences*, 3rd ed. (New York: St. Martin's Press, 1987), 450–452.
7. Based on a chi square at $p<0.05$.
8. The data are compiled from Probe Research press releases from 1999 to 2007. Data for 1999 contains the 1999 election results as broken out by the *Winnipeg Free Press*, 22 September 1999, and one October 1999 Probe Research poll. Annual results are calculated by averaging the results across all quarterly polls done during that year. Results from the June 2003 election (as reported for provincial regions in the *Winnipeg Free Press*, 4 June 2003) and May 2007 election (*Winnipeg Free Press*, 23 May 2007) and are incorporated in the calculations and treated in the same way as a quarterly poll. For additional analysis regard-

ing the Liberal Party in 2006 and its urban support see Chris Adams, "The Liberal Challenge," *Winnipeg Free Press*, 8 December 2006, p. A15.

9. Again, this is based on adding the results for the 2000 to 2007 period in which the surveys were done, and then comparing the differences in Liberal Party support among these three groups. The difference between the under-$30,000 and the $30,000-or-over categories is statistically significant based on a chi square <0.05. Differences between the middle-income category ($30,000 to $59,999) and the highest category ($60,000 and over) are not statistically significant.

10. For the total results for the years in which data were collected, the differences between these population groups are statistically significant at the 95 percent confidence level.

11. Data from 2007 are drawn from two Probe Research surveys done prior to the May 2007 election.

12. Differences between the two education categories and prevalence of NDP support is statistically significant at the $p<0.05$ level for province-wide data and within each of the regions examined.

13. The northern region was extracted from the sample by using respondent postal code categories (the first three digits) and choosing the regions that roughly overlap the five ridings of Rupertsland, Thompson, The Pas, Swan River, and Flin Flon. Other non-Winnipeg ridings are pooled into the South Manitoba category.

14. Further study might reveal that stronger differences exist between party *activists* of the different parties, but this is the subject for future research. For discussions regarding differences between citizens according to their level of political involvement, see William Mishler, *Political Participation in Canada: Prospects for Democratic Citizenship* (Toronto: Macmillan, 1979); Sandra Burt, "The Concept of Political Participation," in Joanna Everitt and Brenda O'Neill, eds., *Citizen Politics: Research and Theory in Canadian Political Behaviour* (Don Mills: Oxford University Press, 2002).

15. Joan Grace, "Has the Manitoba NDP been 'Good' for Women?" (paper presented to the Annual General Meeting of the Canadian Political Science Association, Halifax, 2003), 2–3. See also Joan Grace, "Challenges and Opportunities in Manitoba: The Social Democratic 'Promise' and Women's Equality," in William Carroll and R.S. Ratner, eds., *Challenges and Perils: Social Democracy in Neoliberal Times* (Halifax: Fernwood Publishing, 2005). Grace argues that the governing NDP's track record has focussed on child-development programs and has spent less attention on the needs of Manitoba women.

16. The gender difference among NDP supporters is statistically significant at $p<0.05$ level.

17. Brenda O'Neill, "Sugar and Spice? Political Culture and the Political Behaviour of Canadian Women," in Joanna Everitt and Brenda O'Neill, eds., *Citizen Poli-*

tics: *Research and Theory in Canadian Political Behaviour* (Don Mills: Oxford University Press, 2002), 47.
18. The survey was done with 881 completed interviews in April 1984. Institute for Social and Economic Research, *Research Bulletin: Political Preferences of Manitobans* 1, 5 (30 April 1984): 3. Percentages are recalculated to exclude undecided respondents.
19. The results are statistically significant for the overall period from 2000 to 2006 at p<0.05.
20. Buchart ascribes the "apple cheek" reference to Lindor Reynolds of the *Winnipeg Free Press*. Markus Buchart, interview with author, 3 February 2006.
21. Elections Manitoba, "Historical Summaries," 270–271 and Elections Manitoba, *Statement of Votes for the 38th Provincial General Election* (Winnipeg: Government of Manitoba, 2003), 6–7.
22. Mary Agnes Welch, "Looks like party time," *Winnipeg Free Press*, 18 September 2006, p. B1.
23. Based on results reported in "How We Voted," *Winnipeg Free Press*, 23 May 2007, p. B6.
24. ChristopherAdams, "Canadian Public Opinion and the Environment."

Bibliography

Interviews

Hon. Duff Roblin, Premier of Manitoba, 1958 to 1967. Conducted via telephone, 18 September 2006.

Rt. Hon. Ed Schreyer, Premier of Manitoba, 1969 to 1977. Conducted in person, 7 September 2006.

Markus Buchart, Leader of the Manitoba Green Party, 1998 to 2005. Conducted in person, 12 February 2006.

Andrew Enns, PC Party organizer. Conducted via telephone, 10 September 2006.

Paul Edwards, Leader of the Liberal Party of Manitoba, 1993 to 1996. Conducted in person, 20 October 2006.

Harvey Bostrom, Minister of Cooperative Development and Minister of Renewable Resources and Transportation Services, 1973 to 1977, and appointed to Deputy Minister of Aboriginal and Northern Affairs in 2001. Conducted in person, 16 November 2006.

Stuart Murray, Leader of the PC Party, 2000 to 2006. Conducted in person, 6 July 2007.

Trudy Turner, PC candidate for Riel, 2007 Provincial Election. Conducted in person, 26 October 2007.

Shawn McAffrey, PC candidate for Fort Garry, 2007 Provincial Election. Conducted in person, 23 April 2007.

Hon. Gary Filmon, Premier of Manitoba, 1988 to 1999. Conducted in person, 30 November 2007.

Newspapers

The Winnipeg Daily Times, 1879–1880.

The Winnipeg Free Press (also, *The Manitoba Daily Free Press* and *The Manitoba Free Press*), 1878–2007.

The Winnipeg Tribune, 1942–1980.

SOURCES

Adams, Christopher. "Canadian Public Opinion and the Environment." *Inroads: The Canadian Journal of Opinion,* Summer/Fall 2006.

_____. "Early Manifestations of Globalization: Pre-1930s Farm Policy and Farmer Politics." *Prairie Forum: The Journal of the Canadian Plains Research Center,* Fall 1997.

_____. "The COR and Reform Parties: Locations of Canadian Protest Party Support." Paper presented to the Canadian Political Science Association, Kingston, Ontario, 1991.

_____. "Elections in Manitoba." In Ingeborg Boyens, ed., *The Encyclopedia of Manitoba.* Winnipeg: Great Plains Publications, 2007.

_____. "The Manitoba Liberal Party." In Ingeborg Boyens, ed., *The Encyclopedia of Manitoba.* Winnipeg: Great Plains Publications, 2007.

_____. "The Reform Party and the Roots of Western Protest." *Parliamentary Government,* Fall 1989.

_____. "Interest Groups in the Canadian Grain Sector: Twentieth Century Developments at the National Level." PhD dissertation, Carleton University, 1995.

_____. "Diverging Paths? Why Manitoba Still Likes the NDP and Saskatchewan Doesn't." *Inroads: The Canadian Journal of Opinion* (Summer/Fall 2008)

_____. "The Provincial Political Scene." *Manitoba Reid Report,* Winter 1998.

Adams, Paul. "Manitoba." In R.B. Byers, ed., *Canadian Annual Review of Politics and Public Affairs, 1983.* Toronto: University of Toronto Press, 1985.

_____. "Manitoba." In R.B. Byers, ed., *Canadian Annual Review of Politics and Public Affairs, 1984.* Toronto: University of Toronto Press, 1987.

Allen, Richard. "Social Gospel as the Religion of the Agrarian Revolt." In R. Douglas Francis and Howard Palmer, eds., *The Prairie West: Historical Readings.* Edmonton: Pica Pica, 1985.

Angus Reid Group. *Manitoba Reid Report* [syndicated report]. Winnipeg: Angus Reid Group, 1998.

Anstett, Andy and Paul G. Thomas. "Manitoba: The Role of the Legislature in a Polarized Political System." In Gary Levy and Graham White, eds.,

Provincial and Territorial Legislatures in Canada. Toronto: University of Toronto Press, 1989.

Artibise, Alan. *Winnipeg: A Social History of Urban Growth, 1874–1914.* Montreal: McGill-Queen's University Press, 1975.

_____. *Winnipeg: An Illustrated History.* Toronto: James Lorimer, 1977.

Avakumovic, Ivan. *Socialism in Canada: A Study of the CCF-NDP in Federal and Provincial Politics.* Toronto: McClelland and Stewart, 1978.

_____. *The Communist Party in Canada: A History.* Toronto: McClelland and Stewart, 1975.

Babbie, Earl. *"The Practice of Social Research"* 10th ed. Belmont: Thomson Wadsworth, 2004.

Badgely, Kerry. *Ringing in the Common Love of the Good: The United Farmers of Ontario, 1914–1926.* Montreal: McGill-Queen's University Press, 2003.

Beer, Samuel. *Modern British Politics.* London: Norton, 1982.

Betcherman, Lita-Rose. *The Little Band: The Clashes Between the Communists and the Canadian Establishment, 1928–1932.* Ottawa: Deneau Publishers, 1982.

_____. *The Swastika and the Maple Leaf: Fascist Movements in Canada in the Thirties.* Toronto: Fitzhenry and Whiteside, 1975.

Bickerton, James, Alain Gagnon, and Patrick Smith. *Ties that Bind: Parties and Voters in Canada.* Don Mills: Oxford University Press, 1999.

Black, Errol. "Labour in Manitoba: A Refuge in Social Democracy." In James Silver and Jeremy Hull, eds., *The Political Economy of Manitoba.* Regina: Canadian Plains Research Center, 1990.

Black, Errol, and Tom Mitchell, eds. *A Square Deal for all and No Railroading: Historical Essays on Labour in Brandon.* St. John's: Canadian Committee on Labour History, 2000.

Blair, Tony. *The Third Way: New Politics for the New Century.* London: Fabian Society, 1998.

Blais, Andres, et al. "Do Party Supporters Differ?" In Joanna Everitt and Brenda O'Neill, eds., *Citizen Politics: Research and Theory in Canadian Political Behaviour.* Don Mills: Oxford University Press, 2002.

Blanchard, Jim. *Winnipeg 1912.* Winnipeg: University of Manitoba Press, 2005.

Boyens, Ingeborg. "A Decade of Discontent." In Gregg Shilliday, ed., *Manitoba 125: Volume 3, Decades of Diversity*. Winnipeg: Great Plains Publications, 1995.

Bricker, Darrell, and John Wright. *What Canadians Think*. Toronto: Doubleday, 2005.

Brodie, Janine, and Jane Jenson. *Crisis, Challenge and Change: Party in Class in Canada*. Toronto: Methuen, 1980.

_____. *Crisis, Challenge and Change: Party in Class in Canada Revisited*. Ottawa: Carleton University Press, 1998.

Bumsted, J.M. *Dictionary of Manitoba Biography*. Winnipeg: University of Manitoba Press, 1999.

_____. *The History of Canadian Peoples*. 2nd ed. Don Mills: Oxford University Press, 2003.

_____. *The Red River Rebellion*. Winnipeg: Watson and Dwyer, 1996.

_____. "The Socialist Experiment" In Gregg Shilliday, ed., *Manitoba 125: Volume 3, Decades of Diversity*. Winnipeg: Great Plains Publications, 1995.

Burt, Sandra. "The Concept of Political Participation." In Joanna Everitt and Brenda O'Neill, eds., *Citizen Politics: Research and Theory in Canadian Political Behaviour*. Don Mills: Oxford University Press, 2002.

Cairns, Alan. "The Electoral System and the Party System in Canada, 1921–1965." *Canadian Journal of Political Science* 1 (1968).

Campbell, Robert. *Grand Illusions: The Politics of the Keynesian Experience in Canada, 1945–1975*. Peterborough: Broadview Press, 1987.

Carstairs, Sharon. *Not One of the Boys*. Toronto: Macmillan, 1993.

Carty, R.K., ed. *Canadian Political Party Systems: A Reader*. Peterborough: Broadview Press, 1992.

Chace, James. *1912: Wilson, Roosevelt, Taft and Debs—The Election that Changed the Country*. New York: Simon and Schuster, 2004.

Chambers, William Nisbet. "Party Development and Party Action: The American Origins." *History and Theory* 3, 1 (1963): 90–120.

Clark, W. Leland. *Brandon's Politics and Politicians*. Brandon, MB: Brandon Sun, 1981.

Coates, Ken, and Fred McGuinness. *Manitoba: The Province and The People*. Edmonton: Hurtig Publishers, 1987.

Cooper, Joy. "The Politics of Automobile Insurance: A Case Study." MA thesis, University of Manitoba, 1978.

Corker, Tom. "Winnipeg: Heartbeat of the Province." In John Welsted et al., eds., *The Geography of Manitoba: Its Land and Its People*. Winnipeg: University of Manitoba Press, 1996.

Corrigan, Samuel, and Robert Annis. "Aboriginal Settlement in Manitoba." In John Welsted et al., eds., *The Geography of Manitoba: Its Land and Its People*. Winnipeg: University of Manitoba Press, 1996.

Creighton, Donald. *Canada's First Century: 1867–1967*. Toronto: Macmillan, 1970.

———. *John A. Macdonald: The Old Chieftain*. Toronto: University of Toronto Press, 1998.

———. "John A. Macdonald, Confederation, and the Canadian West." In Donald Swainson, ed., *Historical Essays on the Prairie Provinces*. Toronto: McClelland and Stewart, 1970.

Dafoe, John W. *Clifford Sifton in Relation to His Times*. Toronto: Macmillan, 1931.

Dalton, Russell. *Citizen Politics: Public Opinion and Political Parties in Advanced Industrial Democracies*. 2nd ed. New Jersey: Chatham House, 1996.

Dalton, Russell, et al., eds. *Electoral Change in Advanced Industrial Democracies: Realignment or Dealignment* Princeton: Princeton University Press, 1984.

Dawson, Richard, and James Robinson. "Inter-Party Competition, Economic Variables, and Welfare Policies in the American States." *Journal of Politics* 25 (1963).

Dawson, Robert MacGregor. *The Government of Canada*. Toronto: University of Toronto Press, 1958.

Dewalt, Bryan. "Arthur W. Puttee: Labourism and Working-Class Politics in Winnipeg, 1894–1918." MA thesis, University of Manitoba, 1985.

———. *Challenge and Achievement: The Manitoba New Democratic Party*. Winnipeg: Manitoba New Democratic Party, 1987.

Diefenbaker, John. *One Canada: Volume Two, The Years of Achievement*. Toronto: Macmillan, 1976.

Dobbin, Murray. *Preston Manning and the Reform Party*. Toronto: James Lorimer, 1991.

Doern, Russell. *Wednesdays are Cabinet Days: A Personal Account of the Schreyer Administration*. Winnipeg: Queenston House, 1981.

Donnelly, Murray S. *The Government of Manitoba*. Toronto: University of Toronto Press, 1963.

———. "Manitoba." In John Saywell, ed., *Canadian Annual Review of Politics and Public Affairs, 1977*. Toronto: University of Toronto Press, 1979.

Duverger, Maurice. *Political Parties: Their Organization and Activity in the Modern State*. London: Methuen, 1964.

Dyck, Rand. *Provincial Politics in Canada*. 2nd ed. Scarborough: Prentice-Hall, 1991.

Elections Manitoba. *Statement of Votes for the 38th Provincial General Election*. Winnipeg: Government of Manitoba, 2003.

Errington, Jane. "Pioneers and Suffragists." In Sandra Burt et al., eds., *Changing Patterns: Women in Canada*. 2nd ed. Toronto: University of Toronto Press, 1993.

Finkel, Alvin. *The Social Credit Phenomenon in Alberta*. Toronto: University of Toronto Press, 1989.

Fridfinnson, Lloyd. "Preparing for a New Century." In Gregg Shilliday, ed., *Manitoba 125: Volume 3, Decades of Diversity*. Winnipeg: Great Plains Publications, 1995.

Friesen, Gerald. *The Canadian Prairies: A History*. Toronto: University of Toronto Press, 1984.

———. "John Norquay." *The Dictionary of Canadian Biography*. http://www.biographi.ca (accessed 29 July 2006).

———. *River Road: Essays on Manitoba and Prairie History*. Winnipeg: University of Manitoba Press, 1996.

Friesen, John. "Expansion of Settlement in Manitoba, 1870–1900." In Donald Swainson, ed., *Historical Essays on the Prairie Provinces*. Toronto: McClelland and Stewart, 1970.

Gates, Catherine. "The Influence of Third Way Thinking on Manitoba's Social Policy Agenda." Unpublished graduate research paper, University of Winnipeg, 2005.

Gerrard, Jon. *Battling for a Better Manitoba: A History of The Provincial Liberal Party*. Winnipeg: Heartland Associates, 2006.

Gibbins, Roger. *Prairie Politics and Society: Regionalism in Decline*. Toronto: Butterworths, 1980.

Giddens, Anthony. *The Third Way: A Renewal of Social Democracy*. London: Polity Press, 1998.

Gonick, Cy. "The Manitoba Economy Since World War II." In James Silver and Jeremy Hall, eds., *The Political Economy of Manitoba*. Regina: Canadian Plains Research Center, 1990.

Grace, Joan. "Challenges and Opportunities in Manitoba: The Social Democratic 'Promise' and Women's Equality." In William Carroll and R.S. Ratner, eds., *Challenges and Perils: Social Democracy in Neoliberal Times*. Halifax: Fernwood Publishing, 2005.

_____. "Has the Manitoba NDP been 'Good' for Women?" Paper presented to the Canadian Political Science Association, Halifax, Nova Scotia, 2003.

Granatstein, J.L. *The Politics of Survival: The Conservative Party of Canada, 1939–1945*. Toronto: University of Toronto Press, 1967.

Gray, James H. *Red Lights on the Prairies*. Toronto: Macmillan, 1975.

_____. *The Roar of the Twenties*. Toronto: Macmillan, 1975.

Green, Sidney. *The Rise and Fall of a Political Animal: A Memoir*. Winnipeg: Great Plains Publications, 2003.

Green Party of Manitoba. *Greenprint: The Newsletter of the Green Party of Manitoba*, Issue 4 (August 2006) and Issue 5 (December 2006).

Hall, David. *Clifford Sifton: Volume 1*. Vancouver: University of British Columbia Press, 1981.

Hann, Russell. *The Farmers Confront Industrialism: Some Historical Perspectives on Ontario Agrarian Movements*. Toronto: New Hogtown Press, 1975.

Haque, C. Emdad. "Population of Manitoba: Patterns and Trends." In John Welsted et al., eds., *The Geography of Manitoba: Its Land and Its People*. Winnipeg: University of Manitoba Press, 1996.

Hébert, Raymond M. *Manitoba's French-Language Crisis: A Cautionary Tale*. Montreal: McGill-Queen's University Press, 2004.

Hilts, Joseph Alfred. "The Political Career of Thomas Greenway." PhD dissertation, University of Manitoba, 1974.

Holton, Bob. *British Syndicalism: 1900–1914*. London: Pluto Press, 1976.

Inglehart, Ronald. *The Silent Revolution: Changing Values and Political Styles Among Western Publics*. Princeton: Princeton University Press, 1977.

Institute for Social and Economic Research. *Research Bulletin: Political Preferences of Manitobans* 1, 5 (30 April 1984).

Jackson, Robert, and Doreen Jackson. *Canadian Government in Transition.* 4th ed. Toronto: Pearson, 2006.

Jenson, Jane, and Susan Phillips. "Regime Shift: New Citizenship Practices in Canada." *International Journal of Canadian Studies* 14 (1996).

Kendle, John. *John Bracken: A Political Biography.* Toronto: University of Toronto Press, 1979.

Key, V.O. "A Theory of Critical Elections." *The Journal of Politics* 17 (1955). Reprinted in Peter Woll, *American Government: Readings and Cases.* 8th ed. Boston: Little, Brown, 1984.

Kienetz, Alvin. "Northern Living and Resource Towns." In John Welsted et al., eds., *The Geography of Manitoba: Its Land and Its People.* Winnipeg: University of Manitoba Press, 1996.

Kirchheimer, Otto. "The Transformation of the Western European Party System." In Frederic Burin and Kurt Shell, eds., *Political Law and Social Change: Selected Essays.* New York: Columbia University Press, 1969.

Kruzenga, Len. "Aboriginal people used in vote-splitting scheme." *Windspeaker* (March 1999).

Lambert, Geoffrey. "Manitoba." In R.B. Byers, ed., *Canadian Annual Review of Politics and Public Affairs, 1981.* Toronto: University of Toronto Press, 1984.

———. "Manitoba." In David Leyton-Brown, ed., *Canadian Annual Review of Politics and Public Affairs, 1988.* Toronto: University of Toronto Press, 1995.

———. "Manitoba." In David Leyton-Brown, ed., *Canadian Annual Review of Politics and Public Affairs, 1990.* Toronto: University of Toronto Press, 1997.

———. "Manitoba," In David Mutimer, ed., *Canadian Annual Review of Politics and Public Affairs, 1999.* Toronto: University of Toronto Press, 2005.

———. "Progressive Conservative Party." In David Wishart, ed., *The Encyclopedia of the Great Plains.* Lincoln: University of Nebraska Press, 2004.

———. "Voting Patterns, Canada." In David Wishart, ed., *The Encyclopedia of the Great Plains.* Lincoln: University of Nebraska Press, 2004.

Laschinger, John, and Geoffrey Stevens. *Leaders and Lesser Mortals: Backroom Politics in Canada.* Toronto: Key Porter Books, 1992.

Laycock, David. "Reforming Canadian Democracy? Institutions and Ideology in the Reform Party Project." *Canadian Journal of Political Science* 27, 2 (1994): 213–248.

Leacy, M.C., ed. *Historical Statistics of Canada, 2nd Edition.* Ottawa: Statistics Canada, 1983.

Lehr, John. "Settlement: The Making of a Landscape." In John Welsted et al., eds., *The Geography of Manitoba: Its Land and Its People.* Winnipeg: University of Manitoba Press, 1996.

Levin, Ben. *Governing Education.* Toronto: University of Toronto Press, 2005.

Levine, Allan. "Chicago of the North." In Gregg Shilliday, ed., *Manitoba 125: Volume 2, Gateway to the West.* Winnipeg: Great Plains Publications, 1994.

Liberal Party of Manitoba. "History of the Manitoba Liberal Party." Unpublished document sent to the author, 2005.

Lipset, Seymour Martin. *Agrarian Socialism: The Cooperative Commonwealth Federation in Saskatchewan.* Updated ed. New York: Anchor Books, 1968.

Lipset, Seymour Martin, and Stein Rokkan. "Cleavage Structures, Party Systems, and Voter Alignments." In Seymour Martin Lipset and Stein Rokkan, eds., *Party Systems and Voter Alignments: Cross-National Perspectives.* New York: The Free Press, 1967.

Loxley, John, and Fred Wien. "Urban Aboriginal Economic Development." In David Newhouse and Evelyn Peters, eds., *Not Strangers in These Parts: Urban Aboriginal Peoples.* Ottawa: Policy Research Initiative, 2003.

Lumley, Elizabeth, ed. *Canadian Who's Who: 1995.* Toronto: University of Toronto Press, 1995.

MacEwan, Grant. *Fifty Mighty Men.* Saskatoon: Modern Press, 1958.

Mackintosh, Gordon H.A. "The Parliamentary Tradition in Manitoba." *Canadian Parliamentary Review* 6,2, Summer 1983.

Macpherson, C.B . *Democracy in Alberta: Social Credit and the Party System.* 2nd ed. Toronto: University of Toronto Press, 1962.

_____. *Democracy in Alberta: The Theory and Practice of a Quasi-Party System.* Toronto: University of Toronto Press, 1953.

Manitoba, Legislative Assembly. *Debates and Proceedings*, 1870–2006, various dates.

_____. *The Manitoba Legislative Building Guide* [pamphlet], c. 2000.

Maslove, Allan. "Health and Federal-Provincial Financial Arrangements: Lost Opportunity." In G. Bruce Doern, ed., *How Ottawa Spends: 2005–2006*. Montreal: McGill-Queen's University Press, 2005.

McAllister, James. *The Government of Edward Schreyer: Democratic Socialism in Manitoba*. Montreal: McGill-Queen's University Press, 1984.

McCaffrey, Shaun. "A Study of Policy Continuity Between the Progressive Conservative and the New Democratic Party Governments of Manitoba, 1958–1977." MA thesis, University of Manitoba, 1986.

McCall, Christina, and Stephen Clarkson. *Trudeau and Our Times: Volume 2, The Heroic Delusion*. Toronto: McClelland and Stewart, 1990.

McCall-Newman, Christina. *Grits: An Intimate Portrait of the Liberal Party*. Toronto: Macmillan, 1982.

McCormack, A. Ross. *Reformers, Rebels, and Revolutionaries: The Western Canadian Radical Movement, 1899–1919*. Toronto: University of Toronto Press, 1977.

McInnis, Edgar. *Canada: A Political and Social History*. 3rd ed. Toronto: Holt, Rinehart and Winston, 1969.

McNaught, Kenneth. *A Prophet in Politics: A Biography of J.S. Woodsworth*. Toronto: University of Toronto Press, 1959.

McWilliams, Margaret. *Manitoba Milestones*. Toronto: J.M. Dent and Sons, 1928.

Meisel, John. "The Decline of Party in Canada." In Hugh Thorburn, ed., *Party Politics in Canada*. 5th ed. Scarborough: Prentice-Hall, 1985.

Michels, Roberto. *Political Parties: A Sociological Study of the Oligarchical Tendencies of Modern Democracy*. Trans. Edan and Cedar Paul. New York: Collier, 1962.

Mills, Allen. *Fool for Christ: The Political Thought of J.S. Woodsworth*. Toronto: University of Toronto Press, 1991.

Mishler, William. *Political Participation in Canada: Prospects for Democratic Citizenship*. Toronto: Macmillan, 1979.

Mochoruk, Jim. *Formidable Heritage: Manitoba's North and the Cost of Development, 1870 to 1930*. Winnipeg: University of Manitoba Press, 2004.

Monnin, Alfred M. *Report of the Commission of Inquiry into Allegations of Infractions of The Elections Act and The Elections Finances Act during the*

1995 Manitoba General Election. Winnipeg: Manitoba Queen's Printer, 1999.

Morton, W.L. *Manitoba: A History*. Toronto: University of Toronto Press, 1957.

———. *The Progressive Party in Canada*. Toronto: University of Toronto Press, 1971. (Orig. pub. 1950.)

Nachmias, David and Chava Nachmias. *Research Methods in the Social Sciences*, 3rd ed. New York: St. Martin's Press, 1987.

National Council of Welfare. *Poverty Profile 1995*. Ottawa: Supply and Services Canada, 1997.

Netherton, Alex. "Paradigm and Shift: A Sketch of Manitoba Politics." In Keith Brownsey and Michael Howlett, eds., *The Provincial State in Canada: Politics in the Provinces and Territories*. Peterborough: Broadview Press, 2001.

———. "From Rentiership to Continental Modernization: Shifting Paradigms of State Intervention in Hydro in Manitoba, 1922–1927." PhD dissertation, Carleton University, 1993.

Neville, William. "Climate of Change." In Gregg Shilliday, ed., *Manitoba 125: Volume 3, Decades of Diversity*. Winnipeg: Great Plains Publications, 1999.

Norrie, Kenneth, and Douglas Owram. *A History of the Canadian Economy*. Toronto: Harcourt Brace Jovanovich, 1991.

O'Handley, Kathryn, ed. *Canadian Parliamentary Guide: 2001*. Detroit: Gale Group, 2002.

O'Neill, Brenda. "Sugar and Spice? Political Culture and the Political Behaviour of Canadian Women." In Joanna Everitt and Brenda O'Neill, eds., *Citizen Politics: Research and Theory in Canadian Political Behaviour*. Don Mills: Oxford University Press, 2002.

Ostrogorski, M. *Democracy and the Organization of Political Parties, Vol. 1: England*. Edited by S.M. Lipset. Chicago: Quadrangle Books, 1964.

Pal, Leslie A. "The Cauldron of Leadership: Prime Ministers and Their Parties." In R.K. Carty, ed., *Canadian Political Party Systems: A Reader*. Peterborough: Broadview Press, 1992.

Pammett, Jon. "Behind the Turnout Decline." In Jon Pammett and Christopher Dornan, eds., *The Canadian General Election of 2004*. Toronto: Dundurn, 2004.

PC Party of Manitoba. "Our History." http://www.pcmanitoba.com (accessed 27 July 2006).
_____. "Our Leaders." Unpublished document provided to the author, 27 July 2006.
Perlin, George. *The Tory Syndrome: Leadership Politics in the Progressive Conservative Party*. Montreal: McGill-Queen's University Press, 1980.
Peterson, Tom. "Ethnic and Class Politics in Manitoba." In Martin Robin, ed., *Canadian Provincial Politics: The Party Systems in the Ten Provinces*. Scarborough: Prentice-Hall, 1972.
_____. "Manitoba." In John Saywell, ed., *Canadian Annual Review of Politics and Public Affairs, 1969*. Toronto: University of Toronto Press, 1970.
Phenix, Patricia. *Private Demons: The Tragic Personal Life of John A. Macdonald*. Toronto: McClelland and Stewart, 2006.
Phillips, Paul. "Manitoba in the Agrarian Period: 1870–1940." In James Silver and Jeremy Hall, eds., *The Political Economy of Manitoba*. Regina: Canadian Plains Research Center, 1990.
Pickersgill, Jack. *The Mackenzie King Record: Volume 1, 1939–1944*. Toronto: University of Toronto Pres, 1960.
Piore, Michael, and Charles Sabel. *The Second Industrial Divide*. New York: Basic Books, 1984.
Plamondon, Bob. *Full Circle: Death and Resurrection in Canadian Conservative Politics*. Toronto: Key Porter Books, 2006.
Porter, John. "The Economic Elite and the Social Structure of Canada." *Canadian Journal of Economics and Political Science* 23 (1957).
_____. *The Vertical Mosaic: An Analysis of Social Class and Power in Canada*. Toronto: University of Toronto Press, 1965.
Probe Research Inc. 2004 and 2007 Survey Database (N=4000 per annum).
_____. *Indigenous Voices: Aboriginal People in Manitoba* [syndicated study]. Winnipeg: Probe Research, 2005.
_____. Press releases, 1999–2007.
Przeworski, Adam. "How Many Ways Can Be Third?" In Andrew Glyn, ed., *Social Democracy in Neoliberal Times: The Left and Economic Policy Since 1980*. Oxford: Oxford University Press, 2001.
Rae, Douglas. *The Political Consequences of Electoral Laws*. New Haven: Yale University Press, 1971.
Rea, J.E. *T.A. Crerar: A Political Life*. Montreal: McGill-Queen's University Press, 1997.

_____. "Thomas Greenway." *The Dictionary of Canadian Biography Online*, http://www.biographi.ca (accessed 29 July 2006).

Reid, Escott. "The Rise of National Parties in Canada." *Papers and Proceedings of the Canadian Political Science Association*, 1932. Reprinted in Hugh Thorburn, ed., *Party Politics in Canada*. 5th ed. Scarborough: Prentice-Hall, 1985.

Rice, James, and Michael Prince. "Martin's Moment: The Social Policy Agenda of a New Prime Minister." In G. Bruce Doern, ed., *How Ottawa Spends: 2004–2005*. Montreal: McGill-Queen's University Press, 2004.

Richards, Howard J. "The Prairie Region." In John Warkentin, ed., *Canada: A Geographical Interpretation*. Toronto: Methuen, 1968.

Roblin, Duff. *Speaking for Myself: Politics and Other Pursuits*. Winnipeg: Great Plains Publications, 1999.

Rousseau, Jean-Jacques. *The Social Contract and Discourse on the Origin of Inequality*. New York: Pocket Books, 1967.

Russell, Frances. *The Canadian Crucible: Manitoba's Role in Canada's Great Divide*. Winnipeg: Heartland Associates, 2003.

Safire, William. *Safire's Political Dictionary*. Updated ed. New York: Random House, 1978.

Sartori, Giovanni. *Parties and Party Systems: A Framework for Analysis*, Volume 1. Cambridge: Cambridge University Press, 1976.

Sawatsky, John. *Mulroney: The Politics of Ambition*. Toronto: Macfarlane, Walter and Ross, 1991.

Schulz, Herb. *A View from the Ledge: An Insider's Look at the Schreyer Years*. Winnipeg: Heartland Associates, 2005.

Serfaty, Meir. "Electoral Behaviour in Manitoba: The Convergence of Geography and Politics." In John Welsted et al., eds., *The Geography of Manitoba: Its Land and Its People*. Winnipeg: University of Manitoba Press, 1996.

Shilliday, Gregg, ed. *Manitoba 125: Volume 1, Rupert's Land to Riel*. Winnipeg: Great Plains Publications, 1993.

_____. *Manitoba 125: Volume 2, Gateway to the West*. Winnipeg: Great Plains Publications, 1994.

_____. *Manitoba 125: Volume 3, Decades of Diversity*. Winnipeg: Great Plains Publications, 1995.

Shipley, Nan. *From Slate to Computer in the Transcona-Springfield Area: 1873–1983.* Winnipeg: Transcona-Springfield School Division No. 12, 1983.

Sigurdson, Richard. "Preston Manning and the Politics of Postmodernism in Canada." *Canadian Journal of Political Science* 27, 2 (1994).

Silver, Jim, and Jeremy Hall, eds. *The Political Economy of Manitoba.* Regina: Canadian Plains Research Center, 1990.

Simeon, Richard. "Federalism and Intergovernmental Relations." In Christopher Dunn, ed., *The Handbook of Canadian Public Administration.* Toronto: Oxford University Press, 2002.

Simpson, Jeffrey. *Discipline of Power: The Conservative Interlude and the Liberal Restoration.* Toronto: Personal Library, 1980.

Small, Tamara. "parties@canada: The Internet and the 2004 Cyber-Campaign." In Jon Pammett and Christopher Dunn, ed., *The Canadian General Election of 2004.* Toronto: Dundurn, 2004.

Smiley, Donald, ed. *The Rowell/Sirois Report, Book 1.* Toronto: McClelland and Stewart, 1963.

Smith, David E. *The Regional Decline of a National Party: Liberals on the Prairies.* Toronto: University of Toronto Press, 1981.

———. "Western Canada." In Robert M. Krause and R.H. Wagenberg, eds., *Canadian Government and Politics: Introductory Readings.* 2nd ed. Toronto: Copp Clark, 1995.

Smith, Doug. *As Many Liars: The Story of the 1995 Manitoba Vote-Splitting Scandal.* Winnipeg: Arbeiter Ring, 2003.

———. *Let Us Rise! An Illustrated History of the Manitoba Labour Movement.* Vancouver: New Star Books, 1985.

Stadel, Christopher. "The Non-Metropolitan Settlements of Southern Manitoba." In John Welsted et al., eds., *The Geography of Manitoba: Its Land and Its People.* Winnipeg: University of Manitoba Press, 1996.

Stewart, Walter. *The Life and Political Times of Tommy Douglas.* Toronto: McArthur and Co., 2003.

Stinson, Lloyd. *Political Warriors: Recollections of a Social Democrat.* Winnipeg: Queenston House, 1975.

Strick, J.C. *Canadian Public Finance.* 4th ed. Toronto: Holt Rinehart and Winston, 1992.

Studlar, Donley. "Consequences of the Unreformed Canadian Electoral System." *The American Review of Canadian Studies* 33 (2003).

Swainson, Donald, ed. *Historical Essays on the Prairie Provinces.* Toronto: McClelland and Stewart, 1970.

Thorburn, Hugh G., ed. *Party Politics in Canada.* 5th ed. Scarborough: Prentice-Hall, 1985.

Thorburn, Hugh G., and Alan Whitehorn, eds. *Party Politics in Canada.* 8th ed. Toronto: Prentice-Hall, 2001.

Tomasky, Michael. "The Boss" *The New York Review* (1 December 2005)

Trofimenkoff, Susan Mann. *Stanley Knowles: The Man from Winnipeg North Centre.* Saskatoon: Western Producer Prairie Books, 1982.

Turcotte, André. "Canadians Speak Out." In Jon Pammett and Christopher Dunn, ed., *The Canadian General Election of 2004.* Toronto: Dundurn, 2004.

Wangenheim, Elizabeth. "The Ukrainians: A Case Study of the 'Third Force.'" In P. Russell, ed., *Nationalism in Canada.* Toronto: McGraw-Hill, 1966.

Wearing, Joseph. *The L-Shaped Party: The Liberal Party of Canada, 1958–1980,* Toronto: McGill-Ryerson, 1980.

Welsted, John, et al. "Manitoba: Geographical Identity of a Prairie Province." In John Welsted et al., eds., *The Geography of Manitoba: Its Land and Its People.* Winnipeg: University of Manitoba Press, 1996.

Wesley, Jared, and David Stewart. "Electoral Financing Reform in Manitoba: Advantage Doer?" Paper presented at the Party and Election Finance: Consequences for Democracy Conference, Calgary, Alberta, 2006.

Wesley, Jared. "The Collective Centre: Social Democracy and Red Tory Politics in Manitoba." Paper presented to the Canadian Political Science Association, Toronto, Ontario, 2006.

_____. "Spanning the Spectrum: Political Party Attitudes in Manitoba." MA thesis, University of Manitoba, 2004.

Whitaker, Reginald. *The Government Party: Organizing and Financing the Liberal Party of Canada, 1930–58.* Toronto: University of Toronto Press, 1977.

Wilson, John. "The Decline of the Liberal Party in Manitoba Politics." *Journal of Canadian Studies* 10 (1975).

Wilson, Keith. *Manitobans in Profile: Hugh John Macdonald.* Winnipeg: Peguis Publishers, 1980.

Wiseman, Nelson. "The Pattern of Prairie Politics." *Queen's Quarterly* 88, 2 (1981). Reprinted in Hugh Thorburn, ed., *Party Politics in Canada*. 5th ed. Scarborough: Prentice-Hall, 1985.

_____. *Social Democracy in Manitoba: A History of the CCF/NDP*. Winnipeg: University of Manitoba Press, 1983.

Wishart, David J., ed. *Encyclopedia of the Great Plains*. Lincoln: Nebraska University Press, 2004.

Young, Walter. *Anatomy of a Party: The National CCF, 1932–61*. Toronto: University of Toronto Press, 1969.

Index

Aikins, James 29,
Aikins, James C. 24, 29
Alcock, Reg 61, 93–94, 184n, 200n
Archibald, Adams G. 9
Ashdown, J.H. 74, 196n
Asper, Israel 87–88, 120, 139, 140, 144, 166
Axworthy, Lloyd ix, 43, 84, 87–89, 93–94, 96, 184n, 199n, 201n

Basham, Andrew 166
Basham, Ardythe 166
Beard, Gordon 19
Bend, Robert 84–85, 87, 114, 116, 139, 183n, 197n,198n, 199n, 209n
Benson, Julian 55, 57
Boyd, Alfred 9, 169
Bracken, John 3, 14, 15, 17, 30–33, 65, 75–78, 80–81, 105, 107, 134, 138, 172c, 173, 197n, 209n
Brown, C.P. 194n,
Bruinooge, Rod 61,
Bryce, William "Scottie" 110, 204–205n,
Buchart, Markus xi, 165, 166, 214n,

Cameron, Malcolm 66
Campbell, Douglas 12, 17, 25, 36, 81–82, 87, 108, 173, 174, 183n, 186n, 196n, 197n, 204n,
Carr, Jim 93
Carrol, Jack 117
Carstairs, Sharon 48–49, 51–52, 89, 91–93, 95–96, 127, 137, 140, 142, 200n
Cheema, Gulzar 93
Chrétien, Jean 92, 95
Clarke, Henry Joseph 9, 169
Clubb, W.R. 77
Connolly, Harold 89
Cowan, James 39
Cowan, Jay 117
Craig, Richard 75
Crerar, Thomas 74, 76, 196n

Davidson, John Andrew 26, 194n
Davis, Robert Atkinson / Robert 9, 169
Desjardins, Larry 19, 85–86, 88, 120, 125, 140, 183n, 199n, 200n
Diefenbaker, John 35, 37, 39, 112, 115, 138, 187n,
Dixon, Fred 101, 202n,

Dodick, Doreen 123
Doer, Gary 8, 20, 49, 51, 61–62, 92, 97, 119, 126–131, 134–135, 137, 139–140, 146, 166, 177, 207n
Doern, Russell 124,
Dolin, Mary Beth 123
Doneleyko, Wilbert 110–111
Douglas, Tommy 106
Duguid, Terry 211n

Edmonds, Duncan 84
Edwards, Paul xi, 93–94
Enns, Harry 42
Evans, Sanford 31, 35, 139, 186n, 187n

Farmer, S.J. 105, 106, 109, 187n
Filmon, Gary ix, 20, 24, 46–58, 60–61, 63, 92–93, 127–129, 131, 134, 137–138, 140, 142, 150, 165, 176, 177
Fisher, James 26, 67
Fontaine, Jerry 95
Fox, Peter 40
Fox-Decent, Wally 50
Froese, J.M. 18

Garson, Stuart 78, 80, 81, 108, 173, 197n,
Gerrard, Jon 95–96, 128, 139, 197n, 198n, 201n,
Girard, Marc-Amable 9, 169, 184n
Glass, David 171c, 194n
Green, Sidney 114, 139,
Greenway, Thomas 10, 25–27, 65–71, 74, 133, 137, 156, 170, 194n,

Haig, John 30
Hansford, E.A. 109–110
Harapiak, Leonard 126
Harper, Elijah 51, 123
Harrison, David 25, 67, 169
Hasselfield, Ginny 94–95, 200n
Hemphill, Maureen 123
Hoey, Bob 76
Huband, Charles 43, 88–89, 139

Johnson, George 35, 40
Juba, Stephen ix, 36

Katz, Sam 60
King, William Lyon Mackenzie 77, 107
Knowles, Stanley vii, 99, 106, 112, 205n
Kowalski, Gary 93

Lamoureux, Kevin 93, 95–96, 128, 200n
Laschinger, John 48
Lauchlan, Douglas 89
Laurier, Wilfrid 10, 70, 195n
Lewis, David 105
Loewen, John 61
Lyon, Sterling 20, 24, 37, 40–41, 43, 45–48, 56, 60, 63, 82, 121, 122, 134, 137, 144, 176,189n,

MacCarthy, Dane 83
Macdonald, Hugh John 26, 28, 35, 71
Macdonald, John A. 2, 23–24, 26, 65–66, 137, 184n,
Macdonald, William Alexander 26,
MacKay, Murdoch 78, 140

Major, Bill 77
Manness, Clayton 47–48, 50
Manning, Preston 198n,
Marion, Paul 88, 140, 199n
Martin, Paul 55
McAffrey, Shawn 193n
McBryde, Ron 117
McCaffrey, Beverly 89
McDiarmid, J.S. 17, 78
McFadyen, Hugh 57, 60, 61, 63, 130, 140–141
McLean, Stewart 40
McPherson, Ewen 78
Meighen, Arthur 33, 81
Mills, James 40
Molgat, Gildas 83–87, 139, 198n, 209n
Moran, Hugh 89
Morris, Alexander 9
Morton, William 17
Moss, Peter 199n
Mulroney, Brian 50–53, 91–92, 138,
Munro, John 92
Murray, Stuart vii, 56–59, 61, 63, 130, 140, 154, 192n

Nelson, Holly 166,
Nesbitt, John 87
Norquay, John 1, 2, 10, 24–26, 65–68, 116, 169, 184n, 194n
Norris, T.C. 29, 65, 70–73, 77, 101–103, 107, 123, 137, 157, 171, 196n, 202n
Oleson, Charlotte 123

Olynik, Brent 193n
Orchard, Don 48, 190n

Paulley, Russ 112
Pawley, Howard 20, 45–46, 48–50, 91–92, 112, 119, 122–129, 131, 134, 137, 176
Pearson, Lester 198n,
Pedersen, Blaine 190
Penner, Roland 125
Petursson, Philip 39
Phillips, Myrna 123
Pickersgill, Jack 80
Praznik, Darren 57
Prefontaine, Albert 29–30, 186n
Prendergast, James 70
Price, Norma 123
Puttee, Arthur 100–101

Ransom, Brian 44, 46–48, 60
Richards, Berry 110–111
Richardson, James 43, 96, 184n
Ridgeway, Bill 89, 91, 200n
Riel, Louis 8, 137
Rigg, Richard 101
Roberts, Stan 83, 86, 198n
Roblin, Duff xi, 4, 16–17, 24, 29, 33, 34–35, 37–41, 43–44, 53, 60, 63, 82, 87, 96, 111, 119–20, 127, 131, 134, 137, 138–139, 166, 175, 187n,
Roblin, Rodmond 10, 26–29, 74, 101, 134, 170, 171, 185n
Robson, Hugh 77–78
Rocan, Denis 49, 190n,
Roch, Gilles 92
Ross, J. Arthur 34–35, 187n

Santos, Conrad 123
Schreyer, Edward xi, 6, 18, 20, 39, 41–42, 49, 85, 88, 112–116, 118–123, 129, 131, 134, 137, 139, 140, 142, 161, 165, 176, 183n, 201n,
Schuler, Ron 60
Schulz, Jake 115
Sifton, Clifford vii, 10, 27, 69, 195
Smith, Joy 211n
Smith, Muriel 123
Spivak, Sidney 41–43, 46–47, 59, 63, 89, 120, 122, 139, 144, 188n, 189n
St. Laurent, Louis 81
Stanes, D.M. 84
Stanfield, Robert 40
Staples-Lyon, Bonnie 57
Stinson, Lloyd 82, 107, 110–111, 187n, 204–205n

Talbot, Philippe 196n

Index

Taylor, Fawcett 30–31
Ternette, Nick 165
Trudeau, Pierre 52, 87, 89, 91–92, 94, 96, 121, 138, 157, 201n
Tupper, Charles 27, 70
Turner, Trudy 193n

Waddell, Ken 60
Walding, Jim 125
Weir, Walter xi, 24, 40–41, 63. 84, 113, 115, 140, 175

www.ingramcontent.com/pod-product-compliance
Lightning Source LLC
Chambersburg PA
CBHW020804230426
43666CB00007B/855